FULLY HUMAN

/

FULLY ALIVE

Lyle L. Simpson

Books Academy LLC
5900 Balcones Drive Suite 100
Austin, Texas 78731
Hotline: (254) 800-1183

Ordering Information:
Quantity sales. Special discounts are available on quantity purchases by corporations, associations, and others. For details, contact the publisher at the address above.

Printed in the United States of America.

ISBN-13: Softcover   978-1-964864-33-4
          Hardcover   978-1-964929-22-4
          eBook   978-1-964864-34-1

TABLE OF CONTENTS

Preface xi

You have the power to fully experience your life by giving up all of your conflicting wants and simply fully living and experiencing the circumstances in which you then find yourself.

Introduction xv

A very valid cultural question remains for younger generations today. Do I control my own life, or does God control me? This question has been considered for thousands of years. Previously the answer had been dictated to us by Control People. That is no longer true for many of the younger people in our society today. Many more people today want control of their own lives. How do we accomplish that? Unitarian minister Lester Mondale, and his spouse Maria Mondale, have shown us their Epicurean pathway.

Chapter One: What is Humanism? 1

The history of the philosophy of humanism starts with Epicurus who lived in Athens, Greece. He was born in 341 BCE and died in 270 BCE. In those days almost everyone believed that God ruled their lives on a daily basis. Epicurus felt that we needed to take the responsibility of our own lives and could not blame God for anything that happened to us. Furthermore, he saw no reason to believe in a life after our death. Therefore, our goal should be to make the very most of our own lives while we live on Earth. And the best means for achieving that was to **live in harmony with nature, and to want nothing, and need little.**

The Epicurean philosophy was drowned out by the cultural memes of its day, with God being back in control of the Hellenic people. Epicurean thought would have been forgotten, and no one would know it had ever existed, if it had not been for Lucretius writing his two-thousand-page paper describing Epicurean thinking around 100 BCE. This paper was discovered in a German monastery by a friend of Cosmos Medici of Florence. He gave the paper to Cosmos who had it translated into Italian. They adopted this philosophy for the City State of Florence in the fifteenth century, bringing about the Renaissance that brought European civilization out of the constriction of Catholic control. When the Church regained its status, it shared its control with Protestants.

Chapter Two: The Philosophy of Humanism Today..............17

The Epicurean philosophy surfaced in Spokane, Washington in the first decade of the twentieth century. The name "humanism" was coined as the name of the Epicurean philosophy in Des Moines, Iowa in 1917, barely one hundred years ago. Today the American Humanist Association (AHA) affects the lives of over four million Americans daily, and the philosophy of Humanism can be found around the world.

Chapter Three: Where is our Current Culture?......................35

Our world is in turmoil, with many holding outdated beliefs while over twenty-seven percent of Americans, when asked of their religious affiliation, claim "none." Over forty percent of those who are Millennials or younger say "none", showing that our culture is changing rapidly. The AHA has a significant opportunity to influence a positive alternative for our cultural growth today.

Chapter Four: Why was I Born?...............................49

Are we really alone in our universe? If so, why am I here? There may not be an answer to a "why" question.

Chapter Five: What is "truth" for me? 55

Why do I believe what I believe? How do I determine what is true for myself? We each need to determine what is true for ourselves. Not accepting what a Control Person tells us based on "blind faith".

Chapter Six: Who are Control People? 67

Who are Control People? Why do I accept and believe any of them?

Chapter Seven: How Should We Live Our Life? 71

Psychologist Abraham Maslow shows us a path for actualizing our own existence while we live our life here on Earth today. Using the logic of his hierarchy of needs gives us a model for understanding people, nations, and institutions of every kind as we seek the highest level of living for our own lives. Maslow discovered that our needs can be classified by their drive strength, and that there are six distinct levels. But most Americans cannot get past the third level. Let's discover why. Maslow provides the path to reach the goal of living our own lives to the fullest.

Chapter Eight: Why is achieving Actualization. so Difficult? 93

We live in a world of violence. We Protect our beliefs with scatomas, which are blind spots that block contrary information from even being perceived by us. We cannot see our own blind spots.

Chapter Nine: Who or What Created Humans? 101

Charles Darwin rather dramatically answered the question of how we came to be: we evolved from sea creatures. God had nothing to do with our creation. Humans evolved from very primordial life.

Chapter Ten: What Does our Age Have to do with our Values? 105

The cultural conditions existing when we were born form our values. They have a much greater effect than our parents, the area in which we live, or the status of our family. We are conditioned more by the science and technology existing in our formative days than we are by our family values. Understanding the values of each generation and what caused them is essential if you are trying to influence another's thinking.

Chapter Eleven: What Controls Do We Have for Our Life? 113

Our attitude is the valve to access our brain. A negative attitude defeats learning anything new. A positive attitude creates reception for new ideas and learning. Most people accept their beliefs from those who are members of whatever group with whom they identify. We see this in our grade school days, in our political affiliations, and in the Church where we "belong." It is called "group think" because the group thinks for you, you do not have to think for yourself. Taking responsibility for what you are willing to believe is what turns the valve to improve the quality of your own life.

Chapter Twelve: Live a Happier Life with a Free Mind   121

Lowering your expectations and being more accepting of those events in life that are beyond your control while appreciating the path for fulfilling your goals on life's journey is the is the way to happiness. To do so requires a free mind that you control with expectations and the manner of your reactions to whatever are the circumstances you encounter.

Chapter Thirteen: Why Do We Have all of The Many Beliefs That We Currently Have?..127

Considering the example of why we even have the notion that there is a life available for us following our death shows the effect of historic thinking and the control memes have over our beliefs. Very few of our beliefs are original thinking. Why do we latch on to some and reject others? The millions of new thoughts entering our minds on a daily basis are an important area of study. Using life after death as the example clearly demonstrates why we have many of the beliefs we hold. You can consider all of your beliefs using that technique for their analysis.

Chapter Fourteen: Myths of Faith, The Role of Religion, Varies Within Our Culture..157

Although in some cultures, like China, daily behavior is not controlled by religious faith, for most of the western world, religion is our "social glue". In China, "losing face" with someone who trusts you is equivalent to a mortal sin. For those relying upon the Bible as their source of truth, many accept what they are told without question. Many, without realizing that they read the Bible from a myopic perspective. They accept all verses as absolute truth, ignoring their conflicting provisions in other Chapters. The Bible was written by many people living in a far more primitive culture, with very little knowledge of the means for determining what is true.

In the New Testament, they were doing their best to make the life of Jesus relevant for the Jewish community. Jesus was made into the Christ most probably by St Paul. He never knew Jesus. Paul did know that he was living a better life preaching about Jesus than he had being a tax collector. The New Testament intentionally parallels many prophecies of the Old Testament. Many of the cultural religious beliefs we have today have no basis in reality.

If you look upon religion as a myth that provides you with symbols for enhancing your life, rather than your faith relying upon their truth, those differences really need not matter to you. Religion has a very valid role in the lives of many people. There is no valid reason for attacking their faith beliefs.

Chapter Fifteen: What Happens Next?...................................173

Striving to make the very most of our life while we are here on Earth causes us to encounter many obstacles. How do we measure our own life? What scatomas block conflicting information from even being heard by me?

Chapter Sixteen: What About Religion? 185

What does religion have to do with this discussion? Does everyone need religion? E.O. Wilson tells us everyone has a biological need to relate to nature, a need we identify as spirituality. It is a basic need that the religious would like you to believe it is their exclusive turf. Retired Episcopal Bishop John Shelby Spong tells us humanism can be adapted by most religious people. It could make Christianity relevant in the future.

Chapter Seventeen: What is God's Answer?...........................191

How do we define God? Aristotle says the philosophical question is "why something happens" or exists. We now can accept that there may not be an answer to all "why" questions. We discuss different views of what is God, and whether such perspectives make any difference. The point is that we are left without a universal answer. We each create our own god. God has not answered the question of why we are here for everyone.

Chapter Eighteen: What About Those Who Claim to be Atheists? 195

Looking at the definition of God from Maslow's perspective, people's god concept depends upon the level where they are primarily living. A fear god concept prevails on the basic level, a father god is predominant on the social level. But, by the time a person is actualized, their god concept is generally abstract. If your definition of God is nature, how could you be an atheist? It would no longer make sense. Atheist can validly object to theism, and most theologians would agree with them today. There is no need for a supernatural view of God.

Chapter Nineteen: What is the Role of Religion? 207

Religion became our 'Social glue" when our culture became dominated by agriculture and the domestication of animals. How do we control behavior? Hunter-gather societies of fewer than 150 people could control negative behavior with reputation. Beyond that size society needed a system of control. In early days, each community of city-states among Sumerians had their own god. Priests were appointed to manage their religion. They became powerful, even to the point of anointing their kings to demonstrate they ruled by the power of their God.

Chapter Twenty: This Life May be our Only Opportunity to Exist 215

There is absolutely no valid proof an afterlife exists. Our mind can play tricks on what we perceive. If there is not life hereafter, our goal should be to make the very most of this life that we can.

Chapter Twenty-One: How Do We Face Our own Death? 223

We enjoyed grade school the first time. But we really would not want to go back and start over. Likewise, if we have lived a fulfilled life, we no longer need to fear death. It is as natural to accept as our life has been to live. If our body fails us, death may even be welcomed. Once we have lived a full life, death is no longer an issue. Protecting our loved ones may be the only thing that matters to us.

Chapter Twenty-Two: How Should we Handle Diversity? 227

We expand our horizons when we experience new and different cultures and personalities. Humanists should seek the opportunity to see life from all perspectives in order to enrich their own lives.

Chapter Twenty-Three: Why Do We Need Others? 231

From the day that we were born we were dependent upon others. As we age our needs change but sharing our life with others is no less important for our growth. Meyers-Briggs psychology tells us there are four primary temperament types with different ways to process information. The lens we use to view life makes a difference in what we see.

Chapter Twenty-Four: Why Should We Make Our Lives Significant? 243

If there is no life after our death, the real value of our life comes from whatever we do that lives on after us. That becomes our own immortality.

Chapter Twenty-Five: What Can We Do Collectively?   247

Those who wish to actualize their own existence face all kinds of barriers for growth. Our society is still very primitive in our beliefs. Humanism can build bridges around cultural barriers.

Chapter Twenty-Six: What Values Ultimately Are Important for My life? 253

For me only two aspects of life are really important. My life is "meaningful" to the extent that I can actualize my existence; and my life is "significant" to the extent the world is a better place because I have been here. The healthy person keeps both in balance. Nothing else is as important.

Chapter Twenty-Seven: So, What Can I Do Now That1Have-Discovered: I Am a Humanist?..257

You can seek opportunities where your unique talents and life experiences can make a significant difference in the world. There are all sorts of opportunities that surround each of us daily, if we are only looking for them.

Chapter Twenty-Eight: How Do I Begin My Own Journey?..277

You could join the American Humanist Association to find new opportunities, and to gain literature to advance your humanist education. I have set forth numerous alternatives to "prime the pump." You can create your own. Seeking goals can add significant excitement to your life.

Chapter Twenty-Nine: In Conclusion....................................291

This chapter is intended to tie everything together. That task is impossible. Our life is best summarized by the last statement of *Humanist Manifesto III*. As Humanists, "The responsibility for our lives and the world in which we live is ours and ours alone."

My Poem about life "Our Road Through Life"....................295

Appendix...297

My Goal..301

Humanist Manifesto III..303

Preface

It is amazing the effect that taking a pause to smell the roses can really have upon us. I am, at the time of writing, entombed in my apartment, now approaching two weeks, and I could have longer to go. I flew on an airplane as the coronavirus started to spread. Life in our community has simply stopped, although I am actually enjoying some aspects of this. It allows me to explore my life from a totally different perspective. I now see life as the Epicureans saw theirs. Their goal in life was always to **want nothing and need little, and to fully live each moment. . You gain even more by experiencing wherever you are and whoever is with you with a positive attitude.** You might want to try this too. I find it frees me from useless problems that otherwise would have plagued me.

I have even improved my relationship with my puppy, now ten years old. Living isolated in our condominium is not so bad. We live on the top floor of our building that sits on a high hill, and we are able to look over our entire city. I should do this more often. To make the best use of my time, I think that I shall write a book on what this all really means for each of us.

My subject is all about how we can each make the very most out of our own lives, and why we should do that. This is not a new subject that I just dreamed up. Ancient Greek philosophers developed this thinking over 2,500 years ago. Their view of life was new and different. However, anything new is frightening for people with more ancient views of life. No one wants to have their current beliefs challenged. They are our safety net, and they do make us feel secure. Therefore, challenging their beliefs is threatening. Since the views of these philosophers were not generally accepted, their ideas were soon forgotten—or rather, overridden by priests and those in the public who followed their leadership—so it was as if that view of life had never existed. We still do this today. That behavior in psychology is called "group think." The individual does not have to think for themselves, their group does their thinking for them.

Beliefs viewed from that perspective become a defense mechanism. Many accept what their group thinks, simply because everyone else thinks that and so it must be true. Besides, it is the easiest path. We all have those. You do not have to think for yourself. That is certainly all right if that is all that we want in that area of concern because it is not worth our effort to think for ourselves in that arena. But, if we want to maximize our own existence, for anything that affects our own lives beyond that moment, those beliefs deserve to be carefully considered before being accepted as our lasting truth.

Epicurean thinking was rediscovered three times in human history. Each of the first three times the same thing happened, because people feel safe with whatever they believe, and that is usually what everyone else believes, even if their views are outdated. Many of our current beliefs today no longer make sense in our modern world. Some say "So what? They are rooted in ancient history that adds meaning to our lives. If they were good enough for my grandfather, why wouldn't they be good enough for me?" They may be, and I certainly would not tell anyone they are wrong. If whatever sustains them is necessary for any person, then who am I to insist otherwise? That thinking can be best explained to us by Shakespeare who said, "there is nothing either good nor bad. But thinking makes it so." Therefore, the goal of this book is not to change you, or challenge anything you wish to believe. That is your right. My goal is simply to make you think for yourself. For so long as you think for yourself, instead of merely accepting anyone else's belief simply because they said it, you can control your own life.

My goal is to challenge those people who, by blindly accepting what others tell them, totally miss living their own life to the fullest. This is what is important for each of us because this life is all that we know for certain that we really do have. No one has been proven to have come back to tell us that there really is more. Although some claim otherwise, they offer no credible proof, and that belief requires "blind faith." Why would we want to be "blind"? Blindly accepting something for anything in life that really is important for yourself can seriously hurt you. First, because it may deny you the truth, which could well have produced a much better result for you. Second, because it denies you the opportunity to consider alternative paths when they appear that may enable you to more easily reach your goals in life, and for you to be able to "actualize" your own existence. That should become your primary goal in life.

Group thinking creates "blind spots" that cause you to miss opportunities you would otherwise be able to see. There are so many alternative ways that we can look at our life. Many other paths could make much more of this life for you. You could have them, if you could see them. You owe it to yourself to explore all paths, creating a scotoma blocking those opportunities really does not make sense. For those that really do find a life hereafter, you will not lose that, you will simply have both. Read on and see what all of this really means to you.

Fully Human / Fully Alive
Introduction

Regardless of what we each might want to believe, primarily because it makes us feel better, we will face reality eventually. Many more people today than ever before realize this life is likely our only life. These people recognize there probably is not a life hereafter, regardless of what they may want to believe. We may not want to accept that. But how can you be sure they are not correct? If they are correct, that leaves one of two choices:

1. Those relying upon their unexamined beliefs can simply continue to believe by "blind faith" and continue life as before this question was considered. After all, if we held these beliefs since childhood, why should we believe otherwise now? However, if people who have set aside the notion of an afterlife are correct, those of us who have been relying on a future in Heaven may easily miss living our life to its fullest while we are here on Earth. What a sad loss that would be. Do we really want that for ourselves?

2. We can consider the possibility that they may be correct. Why? It is because there is absolutely no credible evidence that an afterlife exists. When we really consider that belief, we may soon realize that if this is our only life we know for certain we do have, we had better make the most we can out of what remains in this life. Time is fleeting.

Which decision makes the most sense to you? Faced with the question, if there is the slightest possibility that they may be right, we better hurry. Our own lives are passing by each day.

If you agree to try and improve the quality of your life so that you can still fulfil the life that we know that we do have, read on. The point of this book is to help you find your own path so you may "**actualize your own life**." That simply means that your life will be the best if you understand how to get the very most you can out of this life on Earth. You are entitled to the opportunity to make the very most out of your own life. No one can do that for you. To get there you must reach for the highest level of living that you are able to achieve, using the resources available to you to their fullest potential. Those of us who choose to pursue that opportunity, if there is no life hereafter, at the very least, will not miss making the most of our own life that we can achieve while we are here on Earth. You can start that journey today. This book will show you what the path to actualize your own life really means.

In addition, looking at your life from this perspective, you may have the added benefit of contributing meaningful good for others. The good work that you can provide that you would not have even thought about before reading this book can enhance the lives of others long after you are gone. The works of Michelangelo and Leonardo DaVinci are just as important today as they were over 500 years ago. Doing good that lasts for others is a form of acquiring your own immortality that lives on after you that we know really does exist. More importantly, you will not have wasted the only life we are certain that we are able to live in the hope for some life hereafter that may not even be there. Where did the notion that there is a life after our death come from in the first place? We at least owe it to ourselves to try and find this out. This book will help you do that.

Even though it does not require deep thinking to recognize that this may be the right thing for you to do, some people will still take their current path—so sure that they are right—since it appears to be the easiest path for them. So why bother to change? The easy answer is that some people are willing to follow the lead of anybody whose language is consistent with what they were taught in their early childhood before they had the ability to reason for themselves. They do this solely for emotional reasons, not for logical reasons. Simply put, they are willing to allow their life to be controlled by others, Is that you?

It is okay to be content to follow such a path without analyzing it. However, if you read on, you will discover those beliefs for these people persist because they were caused by a scatoma. Scatomas are blind spots in one's mental vision of the world. As a bare Minimum, it is important that you understand that concept if you want to make the very most out of your own life. Most people who give this much thought agree that they want to be able to accomplish all that they can in the time that we have left to live. This starts with your thinking about your unexamined beliefs that were originated in you by others. You can take control of your own life starting today, so that you can truly live your own life, and not theirs. Those people who are controlling your beliefs are probably already dead. Humanists, like most of us, do not like to be viewed as sheep, and we are willing to take extra care to avoid such a control being imposed on us by others. Unless you understand how this occurs, most of our scatomas happen without our own knowledge that we are being controlled. Humanists object to being controlled without our consent because we want control of our own lives. We want to be able to think for ourselves, and to live our own lives. We especially want to be able to make an informed decision about whether we are willing to accept someone else's beliefs as our own.

Sheep continue down their current path because it feels safe, and so they willingly accept that they are being controlled. They are not concerned about being controlled because they no longer want to have to think for themselves. Since they have "faith" in their Control People, they simply are not going to worry about it. That is OK if fully living their own life is not important to them. However, I do get concerned with those members of the clergy who impose our beliefs on us demanding that we accept what they tell us by "blind faith." To merely accept something by faith means that you give up control. As an example, the notion of a life after death being imposed upon you by a Control Person using fear of damnation as their means to maintain their control over you is simply wrong. In effect, these clergy are stealing the potential life of those who are so naive. They do so for them to be able to continue to control their sheep. However, at least for me, it is unacceptable to do so by creating fear, instead of by helping each of us grow through constructive education based solely upon truth that we can verify.

Instead of allowing others to have any control over you that limits your life, the better question for you should be "What will create the very best life for me?" Those providing their control solely for your own good you can choose to accept, just like you do with selecting most of your doctors.

Those who want to control you to bolster their own position or welfare may not be willing to tell you how to achieve the best life. Why should they? Many of those people like having their blind followers. Are you one of their followers? Some of those "Control People" have the nerve to tell you that you are their "Sheep", and they are your shepherd "tending to their flock." Why would you even tolerate that? Is it because they claim they know more than you do? Are you so sure they are right? Did you ever ask, "Why do they do that?" Let us find out why together.

At the same time, let us also learn why we need some Control People. In doing so we need to distinguish those providing us with actual good that we should accept from those attempting to control us who abuse the power we have allowed them to maintain their control. We need to be able to discern the difference so that we only accept those Control People we know really do have our best interests in their endeavors to help guide our lives and stop those who are most interested in keeping you in their fold for you to support them. Most of us have never thought of that distinction before. Why are you told that "you must tithe?" Remember, it is not God that is spending your money.

Reading this book will also help you to understand why people have many of the beliefs that they have, and how those beliefs regulate our lives. We should consider where all our beliefs come from, and, if they are for more than a momentary purpose, we should understand why they were accepted by us. Testing why you might believe in a life after your death will help you become aware of where you may be being controlled. If you defend that belief against evidence to the contrary that will help you understand how a scatoma is blocking any conflicting information. As previously said, we each need to consider all alternative paths available to us by building bridges over our scatomas for us to be able to live our own life to its fullest.

If there is a life hereafter, the people who have actualized their own existence could benefit even more. If there is not a life hereafter, those who have actualized their lives will not have lost fully living the only life we know does exist because they will have made the very most out of it. This book will assist you in making the most of your own life—as you wish to live it. There is not one simple answer for fully living life available for all of us. We each get to make and enjoy our very own lives. But to do that, we must first understand the forces that influence what we do believe.

People will find their answers for fulfilling their own lives in a thousand different ways. Some living on the security low social level will feel that taking what they want from others will provide them with more. But will it in the long run? Do we really want to be remembered as someone who takes from other people in ways that may harm them? There are those who became famous doing that. Bugsy Siegel, John Dillinger, Bonnie and Clyde, and Al Capone were some of those who took what they wanted from others. But consider their life of continual fear. Because they were constantly at risk of being caught, or killed, they lived on a security level for their existence. In this book, you will discover what our levels of living really mean. Those whose behavior is controlled by fear are living their life just like these people. Do you really want that for yourself?

What will produce the highest quality of life for each of us, starting today? In the long run, what really matters the most to us? Is it power, wealth, or fame? Once we die, will we still have any of those to enjoy? Is that goal worth the effort? Are people who attain these goals truly happy with what they have, or do they only seek more to quench an insatiable thirst?

What is the purpose of our own life? Is our life ordained by some supernatural force that controls us like a puppet? Or are we all alone with nine billion other people, living our lives together on a small planet in a universe with billions of other planets? That is what the facts show, so what does this mean for us?

Is there a god that created this universe? There may be, but why would any god even want to control each of our individual lives? What would be the point? Is that God playing a game with us? Even though that notion sounds indefensible, some people still believe that. Or is that notion also only a control device preached by those who want to control us?

For people who really need to believe in seeking direction from God, believing that following God's will is their purpose in life, that belief needs to be fully understood if you are going to be able to have control of your own life. Otherwise, you will be living someone else's life. You need to understand what value does that belief really add to your life? The real question is who controls what you believe God is saying to you? People who have been hypnotized do the will of the person who has hypnotized them. Many times, their behavior is not something they would ever do on their own. They are willingly being controlled by someone else. Why do you think that is not happening to you? The hypnotized person still feels in control. But are they? While they are under the Hypnotist's control, they have no clue that their behavior is being controlled by someone else.

Similarly, the person putting all their faith in God to guide them in everything that they do makes some believers feel safe. This is because they do not have to think for themself. It requires energy to seek out answers. But where do the answers from God really come from? Are others filling those needs for them? Or are their prayers introspection allowing them to become in tune with their inner self, just like what we can accomplish through meditation? Many times, when we are faced with conflicting alternatives, and we let the matter sit for a day we will wake up the next morning with our answer. That is because the conflict within us corrects itself when the surrounding clutter fades away, and the solution becomes apparent. If that is what is happening, then it is you in charge. That is appropriate, and acceptable.

If you feel the need to seek others guidance, that too may be alright if you retain the right to alter or modify what you are told rather than blindly accepting it. If you fear not doing what they tell you, you may have become blind because of your "faith". Your problem is that you have given control of your life to others. Why would you do that? For a large portion of our society today, questions related to the meaning of our lives and the interpretation of what is important are answered by other people. By blindly accepting what you are told you have given control of your life to them. Those who do that really are living a sheep's life. There is nothing wrong with any belief if you put it in its proper perspective. The wrong comes from allowing a belief to block your ability to grow. To become the very best person that you can be during your short lifetime you should not blindly accept what someone else tells you without testing its veracity. That other person sets your goals. Only you know what you really need to accomplish your goals. So why give that power to another person?

Acceptance of other's beliefs without question takes the responsibility for living our own lives away from those who could otherwise choose their own more fulfilling path. The Point of this book is to not let that happen to you. An uninformed life can be a wasted one. That would be so sad, when there are so many better alternatives available to you if you only accept living your own life while you are here on Earth to become the very most that you can become.

This book will consider, in some depth, an overview of life based upon truth and reality, and will show you how not to let yourself rely upon blind faith imposed by others. The goal is to provide a means for each of us to find our own path to actualize our own existence to the fullest for ourselves, in whatever circumstances we may find ourselves. This is true for everyone. Even if the Control Person is your personal doctor, you should still fully understand the advice you receive and the alternatives that are available to you before you merely accept any advice that affects your life more than momentarily.

Even those incarcerated for life can still live a good life for themselves. I have proven, by creating Humanist Chapters in Iowa's maximum-security penitentiary and another in a midlevel prison, which add significant value to the inmates' lives who are members by changing their focus from feeling society has abandoned them, to seeking means for adding value to their own lives through their own endeavors. These Chapters have given the inmates purpose for living even in those circumstances.

One humanist prison Chapter agreed to first clean up their own cell blocks and to start a recycling program for their penitentiary. Their initiative was a meaningful start. It proved to them that what I am saying is true: you can live a higher quality and purposeful life even in limited circumstances. The resulting change in their attitude really impressed their warden. It only requires a little effort to make a real difference in your own life. And it all starts with a positive attitude.

We all start with only the ability to live our own life. Everyone's slate is clean. We are each entitled to live our own life to the fullest, with whatever resources we currently have available. In the United States, we have the freedom to do that. Many other countries deny their citizens that possibility.

"Money cannot buy happiness" is often quoted, but seldom believed. If you do not currently feel that you have what you consider to be enough, I bet that you believe you would be a lot happier if you had more. Life does not come with a guarantee of happiness. But that has never deterred anyone from feeling entitled to it. The real point is that happiness is only a state of the mind. Let us find out together. How do I manage this state of mind so that I can be truly happy?

Lester and Rosemary ("Maria") Mondale were good friends of mine. Lester retired as a Unitarian minister, having been the youngest of thirty-four people who first identified the notion that we are solely responsible for ourselves—originally recognized in the ancient Greek Epicurean philosophy in a modern context that we now call "humanism." They published their view in the first Humanist Manifesto in 1933. That document described the philosophy of John Dietrich, a Unitarian minister who had been considering the view of Epicurus since the first decade of the twentieth century. Lester Mondale was born in Minnesota, and served as a Unitarian minister in Evanston, Illinois. You may have heard the name "Mondale" before. Lester's younger brother, Walter Mondale, became the Vice President of the United States.

Following their retirement, Lester and Maria lived on eighty acres of wooded Ozark hills in southeast Missouri. They named their little bit of heaven on Earth 'Copperhead Cliffs." There was a good reason for that name: I met a copperhead snake slithering under their kitchen wooden stove. They also accepted it as their houseguest. They lived daily with nature.

A creek ran through their property and ponded three times, the largest having an eight-foot cliff on one side that they could easily dive off into their pond, and a fifteen-foot cliff across that pond upon which Native American Indians used for council fires where they could see their Surroundings to best protect themselves. This creek ended in a small river that crossed within the Mondale property where beavers had built a dam that created an eight-acre lake the Mondale's originally stocked and were then able to fish in their canoe.

The woods were dense, but they built trails, and cleared three separated one-acre areas where they raised most of the food that they canned and were then able to eat throughout the whole next year. Lester was still cutting down trees for firewood for their kitchen stove to warm their log cabin at age ninety-eight. They were able to live a very happy and peaceful life on fifty percent of their social security. They wanted nothing and needed little. That was because they were truly in tune with nature.

The Mondale's prove that it does not take great wealth to be happy. It only takes being in tune with yourself and your environment. Let us find out how to do that for ourselves.

Chapter One

What is Humanism?

For those in the Western world, Michelangelo arguably created the very first historic symbol of humanism. He carved "the David" out of marble between 1501 and 1504. This statue was commissioned as a symbol of the Epicurean philosophy adopted for the city-state of Florence, Italy. This philosophy was Introduced by the Medici family who were very wealthy Italian banker-statesmen and the de facto leaders of the City-State of the Florentine Republic. They had no King ruling over their people. They elected their own "mayor" to manage their Province.

Even though Catholic priests in Florence still exercised power, the control of their society came from the people. Even though they were in the fifteenth century, they were not ruled by God. That was very unusual in those days.

The people living in the Provence around Florence participated in electing who ran the government subject to the policies being set by a governing council. This was a noteworthy contrast to those living throughout Europe under the control of kings. A king's power was the result of being "anointed by God" through their priests who generally ruled throughout the rest of Europe in those days. In contrast to a democracy where the will of the people prevailed, kings had absolute power which came solely from God, not from the consent of the people. Since power to rule coming from God was an accepted cultural belief in that era, it was seldom challenged. Many Europeans were taught from early childhood that God controls us, so any leader the priest anointed had the exclusive right to serve. It took courage to challenge God. After all, those that did faced death.

Our United States Constitution was an early test for a country of our size of the concept that the power to rule comes from the people, rather than the right to rule descending upon us from God. Most people in the world, even today, do not have significant control over their own life, let alone their government. Americans are very fortunate for us as individuals to have some degree of influence.

The people of the region controlled by Florence were economically supported primarily by the Medici family. They were very powerful and became enthusiastic patrons of Renaissance culture. The Renaissance was their revival of intellectual thought that brought Western civilization out of a period where the Roman Catholic Church had controlled human existence in Europe for over a thousand years, many times burning at the stake those who challenged the beliefs of "the Church," even if that belief has no foundation. The Catholic Church may no longer kill their opponents, but they still have a very strong influence for what over one half of the Christian population in the world believes today. Some congregants are still perceived as mere sheep. We earlier questioned why do people put up with that existence? Let us find out why together.

The notion that our lives were controlled daily by Gods was the common public belief, as it had been for tens of thousands of years. The public just did not all agree upon which God. But not everyone adhered to these beliefs, As understanding of the natural sciences slowly advanced, supernaturalism began to lose its grip. During the fifth century BCE, Leucippus did not believe that people were molded out of clay in God's image as was the current view of most people in Athens. Leucippus felt that we were made of indestructible tiny particles. He believed that these particles would exist forever, even if we did not.

Democritus, born in 460 BCE, labeled and described the particles that Leucippus postulated. He was the first person to believe everything is composed of atoms, which were thought to be physically indivisible Particles. He reasoned that the world of atoms looks like the stars in our universe. Between atoms, there lies empty space. He also believed that atoms are indestructible and have always been—and always will be—in motion. He reasoned that there is an infinite number and many kinds of atoms, which differ in shape and size. Democritus view remains very close to that of our science today. The concept originated from the development of philosophy, not through science, as a scientific method of developing our truths did not effectively exist until more recently.

Epicurus (341 to 270 BCE) came along a hundred years later and intellectually carried the emancipation of humans from the control of their gods to a logical conclusion. He felt we were not each controlled by a "Supernatural" God for which there was no credible evidence even existed. Although vocal atheists periodically surfaced back then, most people believed God, or gods, existed because other people told them so. Few people in those days ever questioned someone who claimed authority. That made no sense. But the public can be gullible, or at least ignorant, on any given subject. Many people are sheeplike, allowing themselves to follow rather than tackle the hard questions of our origin and destiny. This is still true today.

Epicurus was one of the first who rose above the uninformed masses realizing that we are each solely responsible for ourselves. He felt life was about pursuing pleasure and avoiding pain. Furthermore, he said that he saw no reason to assume that there is any life after our death. Epicurus realized that belief is only a delusion that keeps us from taking responsibility for our own lives. Epicurus offered a contrast to the prevailing culturally accepted view of the Control People of his day who felt their control was necessary to maintain an organized society. That dichotomy still exists today. It was not long, however, before the generally accepted public view prevailed, and the alternative voice of Epicurus was lost to the public.

Most members of the clergy honestly believe they are providing their followers their best by being their shepherd. Epicurus simply could not accept such a simplistic belief. He saw no valid reason for needing a shepherd for a question so important for him to understand why he is here on Earth. He felt that any God who could create the universe would only be in the background watching to see his world as it actually existed. The belief that God would exercise control over his creation would mean our individual lives mean nothing. We would be mere puppets. Instead, Epicurus thought that if our lives are to mean anything, we must accept that we are here all alone. It is up to us to accept the responsibility for our own lives. Therefore, Epicurus concluded you had better make the very most of this life while you are here on Earth, because if there is not another life hereafter, making your own life significant to others is the only way for your own life to really mean anything.

Many people today agree with Epicurus. But many of those today who hold that view have only rediscovered this philosophy in the very recent past. Why is that so? It is because this belief conflicts with those Control People who still today want you to believe there is a life after death, and that only they hold your ticket for you to get there. We have pointed out that notion is a control device created by humans, but what perpetuates that belief are those who were told that early in their life. Since they accepted it before they had the ability to reason for themselves, most will not question that belief for their entire lifetime. It stays entrenched because most people really want to believe it. That belief is accepted for emotional reasons, by those not looking at that issue from the view of logic and verifiable truth. They remain in "La La Land" of their childhood, because it feels safe for them.

When you really consider that issue, ask yourself: Why would any God that really had created all people alive today deny access to heaven to those of a different religion, especially if those in question never were exposed to the "true" religion? Can you now see how religious exclusivity is only a device to control you? Do you really believe any God capable of creating life on Earth would have any good reason for doing that? Or is that a simply means for Control People for them controlling you?

Even though there is absolutely no evidence justifying that belief of exclusivity, and even though there is no valid doubt that such beliefs are used as control devices, true believers relying upon their own "blind faith" cannot see that. This is also a pretty good test for you of whether your beliefs are being controlled. If you feel the urge to defend that belief, that is pretty good evidence that your own narrow fixed beliefs have hardened into a "scatoma." Remember that scatomas are mental blocks, acting like spam blockers, fervently preventing any other belief from being considered, let alone accepted by you. Why is that so? This book will help you answer that for yourself.

First you need to understand that you cannot hit a Scotoma head on. These are security level beliefs and hitting them head on produces an angry reaction. You need to build a bridge around it through logical education showing you the alternative paths to that belief. One will become acceptable for you and even though the scatoma does not go away, it is just no longer controlling you. Much like the path around a barricade in the road no longer stops you from proceeding down the road. That is a major purpose for a college education. It forces you to think beyond your defense mechanisms.

As awareness of nature and an understanding of the scientific approach for discovering knowledge advanced, supernatural answers were frequently modified just enough to allow for the science, thus rendering conflict between religion and science on that matter making it, for the moment, a non-issue. That is how all memes work until they ultimately become irrelevant. Consider the challenge of Galileo by the Catholic Church. It took several hundred years before the Church finally acknowledged that the Earth actually revolves around the Sun.

Such supernatural beliefs expressed by Control People of fundamentalist faiths today are becoming as archaic as the idea that the Earth is flat, and if we approach the edge, we risk falling off. Those accepting that view of their life are not aware of how out of touch their blind faith really is today. They are blinded by their scatomas put in place by strong influential Control People. Their scatoma keeps them from seeing beyond those beliefs. Hopefully, their grandchildren will be able to grow out of their grandparents' outdated dogma.

For many faith beliefs, our religious views are woven into our identities before the age where we have developed the ability to reason for ourselves. Many people cannot escape from that view during their life because they fear that the Control People who imposed those beliefs on them may be right, and no other alternative offers that same level of security. If the promise of a good life hereafter is not enough to control you, those people also invented "hell." The combination of reward and punishment used effectively by Control People is potent. "If I do not believe by blind faith, I will go to hell." This belief is one of the strongest social tools to control naive people remaining in existence today. Charles Darwin said that "Hell is the most damnable belief imposed on mankind." Which view is right: Darwin's view, or the view of the Control People? What difference does that make in how we live our own lives? It makes a very big difference. This issue merits our own consideration. After all, as you have heard many times, our life today may well be the only life for us to live.

If Epicurus is right, we will have wasted our own lives if we do not live it to the fullest while we are here. How do we do that? We know that we are Fully Human. Yet do we really know how we become Fully Alive? Can we do that and still hold on to our wish for a life hereafter? Of course! But these questions merit further thought for those willing to improve the quality of their own life.

I am not saying you cannot hold on to any belief for whatever reason is important to you. If it gives you comfort, why should anyone tell you that you are wrong? You can hold onto that belief and still make the most of your life while you are here. Making the very most of this life is important, so that you will not have missed fully living your life no matter what beliefs you choose to accept, including the possibility of having a life hereafter. If you do not allow the wish for a life hereafter to control your life on Earth, there is no reason that you cannot hold on to that belief. Then it will not interfere with you living your life on Earth to the fullest that you can achieve. Each of us will arrive at our own conclusions; and no one should really care which path appeals to you. However, those who hang onto that belief, causing them to neglect to make the very most of this life, will lose either way. That makes little intelligent sense for many more people today.

Since the purpose of this book is to help you gain the very most that you can from the only life that we know for certain that we have, let us consider that if Epicurus is correct, and you also meet what you feel is required for you to qualify for a life hereafter, you will have gotten the most from life that you can. To accomplish that you must have control of your own life so that you can grow to the highest level of living as described by psychologist, Abraham Maslow, that you can obtain for yourself. The problem then is that you cannot get there if someone else is in control of what you believe, If you allow others to control what you believe, you will be living their life and not your own, You must be in control of your own life for you to be able to choose your own path if you are to be able to grow as you deem appropriate. To fulfill your own existence, you need to achieve your level of living that actualizes your own life for you to be able to make the most that you can out living your own life today. No one else can do it for you. Let us read on to find out what all of that really means for you.

If the Control People who are influencing your life are correct, you will still have gained more in your life, especially to the degree your life has become significant for those who live better lives because you were here. Even if the Control People are not honest in their approach but are merely controlling you as a means of creating the social glue that allows us to successfully live together, this book will not destroy those beliefs. This book aims to enlarge your view of the reality in which you live.

And, hopefully, you will not have missed truly living the only life we really do know for sure exists. The problem is a matter of who is in control of your life, not a matter of what you might choose to believe.

Those feeling their religious control of people was threatened by Epicurus, attempted to discredit him by claiming that he was "a hedonist." They said Epicurus claimed our goal was "to eat, drink, and be merry, for tomorrow you will die"—and because without a life hereafter, there obviously is no "hell" to punish you for your sins. Those threatened by that view also claimed Epicurus was saying that "you can freely sin all you want to sin." Epicurus was a hedonist in the literal sense of the word, but his beliefs were the exact opposite of those attempting to discredit him. He believed living your life fully in tune with your own environment. *For Epicurus, the good life was "to want nothing, and to need little, and to fully experience each moment."* He also believed that to the extent that your life was guided by lust or a goal of over-indulging in anything, you were led by your own needs and wants, instead of allowing your life to be guided by your environment. The good life was the life that fully enjoyed or appreciated each moment to its fullest, without seeking anything. His distractors looked at life from the wrong perspective. Epicurus would not want to have anything to do with the people they described.

Like the life of Lester and Maria Mondale, the simple life produces the most happiness, because you have no need driving you to acquire anything. You simply enjoyed everything to the fullest that is around you, whatever there was available for you to then enjoy, like a beautiful sunset. Epicurus believed that you must take control of your own life. For Epicurus, the gods were not controlling you; they were merely in the background watching. They are merely hoping that you will get the very most of the life that they gave you. They will not help you get there; you must accomplish that on your own.

Because of the overwhelming beliefs in the many gods thought to be controlling the people of Athens in the fourth century BCE, their cultural meme overtook the philosophy of humanism expressed by Epicurus and the belief of Epicurus diminished in Europe. Fortunately, it was immortalized in an epic poem by Titus Lucretius Carus, who was a Roman poet and philosopher, living around 100 BCE. His only known written work is the didactic philosophical poem, *De Rerum Natura*, about science which included the tenets and philosophy of Epicureanism, which is usually translated into English as "On the Nature of Things."

Lucretius was far more provocative than Epicurus. He claimed Epicurean philosophy turns religion on its head. His interpretation was that it exalts human existence and tramples religion. He believed that for all of eternity after our death, we simply will not exist. Only the effect of our life here on Earth remains after us, and therefore creates our only immortality. If we want to make the most of this life, we must seek our own happiness while we are here. However, close to Epicurus's belief, Lucretius claimed the only impediment to our happiness is desire. We have the exclusive power to control our own desires. This power is dependent upon our having free will to make our own choices.

If it had not been for Lucretius, we might not have known of the Epicurean philosophy even today. We, too, could still be living in the past, fearing for our very lives if we disagreed with the Control People within the Church that still dominates the lives of billions of people living today. Some might even feel that kind of life is analogous today to that described by George Orwell's *Nineteen Eighty-Four*.

Lucretius' poem lay dormant for 1,500 years in a German Monastery until it was discovered by Peggio Bracciolini, who was a classmate and friend of Cosmo Medici. He was an avid searcher for ancient manuscripts. He was from the city-state of Florence in northern Italy. He sold the manuscript to Cosmos Medici in the very early part of the fifteenth century ACE. Cosmo asked Nicol Medici, who was Secretary to the Pope, to translate Lucretius' poem from Greek into the Tuscan Italian language rather than Latin, which was the language of religion used by the Church for everything else that he translated.

The Medici family read, and the people of Florence adopted, the Epicurean philosophy as the philosophical approach for the lives of those living in their region of influence surrounding the city-state of Florence. This poem, and the philosophy of life it described, caused the Renaissance to occur that embraced the arts and improved the culture, and they adopted the Epicurean philosophy for Providing individual freedom. The culture around Florence flourished, and out of that came the important works of Michelangelo and Leonardo DaVinci, among others.

The Church controlled the prevalent Western cultural belief of that day, as it had for well over 1,200 years prior. Many theists embraced the cultural change the Renaissance ushered in, although they muddied the waters for what was otherwise a significant contrast to their accepted beliefs that preceded it. Nevertheless, the Epicurean view of life challenged the current philosophy of life, which had become a cultural meme accepted by most people living throughout Medieval Europe. It was more than a challenge; it sparked a brushfire. The Floridians' adoption of the Epicurean view of life in the Chianti region of Italy had initiated the Renaissance period that brought Western civilization out of the dark ages dominated by strict control of the Roman Catholic Church spread throughout much of Europe.

Michelangelo lived in Florence and served the Pope in the Vatican in Rome. The Church and the Medici were his primary patrons. For the Church he was asked to design the dome of St. Peters Basilica, and then to paint the ceiling and the alter wall of the Sistine Chapel. I have often wondered how many Catholics today realized those and the marble sculpture of the Virgin Mary and Child statute sitting in the sanctuary of St Peters in the Vatican, were created by a Humanist?

Although he was very religious, he was greatly influenced by the Medici philosophy of life. When Michelangelo was asked to make a sculpture representing the Epicurean philosophy of Florence that created the renaissance, Michelangelo chose a discarded piece of white marble that was quarried nearby—a little over seventeen feet long and about five feet square. It was sold at a discount because a corner of the block had been broken off by another artist. Since it had a defect Michelangelo got it for a bargain price. He did not complain even though he then had to carve "The David" diagonally through his block of marble.

Since the Epicurean philosophy recognized each individual, instead of a god, as the center of "the nature of things." Michelangelo decided

King David was the best representation of man conquering his own life, instead of humans being controlled by God. Michelangelo's statue was ultimately placed in the courtyard next to the offices of the government (now the Uffizi Art Gallery). Connecting this building to the offices and palace of the Medici was the world's first skywalk. Running over a mile long, it crossed over the Arno river through the Ponte Vecchio Bridge, two stories above the public way on the bridge through the community meat markets, then located on the ground floor of the bridge where merchants could dispose of their waste in the river's waters, while those passing on the floor two stories above walked safely to the Medici residence. Today the Ponte Vecchio houses the gold merchants, since the Medici finally dictated that the meat markets must move because of the smell of rotting meat the market produced had reached the top level of the bridge.

As a result of this new freedom to challenge the Church, the cultural climate changed and resulted in the Protestant Reformation. The expansion of an alternative to the strict control of the Church caught on rapidly in Western Europe. This freedom from the fear of the Inquisitions, and their threat of death by the Church that previously had prevailed throughout Europe was a breath of spring for the public. Thus, Martin Luther felt free to post his Ninety-Five Theses to the door of All Saints' Catholic Church in Wittenberg, Germany, objecting to some of the canons of the Church. That resulted in the Protestant Reformation when Luther and his followers were excommunicated from the Catholic Church. Their solution was to create their own church. But that only changed who ruled the religion that ruled the people. The masses were still being told by Control People what they must believe. Protestants were still within the Christian faith. Those People just have a different set of clergy and order of service.

Those who adopted the Epicurean Philosophy of life lived as humanists, free of external control of their life for about two centuries before the cultural belief memes, created by the Church, again overtook control of public beliefs. Ignorance and blind faith once again for the third time, influenced the public to predominantly accept the traditional cultural belief that God ruled the life of each person. Those with that belief also accepted that the Church spoke for God. Priests were back in control of life in the region, although many of their controlled people were now labeled "Protestants."

The Printing press, which was invented close to the end of the fifteenth century, mass produced the Bible. And for the first time, the masses of the public were able to read the Bible for themselves. This reduced the perceived necessary role that the Priests had filled for 1,500 years.

Now it was harder for them to claim they were the public's interceder with God, since the Public soon learned to read, and they could then interpret the Bible for themselves. Now there were also many faiths aiming to fill that role. Combined with the effect of the Renaissance causing the public to have a sense of control over their own lives, the power of the Catholic Church now shared the stage with Protestants, so that their control of religion was significantly reduced. However, the meme creating the cultural belief of the public in God, of whatever form, was so strong that the public belief merely readjusted how this God was expressed in a more modern form that still exists today.

Leonardo de Vinci, twenty-two years older than Michelangelo, also lived in the Florentine Republic. He painted *The Last Supper*, which is well known today. Leonardo was a much stronger humanist than Michelangelo. In fact, Leonardo became a leader among those with the more liberal humanistic view of life, suggesting that we all need to make the most of our life here on Earth today, because that easily could be all that there is for us to enjoy. Leonardo became one of the most famous artists, scientists, and forward thinkers of his day. His work is still revered today, even by those within the Catholic faith. Leonardo and Michelangelo have both become immortal. Their lives still affect all of us today more than 500 years after they died. That is a significant immortality, even though nothing more exists for them as individuals.

However, the shifting power and new uncertainties allowed many people to emerge to contribute to the public's alternative views of religion. In addition to Martin Luther, another person with significant influence was Erasmus. He felt compelled to challenge the organized Church. He was trained as a Catholic priest but ultimately became a Dutch Christian Humanist whose extensive writings significantly influenced the Renaissance that altered the extensive control previously existing for the Church. Even though he challenged the thinking of the Church, he did so within religion.

Although the Church's control that had prevailed for more than a millennium, dictating what we each person must believe diminished, it was merely shared with other religious faiths, some even exceeded the Church's bold hold on the lives of their sheep. Before you feel pious and above the fray, we were not immune in the United States. In more "modern" times we had the Salem witch hunt, which showed, even in the "land of the free," the power for false beliefs to hurt people had not gone away. Many cultural beliefs, even today, are still quite primitive.

Church control over what we must believe was so strong that it easily overwhelmed the change in view adopted in Florence that contributed to the Renaissance. The historic memory of the masses throughout the rest of Italy had been well cemented in their previous culture, especially after it had been reinforced by the Church's threats on the lives of those that denied their control. The Renaissance did cause the Church to modify its control techniques, but it did not eliminate its dominance in the lives of most people living in other Christian regions of Europe, and soon would be introduced to the Americas as a part of our culture. Today, you are merely told that if you do not believe "You are going to hell," but the Church no longer helps you get there like they did by burning disbelievers at the stake.

The Renaissance merely reduced the power of the Church and nudged the Church toward a more liberal view of life. Like all memes, the Church simply adapted to the change in the cultural view. Therefore, the Church's control survived. And those who adopted the Epicurean philosophy faded from prominent existence affecting cultural change for a third time, but it had made a difference. Fortunately, the societal advancement that came with enlightenment also brought with it the study of science in the eighteenth century.

It expanded the public's awareness of the benefit of knowledge and philosophy. Knowledge and truth became popular. However, even that climate did not last. Many people today recognize that the masses of the public can be gullible and are uninformed, if not ignorant, on almost any given subject. Our own society still determines what people "ought to believe".

Even with this Momentum, the Epicurean philosophy of life did not have enough strength to overcome the publicly accepted meme of Christianity that, after generations of growth, now had acquired producing an independent life of its own. There is no question that religion had become a meme, adapting with change in our culture of that day. We will learn in this book what the effect of memes truly has upon our beliefs.

With all the religious turmoil existing at that time, Epicureanism did not have sufficient strength to sustain itself. Thus, the predominant cultural religious beliefs of the Church that have existed for over 2,000 years have remained predominant up to our modern time.

This book does not intend to tell you that you must give up your religious beliefs. Your personal religion provides the symbols that you have learned from early childhood and includes emotional ties that bind you. Logic cannot easily replace deeply felt beliefs that we acquired before our age of reason, since those acquired in our early childhood are accepted for emotional, and not logical reasons based on provable facts.

Many people use symbols to express themselves in ways that we currently have no other better means of addressing. Religion fills the lower levels of security needs for most people. The goal of humanism is to provide an approach for maximizing your life here on Earth. It has no need for a life hereafter. There are Humanists today that may believe in a hereafter to fulfill their objective of maximizing our life while we are here on Earth. If that really adds value to your life, that should be up to you. Humanism means not giving up the right to control your own life, and the ability to live your own life to the fullest that you can achieve. The concern for Humanists with religion is when it causes scatomas that interferes with its members ability to actualize their own lives.

Humanism does not tell you that you cannot believe whatever you chose to believe. It is your own life for you to live as you want to live. Our concern is with religious Control People who feel threatened when you think for yourself. Especially if they use fear or guilt as tools to maintain their control over you. Humanism's goal is to show you how to make the very most of your life on Earth as you want to live it. To do that you have to be able to make your own informed decisions without blindly accepting what others tell you. Do not let them deny you the chance to validate their truth for yourself if their belief is to be accepted by you more than momentarily. The edict that you must "have faith" creates a barrier many can never overcome.

Many people can place their religion on top of the humanist philosophy of life because most religion focuses on a life hereafter, and only marginally on how we live our life here on Earth. The path to get to heaven is what the Church claims to provide if you really want to achieve an afterlife existence. No humanist should object if that is important to any person. But most humanists find no reason for them to accept such a belief in the first place, since there is no valid evidence that it exists— let alone the commitment of time required if you do want to accept that belief, and therefore must follow the prescribed path of your Control Person they claim is necessary for you to get to Heaven. Humanists believe only what they can accept as true for themselves. How we determine what is true for ourselves is a subject we must now address.

One point of this book is whether you can realize what is happening to you that denies you the ability to live your own life to its fullest because you are willing to be led. As a result, you are willing to rely upon Control People's beliefs without verification. The issue becomes whether you wish to maintain control over your own life. No one has probably asked that question of you before, but how you do answer that question can change your life. If you want to fully control your own life, it will free you to become the best person that you can become. And it will save you from wasting your time that creates barriers for you if you wish to create a path of your own.

Many people older than Millennials no longer find a need to control their own beliefs because of their own socially developed "scatomas" have hardened into cement, and the fact that they have become comfortable in their own limited niche in life. Therefore, many take the stance, "Do not tell me that I am wrong, as I really do not want to believe you." If you are a content sheep, this book is not for you. Pass this on to someone who is younger, a person more open-minded. This book is intended for the people who, like Epicurus, believe that everyone should take control of their own life.

Even more important is learning how to maximize the only life that we know for certain does exist. If you are one of these people, this book will tell you how you too can accomplish that goal so that you can actualize your own existence.

Chapter Two

The Philosophy of Humanism Today

Knowledge and awareness of reality in any depth requires life-long experience, or a higher level of education, often unavailable or beyond the reach of the medieval public in the past, as many were unable to read. Most people who had the ability to read in our earlier history were monks and priests who worked within the Church. Humanist philosophy was again subverted a third time, this time for close to 500 years. Remember it was not until 1440, when Johannes Gutenberg invented the printing press using moveable type making books more available to the public, that people could learn to read. Gutenberg's creation would change the entire religious playing field in the future as the public could for the first time, read the Bible for themselves.

Epicurean philosophy re-surfaced formally in America during the first decade of the 1900's, initially with a Unitarian minister living west of the Mississippi River. At that time, those who moved west had to be self-reliant to survive. By then, for most people living east of the Mississippi, cultural civilization had developed to a point that society provided the answers to most issues for a majority of the public, and "Group Think" significantly controlled their beliefs. People living east of the Mississippi no longer really needed to think for themselves, if they were willing to accept what society believed. Because all necessary knowledge for the public was within religious institutions and cultural memes, life did not require an individual to think for themselves.

People who moved West had to be more self-reliant, since society was not as organized as it was in the East. The Reverend John Dietrich was an innovative thinker. He was the minister of the Unitarian Church in Spokane, Washington. That is about as far west as you could then get in the continental United States. Dietrich rediscovered the concept that "man is the center of his own human life, and we are not controlled by any "god." This is the same philosophy first interpreted in recorded history by Epicurus. Dietrich preached this concept of personal autonomy in his sermons for several years before he was called to move on to another congregation in his career, typical for clergy. Rev. Dietrich became the minister of the First Unitarian Church in Minneapolis. He discussed his thinking with other Unitarian ministers in the Midwest. Rev. Curtis W. Reese, minister of the First Unitarian Church in Des Moines, Iowa, liked Dietrich's view of life. Reese's Unitarian congregation did not meet in the summer months of June, July, and August. Before air- conditioning, it was too hot in Iowa to want to sit in a church pew on Sundays. Besides, many living in Iowa at that time were farmers who worked seven days a week during the growing season.

Unlike most other church faiths, the Control People of the Unitarian church do not worry that they could not control you if you took a summer break. That is because in the Unitarian Church you must think for yourself. No one gives you an answer to anything that you are expected to accept as your personal belief. Its members are presented social issues to consider in their sermons, and each person needs to think of an appropriate response for themselves. Accepting anything by having "Faith" is not a requirement in most Unitarian congregations. In fact, any requirement for your believing anything by "blind faith" would generally be looked upon as insulting, and as a denial of the intelligence of its members. Those in the Des Moines Unitarian Church who were there were seeking knowledge, not prescribed answers.

To rekindle his congregation in the first week of September, Reese's sermon had to be a "barn burner" to recapture the attention of his members. Unitarian members of his church were certainly anything but sheep. Reese shared his Proposed sermon with Dietrich, who approved, except for the title. He said the title should be something that the congregation would remember. He Suggested that Reese might call it something simple, like "Human" or "Humanism."

Thus, the first time Epicurean Philosophy was labelled "Humanism," was in Curtis Reese's sermon delivered in the Des Moines First Unitarian Church in 1917, only a little over one hundred years ago. This sermon centered on the individual being the sole decision maker in their own life, rather than a supernatural god for whom no evidence even exists, making their decisions for them. This Philosophy is what was formally defined in the *Humanist Manifesto I*, by Lester Mondale, John Dietrich, Curtis Reese and thirty-one other philosophers and ministers when it was first published as the Humanist Manifesto in 1933. Thus, this awareness of the Epicurean philosophy occurred somewhat recently, within the lifetime of some of us still living today. But changing the public's awareness of any view of reality takes time. The growth of our ideas accelerates by an algorithm, not in a straight line.

Dietrich and Reese next formed the American Humanist Association (AHA) in 1941 with its first office located in Yellow Springs, Ohio, when they appointed that community's Unitarian minister, the Reverend Edwin H. Wilson, as the AHA's first Executive Director. The AHA's first Board of Directors elected Raymond Bragg, then the current Unitarian minister for Minneapolis, as the first president of the AHA. Their purpose was to ensure that the voice of the Epicurean philosophy be heard by the public, since it had been drowned out three times before by the ancient religious dogmas of cultural faith beliefs. They wanted their great grandchildren to know that an intelligent alternative to blind faith religious beliefs was available to them which was based upon verifiable truth and reality if they would only listen. Just like it was for the people of ancient Greece 2,500 years earlier, this was a unique way of thinking about what their lives really meant for them.

Wilson began publishing a periodic newsletter entitled Free Mind, addressing those who identified with this newly resurrected philosophy of life. The AHA became "the mouse that roared." It might have been small. But from its inception, the AHA's philosophy was mighty, and it spoke the truth about reality. Wilson was still serving as an AHA board member when I became it's twelfth president thirty-eight years after its formation.

Today humanism is known around the world. My wine steward aboard a Viking River cruise ship in Russia traveling from St. Petersburg to Moscow, had taken a college course in Vladivostok, Russia, located in a far corner of our world seven time zones east of Moscow, which had taught her about humanism. That community is only about 100 miles from the Alaska islands.

In some European countries today, humanism is the predominant belief. The humanist message that originated in my Unitarian Church in Des Moines, Iowa, has been heard around the world in less than 100 years. Our cultural control of the Blind Faith beliefs still predominant in America is viewed as primitive in some parts of the western world today.

Truth should ultimately prevail if it has strong advocates who are organized until truth prevails and becomes its own cultural meme. The bully versus the altruist dichotomy we will discuss later will elucidate this. When there are only individuals advocating for truth, their belief will easily ultimately be drowned out by the much stronger religious cultural memes surrounding that person. The voice of Robert Ingersoll, a humanist who was publicly so very popular a century and a half ago, spoke this truth, but his message did not last. Thus, the formation of the AHA was a turning point for humanism. Our objective today is for its voice to be sustained so that it is heard by future generations.

Humanism attracts all sorts of intellectual people, including academics and scientists. Charles Darwin was a humanist at a time when Epicurean philosophy was not publicly recognized. He was afraid for his life when he disclosed his proof that human life evolved naturally from sea creatures, and was not uniquely created by God, so he postponed publishing until he was elderly. More recent humanists range from Albert Einstein, and Theodor Seuss Geisel (as "Dr Seuss"), to the astronomer, who created the TV series, "Cosmos", Carl Sagan, and Bill Nye 'the Science Guy", Jonas Salk, who provided a cure for polio, to Betty Friedan who brought women out of the cultural dark as second-class Citizens, and her successor, Gloria Steinem, who currently leads the National Organization of Women.

I have known most of these people personally. Those people would resent Control People who would treat us as sheep.

We are seeing in America the same personal awareness and desire for autonomy today from millennials and those who are younger. Soon, everyone who accepts the responsibility for their own life will realize it is time that people understand that those who are puppets, subject to the control of others, are no longer the majority. Humanism will have reached the point where it also becomes a meme that can no longer be eradicated from public acceptance. And the current cultural belief that religion is immune from public criticism and challenge will no longer be tolerated. Religion will have to stand up to the test of truth. Those religions adding value to their members will continue to exist. Those attempting to control their members using fear and guilt as control devices will become unpopular and wither.

Many religious Control People who felt it was important that they tend to their flock for their own survival, will have to add real value based upon significant education and recognized personal benefit for the people they serve. No longer will their flocks being told they must "tithe" by those dependent upon their gifts to sustain themselves so that they can maintain their church be tolerated. They will have to earn their right by providing their members value their members feel they really do need, instead of only being necessary for their promised reward in a life hereafter that they have no means to prove even exists.

Historically, that has not been true. Ever wonder why, in a poor community in Mexico and Central America, frequently the only show of wealth is in the Church? The Church should contribute leadership, providing opportunity to succeed for all their parishioners so that they too can participate at the same economic level to justify the Church's show of wealth.

It is now time that the older members wake up, and the cultural protection for religion previously sustaining those Control People who have been abusing their privilege will no longer protect them. You see the start of this with the Church having to deal with public concern with priest's sexual abuse of their children. Other challenges will follow. Their clergy will now have to add real measurable value recognized by the people they serve, or their church will wither and die because their younger members will simply not be there.

The path from the Sistine Chapel to St. Peter's Basilica takes the public through a hallway lined with glass so that the public can see into the Vatican Museum, which is filled with objects of great value, while poor people sit against the outside of the wall surrounding the Vatican pleading for "Alms for the Poor" from those lined up to tour the Sistine Chapel. Yet no one inside the walls of the Vatican is paying any attention to them. Why not? This is an example of what I am talking about that you might want to consider.

Today the AHA offices are in Washington, DC, less than a mile north of the White House. The AHA recently formed the Congressional Freethought Caucus, for which it provides support, and where they meet today. As a result, the AHA wrote a legislative bill related to human rights which has now passed through Congress. The AHA is making a substantial difference in the lives of people today. There are millions of humanists around the world, in part because Dietrich and Reese created the "mouse that roared," and its voice is being heard. There is still much work for the AHA to do. Our 2020 US Census told us that there are at least twenty-seven percent of adult Americans who claim 'none" when asked of their religion. Over forty percent of the younger generations, primarily millennials and younger, claim they have no religious faith affiliation. Many of these people would identify as humanists if they knew this philosophy of life exists. The goal of the AHA is to make sure that these "none's" hear the voice of humanism. That is one purpose for writing this book.

Recognizing that today it is finally culturally acceptable for each of us to be responsible for our own lives. We can safely become the center of our own existence without fear of being excommunicated. Or, even worse, fear of being sent to "hell." (As if those able to rise above the naive public's beliefs could even accept such a place exists.) Today, even though many people still allow their lives to be regulated by those Control People, a larger number accept their Control People as having valid authority because it is a valid fact that we all benefit from living peacefully together in our society, because religion still provides our social glue. But at the same time, more people than ever before no longer are willing to give up control and responsibility for their own lives to these Control People. Those people do not want to be treated as sheep.

Today humanists are not controlled by any external "supernatural" God, and we certainly do not have to account to any Control People if we do not want to. We reserve the right to challenge all who want to control us, unless we understand that what they are doing is for our own good, or that our society dictates that we must so that we can all live safely together. Humanists realize that we do not have to accept any cultural meme that has little valid root unless we choose to do so.

Today we can ignore those Control People who claim that a god, or gods, rule our lives. Nor do we have to accept their claim that we must accept the authority of these purported Control People, since they are our only available path to intercede with God, and if we do not accept their belief, we will suffer the consequences of God's wrath. There is no longer a threat today of being burned alive at the stake living in the United States. Yet today there are many regions, particularly in Islamic nations in the Near East, where there is little tolerance for different conflicting beliefs. Even though many beliefs, still accepted by a naive public today, are irrational.

Fortunately, more people are becoming aware that our group thinking is primitive and does not stand up against any test for truth.

Perhaps this example will make my point: Would you normally think that someone who "hears voices," resulting in him mutilating his genitals and tempting to kill his own child, has a problem? You would think that a person doing that has serious mental issues. Instead,

Abraham was the creator of a faith belief affecting the lives of billions of people living today who still think that it was alright for him to do that, and that his beliefs should be followed because he speaks "the word of God". Religion has created our cultural cloudy lens blocking our ability to see in a way that would otherwise raise such awareness. The cloudy lens of cultural beliefs protects all religious beliefs from public criticism. It is time that society cleans the lens through which we view life.

For many humanists today, when it comes to freedom of belief, we feel that we, in America, have finally become free. That right is sufficient reason to defend such freedom from anyone, or any faith belief, or any politician, treading upon our right to be free from their control.

No longer should religion be free to ignore that it is culturally unacceptable to question how religion controls its people. Religion can no longer hide behind its veil by claiming it is immune to criticism. It is our constitutional right, and maybe our duty, to challenge anything controlling our lives or those of people we love. People today understand that they can live more fulfilled lives without the need to accept anything by "blind faith." When a Control Person claims: "You must have faith." That should be a red flag for you. Stop the Control Person right then and demand to know why? Push that question until you hear all of their answers, and when they tell you that you simply must believe "on faith" because there is no proof, you should by then realize that you are being controlled.

It is time that all people have the right to live their own lives, as they wish to live, without Control People making threats of eternal damnation, or their denial of rewards in heaven for which there is absolutely no proof even exists. These are primitive beliefs that only exist as a "social glue" necessary for those people who must have external control for them to even be able to exist in our society. For many living among lower-level needs, and those unable or unwilling to see beyond their current cultural beliefs, external control remains essential for their purpose to sustain their living within our society. But those people are becoming a minority of our population today. If our society taught Maslow's hierarchy of needs to everyone so that people realized that they could live on higher need levels than their current existence, many would reach for the stars. By the time you get above the ego level of existence, the social glue provided by religion is no longer necessary.

The cultural belief that it is wrong to criticize religion is no longer acceptable. That belief has protected religious beliefs from scrutiny for centuries; and it should no longer be tolerated. That is what has protected religion from truth. People are dying in unnecessary wars, even today, in the name of their religion. That is the worst kind of primitive thinking because it hurts people for no valid reason. However, it is still accepted by many even today because it is being performed in the name of their God. It is accepted by "blind faith". That should no longer be tolerated. Yet those that still do are accepting something as true, without any valid evidence that supports that belief. That is primitive thinking, yet it still exists. If we do away with the cloudy lens, everyone could then see the truth. The problem that would cause for those who cannot rise above the social level is not something that our society can currently accept because we offer no substitute. Those are security level beliefs, and the humanist philosophy does not provide anything on that level.

This freedom from religion has only been available for any of us relatively recently. The philosophy of Epicurus originated close to five centuries before Jesus, and over a millennium before the birth of Muhammad. Overtaken by the more prevalent cultural memes of the primitive masses, Epicurean philosophy later resurfaced in Rome close to the start of the modern calendar. Epicurean philosophy was again lost for 1,500 years until the Renaissance, where it contributed heavily to lifting the Western world from the Dark Ages of Medieval times. After a few hundred years, it slipped from public awareness for a third time because of the more dominant cultural meme that, except for a few small, barely noticeable pockets, remained drowned out, until it arose again during the last century.

Epicurean philosophy, from our cultural perspective, is new, but it is much older than many faiths that are embraced by the public today. More importantly, for those of us involved in organized humanism, our philosophy of life is growing more rapidly than any religious belief, or any religious denomination is currently growing.

Today, particularly through social media, over four million Americans are connected to the American Humanist Association in some form or another daily. Public awareness has grown from less than 100,000 People only twenty years ago. Hopefully, this fourth time for the evolution of our humanistic philosophy we can generate momentum to become a cultural "meme," having an independent life of our own comparable to that of any religion existing today.

Social media allows humanism to resound with a public that has become large enough that it can no longer be drowned out by competing religious philosophies that feel threatened. Humanists find truth and reality easier to accept, instead of relying upon cultural myths for which there is no valid evidence to support them other than authorities who are validated only by other authorities. To a humanist, most faith beliefs do not have reliable evidence supporting a truth that can be confirmed, thus necessitating acceptance solely by "blind faith". To humanists, this makes no intelligent sense, yet billions of people are still willing to accept their own beliefs by "blind faith" today. Why would they even want to do that? Is it because then they do not have to think for themselves? With that attitude, someone else will tell them what they must believe. They will no longer be living their own lives. They are then living the life of a sheep.

In the 1980s, Richard Dawkins coined the original concept of "memes." Memes are identified human beliefs that have become self-replicating and are passed from brain to brain that now take on life of their own. The people that hold that belief are only that beliefs temporary hosts, and they pass that information onto others as their truth, without the necessity of validation. This self-replication keeps memes culturally alive in society. We will discover later on some memes we each know personally. Yet we have never considered why we even know them. Why not?

It is interesting how young people have made Dawkins' concept of the meme popular today. Understanding that beliefs have a perpetual life of their own, separate from the truth, is a powerful concept. Hopefully. young people are much more apt to understand this. Do you suppose the very people fearful the public might come to understand concepts that challenge their "blind faith" beliefs are also the ones who contributed to diminishing today's understanding of the meme concept? Interesting thought, isn't it?

Perhaps some people with more ancient cultural beliefs who felt threatened have tried to discourage their flock from discovering other ways of thinking, therefore they have reduced the cultural permeability of memes for the more religiously inclined by making it an everyday part of our language, without understanding its true meaning. That may not be a coincidence.

The accomplishment is the equivalent of what grade school bullies do on the playground. They call another peer an innocuous name like "shorty," evolving into mockery when others join in the teasing. Instead of using mean names those attempting to distance religion from being recognized as a meme accomplish the same result by diluting the meaning of the word meme in their attempt to make it less meaningful. A brilliant move that may have worked. Truth now has a strong voice, and it will be heard.

No one should reject all religion because religion offers a valuable "social glue" that is essential for many people around the world. Religion contributes to the ability for large numbers of people, particularly in our Western culture, to successfully live alongside each other. That is an important and necessary cultural role. No better means of fulfilling that necessary role in our society exists today for many people whose lives have not risen above the mid-social level of Maslow's hierarchy of needs, which we will soon understand. Perhaps there will be a time when almost all people have actualized their own existence; when their innate values are accepted by everyone simply because they are the most valid and produce the right behaviors for everyone. At that point, religion may no longer be necessary in our society. Those of us living today will never see that, because we are currently still living in a very primitive society.

Most people participating in a religious faith in America today do so primarily for social reasons that have little to do with underlying religious myth, or the religion's history. I will attempt to prove that in a later chapter. For many, their religious history serves only as symbols for expressing the values necessary to sustain our organized society. For instance, requiring confessions, historically accepted as a necessary part of some religious faiths, becomes relevant only because it reinforces the participants role in correcting their negative behaviors so that they can successfully live in our society. God may not be directly involved with that, only symbolically. But for many, even for some within that faith, the concept is no longer accepted by them as being necessary, or even beneficial.

However, religion in the large picture as an institution is still a necessary part of our Society for a majority of people. Religion as an institution must still be supported today, not condemned, for what good it does provide. Religion as our social glue remains important to us in the Western World to sustain our society for a majority of our people. But that does not mean that some techniques used within their faith by some Control People need to be tolerated. Some religious practices may be very objectionable and should not be tolerated by the larger percent of our society that can see the damage they have created.

It is the overt control by some Control People in the name of their religion where humanists should object; especially when guilt and fear are used as means of imposing a control device. Those techniques frequently, even today, psychologically stop some people from living their own lives for themselves to the fullest they could otherwise achieve. Humanists find no acceptable, let alone a valid, reason for creating these psychological barriers on a naive public.

Humanist philosophy is now widely accepted. For many in our younger generations, it is perhaps the most acceptable philosophy of life for human beings, and no longer just tentatively tolerated by our current society. It is the closest philosophy related to provable reality. It requires nothing more for it to be accepted. Humanism is based only upon provable knowledge, most often validated by science. Today there are more new people annually identifying with humanism in America than any of the organized religions. Humanists do not require faith to be able to accept our philosophy, which is a major reason the belief is growing.

Humanists accept that all knowledge is tentative. The only absolute truth we know for certain today is that someday we are each going to die. All other knowledge is only the best information that is currently available. As more information becomes available, a humanist easily modifies what they are willing to believe. But that too is only temporary until a deeper understanding of our knowledge surfaces.

As late as 1985, humanists were looked upon by the general public in the United States as the "Devil Incarnate" thanks to Jerry Falwell, a TV "Bible bigot" who had thirty-seven television stations covering a gullible public every Sunday morning. His point was that if you did not believe as he preached, you could not live a good life controlled by God. To him, you were "a sinner." This is ignorant, and certainly not true, but the masses of the public are gullible. The public is often uninformed, if not ignorant, on almost any given subject, and everyone wants to believe in something. So, many people blindly accept what they are told by those they regard as more knowledgeable than they are. Falwell's message was clear on one issue: "Just send me money." Television evangelists feed on this need by making you feel good that they have answers, and that you found them.

They will teach you how you can be "saved." That is the epidemy of gobbleygook. Many speak in simplistic language presenting themselves as an "authority." As a televangelist, Falwell alone took $54 million from the naive public annually as early as 1984. That is more than one million dollars a week! The President of the Presbyterian Church said that year, "think what we could do for others with that money." Other than providing his broadcast, Falwell did little real public good with the tax-free income he acquired. Except for what little he declared in salary, Falwell had to answer to no one for the wealth he acquired, including to the Internal Revenue Service. My own mother once sent five dollars to Falwell that she could not afford to spend. When I asked her why, she said, 'he speaks with such authority."

I could not garner the media to overcome the negative image of humanism that Farwell painted using his thirty-seven television stations to spread his message across America, which was essentially his only primary expense. I could not accept being honored as the "Senior Devil" since I do not believe in the Devil, nor that Hell even exists except in the minds of religious zealots who want to control you. I spent a great deal of time thinking about this. I was having dinner with Isaac Asimov and his wife, the psychiatrist, Janet Jepsen, who were sitting across the table from me next to Steven Jay Gould, the Harvard professor of geologic history and the two of them were arguing over the proof for the reason for the extinction of the dinosaurs. Iridium is an element found only at the 66-million- year geological level, which Gould was claiming proves that it was a meteor that killed the dinosaurs. My thoughts were on how to deal with Falwell, when a lightning bolt struck me. I could not garner the press to overcome Falwell, but Asimov could. So, I sat in his hotel room the next morning and convinced him to become the spokesperson for humanism, Asimov's voice would be heard to overcome Falwell. To accomplish that, I talked Isaac Asimov into agreeing to become my successor as the President of the American Humanist Association.

Dr. Asimov was a renowned author, having published 480 books during his lifetime, ranging from *Asimov's Guide to Science: to Asimov's Guide to Physics: to Asimov's Guide to the Bible.* The latter takes two volumes to cover each chapter of the Bible to show historically why that Bible chapter was written. In addition, one third of his books were science fiction. Even though he was the foremost science fiction writer of his day, Asimov Would not fly in an airplane. If he could not travel by car or train, he would not leave his Central Park apartment.

Dr. Asimov agreed to serve as my successor if I would see that he did not have to fly in an airplane to attend AHA board Meetings. I agreed to chair board meetings, so he did not have to attend. He agreed to my request because he knew that he could garner the press necessary to overcome Jerry Falwell. He also realized how Falwell was abusing the public he served. Falwell immediately knew that his days of unaccountable wealth would be numbered if he challenged Asimov. Therefore, we humanists believed that he shifted his message from using "secular humanism" as his "scarecrow," and instead he used his pulpit to create what he labelled the "Moral Majority" (which Edwin Wilson told me "Is neither."). Falwell used his Sunday service to empower his religious fundamentalist sheep to become politically active. As a result of creating far-right political activists, religious fundamentalists have now ruined the Republican Party for many mainstream Republicans. I have often wondered if I should feel responsible for causing that to happen?

One of the better things I accomplished to benefit our society is that I contacted my friend, U.S. Senator Chuck Grassley, who then chaired the Senate Finance Committee. I asked that he explain to me why TV Evangelists can even qualify for tax exempt status when they do little good that benefits the general public? Senator Grassley pursued that question. Many of those TV "Bible bigots" who were undeservedly taking advantage of our tax law, ceased milking the naïve public out of millions of dollars annually that primarily only lined their own pockets. Falwell created his own university to produce even more people who thought like he does. Did I really accomplish any good?

Some TV evangelists are still active today, but they know that attacking humanism directly will backfire. The AHA has become aggressive in legal and legislative advocacy and it is making significant inroads challenging those who would use government to promote their religious beliefs to the detriment of those with other beliefs. As I mentioned earlier, the American Humanist Association has also created a Freethought Caucus in the United States Congress to speak for those who choose to be responsible for their own lives. Humanists are even taking their challenges to the United States Supreme Court to stand up for the country's secular foundation. I would never have thought that possible when I joined the Supreme Court fifty years ago. I joined it because I was a military judge at that time.

In contrast to individuals guided from a fundamentalist religious perspective, preparing themselves for a life hereafter that most probably does not even exist, the philosophy of humanism is all about each person having the uninhibited ability to maximize our own life while we are living on this Earth. Instead of our worrying about an afterlife, most humanists realize that our only provable form of immortality that we know really does exist, is the degree to which we are *leaving our Earth a better place because we have been here.*

Control People do not cause humanists to spend the only life they have seeking a ticket to an afterlife for which we have no valid evidence even exists. Some Control People not only insist that we each must tithe but require our following their directions for the path to heaven. At least in one prominent faith, its sheep are told that they should spend their families' limited resources for elaborate funerals that barely memorialize the meaning of the deceased's own life. Their ability to extort these "contributions" from a gullible public is because they claim that they are the only ones who can provide us with the ticket to assure that we get into Heaven. Therefore, "for a little larger contribution, we can buy the way out of Purgatory for those that we love." Come on people!

That makes absolutely no intelligent sense. Yet intelligent people, having those beliefs instilled in them before their age of reason, cannot simply ignore their emotions that compel them to comply. If it were not for the cloudy lens created by Control People, we would all see that it truly does not make any good sense. Those who comply do so for emotional, not for intelligent reasons. Emotions trump intelligence every time.

Isaac Asimov's wife, Janet Jepson, just died as I am writing this. She was a psychiatrist, and she personally was the published author of twenty-seven books, six of which are novels. Dr Jepson responded a few years ago in an interview for *The Humanist* magazine when asked her view of Heaven:

"There are actually only a few of my loved ones I'd want to see again, much less in some conventional notion of heaven. In fact, perhaps only one, but my husband didn't believe in heaven either, so perhaps we will meet in limbo. Surrounded by all the most intelligent of Homo Sapiens."

In a prior published writing on religion Dr. Jepson wrote:

"I admit that it's cold shivering in the draft of an open mind while trying to be a decent human being without the prospect of supernaturally induced punishment or reward, facing nothingness with whatever courage it's possible to muster. In between shivers, I can respect people able to keep their minds open while enjoying whatever conventional organized religion that they need— provided they don't depend on their religious organizations to do their thinking for them and telling them what to do."

It does require strength of character to assume the responsibility for your own life, and courage to think for yourself, but the ultimate reward for doing so is that you will invest your energy, and the remainder of your lifetime, ensuring that the world will be a better place because you have lived. You will thereby assure your own immortality in the only form that we are certain actually does exist. You will also make your own life worth living for yourself.

Chapter Three

Where is our Current Culture?

Since our religious beliefs were introduced to us before our age of reason, our early beliefs are reinforced with the emotions experienced when they were created. Many people feel safe and loved at the time we acquired those beliefs. Their family is their life. For those people, those beliefs became a very positive part of us as a person and cannot simply be ignored, whether they are true or not. As a result, many intelligent people simply continue in life as they were trained as children, rather than take what, for them, may be viewed as a risk if they deny those beliefs. For maintenance of our society and our ability for us all to live together, there is a very important role for these beliefs as our "social glue."

Obviously, most Control People working within organized religion provide a lot of good for the people they serve. They feel that they are necessary to sustain our society today at our current level of our cultural evolution. As previously stated, most important for all of us, religion is a major factor as our "social glue" that maintains our society. It was essential for the ability of the masses to safely live together on the same psychological need level in our early society, and it remains so today. We have not survived long enough for our society to have outgrown that need. We sustain religion within our society for all of us to safely live together. Therefore, most Humanists do not challenge religion itself, regardless of its level of truth. However, we can challenge those that abuse the privilege or those who remain in control using threats and fear as a means of maintaining their control. That may be an easy tool for some faiths, but it is an abuse of their power, and it causes significant harm to the people they serve.

Our United States Constitution was designed by people from families who were relatively recent immigrants who came to America to get away from the strict religious control of the Church. Even those from England that had abandoned the Catholic faith had only replaced it with the King instead of the Pope in power. Therefore, our American constitution was intended to protect us from religion, by clearly separating the powers of the church from those of the state. The separation of the public and our government from religion is essential for people to be free so that they can live their own lives. Those that thought America was formed as a Christian country because of the story of the Mayflower are simply wrong. That is why the Mayflower went as far north as it did to avoid the more populated areas of the colonies, so that the pilgrims could live in their own community and express their own faith uninhibited.

Dr. E.O. Wilson is a Humanist who retired as Professor Emeritus of biology at Harvard, where he created the science of "socio- biology." Dr. Wilson proved that biology does not end at the point of birth and sociology becomes the exclusive science from that point forward. He found that many of our biological needs prevail to control our behavior after birth. As an example, the need for spirituality is a human need. Our religious faith has nothing to do with creating that need, even though religion has claimed it as their province. No one is immune from the need. How you might express it is a personal matter that does not require religion. Even watching a beautiful sunset can fulfill that need. Spirituality may be fulfilled by essentially tuning yourself to nature. It is a natural phenomenon, not the exclusive province for the supernatural.

Dr. Wilson pointed out that societies of fewer than 150 people during the hunter-gatherer era could exist without any external control of their society—because people knew each other, and the fear of rejection by their friends maintained social control of each member's behavior.

Dr. Wilson explained that once society moved from being hunter-gatherers toward permanent locations as they became agrarian farmers, creating a society dependent upon growing crops and domesticating animals, Organized societies increased in size to encompass thousands of people. No longer was society able to control behavior by everyone knowing everyone else. To maintain a society that large were benefited by social controls that were more sophisticated to serve as our "social glue" that controlled behavior so that we could successfully live together.

The first recorded history tells us that the religiously advanced society, using this means for creating the social glue holding together their society was going strong about 15,000 years ago. These were the people living in Sumer, located in Mesopotamia. They recorded their life in writing. Sumerians were one of the first agrarian cultural civilizations. Sumerians had numerous city-states located between the Tigris and Euphrates rivers in an area about the size of Massachusetts in what is now southern Iraq. Their concept of religion evolved as an integral part of their societies. Each city-state had its own god.

Sustaining religion necessitated creating a class of people to maintain such a society. These Control People were socially empowered as "Priests." As their role evolved in subsequent generations, they magnified their authority, even to the point of assuming the responsibility to coronet their society's Kings, claiming the King's power comes from God. Eventually, as in many cultures, they caused the public to believe that the Priests' authority was paramount in society, even acting collectively Priests claimed their authority surpassed the power of the King. This dichotomy kept society in balance.

Those responsible for the excavation of Sumer claim Abraham came from the city-state of Id, in this ancient society of Sumer. Their tour guides will show you what they claim was Abraham's home. That community was excavated in what is now southern Iraq by Saddam Hussain's archeologists.

Sumerians were a well-organized culture. They invented the first wheels, built chariots, and captured the western Mediterranean as far around as Egypt. Because the Babylonians invaded their lands and absorbed their culture, no one knew of their previous existence until an engraved rock found in Iran approximately 250 years ago conveyed the same message with three languages. We were finally able to read the thousands of clay tablets found in the sands of southern Iraq, which disclosed that an advanced society inhabited that land 15,000 years ago. They actually had schools for their children with teachers, there were doctors, and, in effect, lawyers in an organized society.

Egyptian culture provides a good example of the relationship of Kings and Priests, where the Kings ruled from Memphis as Pharaohs, and the Priests from Thebes. Each had an Obelisk representing their authority reaching one-hundred twenty feet high showing their power for all to see. How they carved those obelisks in one piece from stone, transported them over a hundred miles from their quarry, and then stood them up vertically with their primitive tools, remains a debate among scholars. I stood on one obelisk that was being carved in its quarry that had split in the process and so it was abandoned. The thought that it could even be transported in ancient times, let alone stood up vertical was overwhelming. I could not even comprehend how the one I stood on still in the quarry could even be moved today, let alone how it could be severed from the rock beneath it.

The Egyptians called their concept of peace between their Pharaoh and Priest "Maat." When both columns were standing, the people had peace and prosperity. When either column faltered, the people suffered, To the Egyptians the Obelisk was a very important symbol of power. The first Jewish Temple built in Jerusalem had two columns at the entrance. The tomb of the Apostle John has two columns at the entrance. This symbol survives today on the pedestal of the Senior and Junior Warden in every Masonic Lodge. Yet very few Masons know why. The cultural traditions we inherited since those days are no longer serving the needs of everyone in our society today. We have now acquired knowledge through science that conveys truths that allow us to understand our role in evolution and our relationship to nature that no longer depend upon our previous primitive beliefs.

We know now that the Earth really is not flat, and that our universe has existed for over eleven billion years. It was not formed just 6,000 years ago, even though some people still believe that. Their "Control People" should be banned from the benefits of our modern society for denying their sheep the ability to see the truth of reality that lies all around them, if they would only be allowed to open their eyes and see for themselves. The human mind can be controlled. We have proven that hypnotists can control what you believe, whether that person is a psychologist helping us overcome scatomas that deny our ability to see the truth, or whether that person is a priest.

The fact still is that some people cannot accept knowledge that is evident right in front of them, including a current belief so baseless the truth should be apparent that the world is not flat. The fact that some still fear falling off the earth if they were to travel to the edge is beyond belief. Since we are now able to fly around the world it does not take much intelligence to see the truth. Yet some people deny the truth. That is pretty good evidence of the damage that can be done by someone whose sheep have given their Control People that level of power over them. There are many other examples, but this should make my point apparent to you.

It is now finally time for all humans to have the cultural freedom for those capable of living their life more comfortably that is in tune with provable reality to have the freedom from religion to accept reality as their truth. That would allow those people to be able to see a better life, instead of our cultural more ancient religious constraints controlling their existence. The problem is that those people who are being controlled since early childhood cannot see that they are, even though the facts are just as apparent as the proof that the world is not flat. I used that example because most people who are still being controlled can see the person holding that belief is being controlled, and yet they may not recognize that they are also being controlled. It is unfortunate that some religions still demand control by their adherents to "have faith," in contrast to those mainstream Christian religions in America that only intend to provide support, instead of control, over the people they serve. When you are told that you must have faith, you are being controlled. Do not allow yourself to be "blind."

Instead of perpetuating unfounded beliefs that originated in a more primitive age when people lived their life based upon ancient myths and fears that we now know did not validly exist, at least in the form as the public accepts them today, religions that encourage individual growth instead of restricting freedom and demanding conformity will remain relevant for generations to come.

Humanists find that their philosophy provides all the necessary social control without the need for threats of damnation, or rewards of an afterlife that no legitimate evidence supports. Such beliefs can only exist by our accepting "blind faith" imposed by Control People. Humanists see no reason for such "blind faith" when a better, more responsible life exists without it. Ranging from mainstream Protestant Christianity to Buddhism, many of their clergy, and members deep down inside agree with that today.

The Dead Sea Scrolls were discovered in 1947 in the West Bank of what previously was Israel. They were written in Qumran on the northwest corner of the Dead Sea from about 250 BCE through 67 AD. They were being written daily during the entire lifetime of Jesus.

Many of the scrolls were copies of those written from the time of Moses up to the current times. They were hidden in caves under the Second Jewish Temple on Mt. Moriah, where Abraham was to sacrifice his son. That is the site selected by King David to build the Jewish Temple, because it is where God first spoke to Man when God spoke to Abraham. This is the site today of the Islamic Shrine with its Gold Dome; a landmark of Jerusalem, covering the footprint in the rock where Muslims believe Muhammad on his horse ascended into Heaven. You can experience all the conflict of the Middle East today in an area the size of a square block, at the Western wall of the Temple Mount.

When the Romans expelled the Jews out of Israel, the scrolls being written in Qumran were hidden in caves. They remained there for almost two thousand years before they were discovered in 1947 by a bored Bedouin shepherd entertaining himself by throwing a rock in the mouth of a cave thirty feet above him. The rock went "tink" and not "thud." He had to find out why. He climbed up to the cave and found hundreds of scrolls hidden in earthen jars.

History has not touched them for over two thousand years. The fact that they tell us a story differing from our current religious traditions has many Christians and Jews troubled. What has become apparent is that one important lesson the scrolls tell us is that our current religious traditions have been seriously molded over the past two thousand years. Because of well-intentioned Control People, our beliefs today differ from many historic facts the Dead Sea Scrolls reveal. Our current Christian and Jewish faith traditions seem to serve our society today, so why should we care?

The problem is that this new knowledge has caused many people to question their own faith. Since many of our traditional assumptions regarding our purpose on Earth are not "Immutable truths," upon what authority do we base our very existence? There may be no singular historic truth that guides our lives. We may be here on Earth all alone. The subject of *"Why Was I Born?"* is a question we must now all answer for ourselves. I wrote a book with that title, now available on Kindle and Nook. Most of its contents are included in this essay. The point being this question has also affected me.

All the books of the Old Testament were found in ten of the caves around Qumran where the Scrolls were written, except for the Book of Esther. One book of the Bible had forty-one copies, and they were all different. Which one did God ordain?

These Scrolls were being written daily only twelve air miles from Jerusalem. Why is there no mention of Jesus' resurrection? You would think an event like that would have been noticed. There was a story of a resurrection some hundred years earlier of a Messiah with twelve disciples, that never got traction. Apparently, it was not believable. So, there was some history of such a claim in Jewish history that the writers of Jesus life might have captured as a part of his story to help make Jesus acceptable to all Jews.

The fact that we culturally even have that belief today means the information supporting that claim came from someone who either observed those facts, or knew someone who had, or more likely, since the story that was written more than forty years after Jesus death, the author was someone who had not personally known Jesus, but he wanted to make the life of Jesus more acceptable to the Jewish community. So, the story of his life Jesus life was embellished to impress them. That story did in fact separate Jesus from others who also claimed to be the Messiah. It was rather popular in those days to make the claim of being the Messiah because the Jewish tradition of that day was their waiting for a Messiah who would come because they believed that was necessary for all deceased Jews to ascend to their afterlife at the same time at "the end of days". But since there is no mention of Jesus, nor of a resurrection, in the Dead Sea Scrolls that were being written by people wanting to believe that a Messiah was living during the life of Jesus, that is pretty good evidence that it simply did not happen.

The monks living in Qumran were seeking a Messiah because they believed that the Messiah would come immediately before the "end of days," when all Jews would at the same time ascend into heaven. They believed that should happen next week because they were ready to go. In fact, they were looking for two Messiahs: A Kingly Messiah and a Religious Messiah. Yet they did not recognize Jesus as that Messiah. Why not, if he in fact was one? There are many other issues that facts challenge our current cultural religious traditions.

Those writing about Jesus's life long after his death tell the story of Jesus throwing out the money changers of the Temple. They also claim that Jesus was a descendant of King David. Their point being that Jesus was both a Kingly Messiah and that he had equal power of the Priests when he threw their money changers out of the Temple. Episcopal Bishop John Shelby Spong, who only recently died, believed the goal of early Biblical writers was merely to make Jesus relevant for Jews. We will discuss his beliefs further later.

The point is that even though our religions express our beliefs—our beliefs do not have to be based upon historical facts for us to be able to accept them, or for their stories to add value to our lives.

Religion has become a meme with a life of its own. Memes modify themselves to sustain their independent life as they replicate. Just like humans evolve as our genes are passed from us to the next generation, memes evolve to be accepted in their current cultural environment by being modified by the person passing on the belief.

Even though many Humanists may still participate within their own religious society from their childhood, most do so for family or cultural reasons. Religion fills the security and social level of our needs for most people, having nothing to do with its unifying myth. Participation for many people is because of the social network of associating in a smaller group of people sharing similar values and mutual support that has nothing to do with the myth that unites them. There is nothing wrong with that. Those Humanists that accept identifying with a faith belief have made an informed decision to do so for their own reasons. Those Humanists who do participate place their religious beliefs on top of the Humanist philosophy. Humanism does not address those issues, nor does humanism fill the needs of anyone on the security or lower social levels. Humanists who elect to retain their religion do so for valid personal reasons, not because they are being controlled by others who insist that they must believe what they believe.

To be able to really accept humanism as the philosophy for guiding their life, Humanists must be able to live psychologically above Maslow's mid-social level, normally above the mid ego level. They must at least feel secure within themselves. Let us find out what that means. The point for this chapter is that humanism does not intend to attack any religion for those who need those beliefs to sustain their own existence.

Humanism's only beneficial interface with religion as a philosophy is to object when religious zealots who serve as Control People create cultural barriers for their own reasons which result in inhibiting anyone from becoming fully actualized humans, fully living their own individual existence today. In America we have the Constitutional right to be free of religion if we want to be free. Read on, let us find out what this means.

For those who are not capable of rising above their current level of life, why should Humanists care if those beliefs are enough for themselves if outside individuals are not causing that decision for them using fear as a means of their control? We do not object to anything you chose to believe, even though we may not agree with that belief. You have the right to believe whatever you want to believe. We are only concerned if you are afraid not to believe something because you are being controlled. The philosophy of humanism accepts that all people should be free to live their own life to the fullest existence that they can achieve, as they wish to live their own life. We are concerned for those people in our society who are bound by scatomas that block their ability to live a more fulfilled life. Our concern is for those who, because of their scatomas, cannot rise to the level of even comprehending that humans could live a better, more fulfilling life if they are not inhibited.

As an example, two people may be sitting next to each other in the same church pew, but they may be there for significantly different reasons. One might be that he or she feels it is a mortal sin not to be there, because attending every Sunday has been proscribed for them. The other person may be there simply because he or she seeks enlightenment, or wishes to support others in his or her family. The person who attends out of fear cannot rise above their current level of living for so long as that scatoma exists, or at least has not otherwise been bridged. The person there to learn or support their family can rises above their religion so that it does not keep them from becoming Fully Alive.

Even with atheists, there are those who tolerate the beliefs of the person sitting next to them because they appreciate that everyone has the right to live their own life. They realize that threatening the belief of another person is un-humanistic behavior. Most Atheists who are

44

Humanist, are tolerant of others having the right to whatever they wish to believe for any reason that is important to them.

However, many mainstream Humanists have a problem with those highly activist Atheists that carry their zeal beyond their personal belief by insisting that no one should believe in any "God," instead of limiting their objection to only those with more primitive supernatural god concepts. Instead, they insist that you must also accept their belief that "there is no God, so get over it." That behavior is clearly "un-humanistic." The same objection exists for religious fundamentalists that insist that everyone must share their belief. Both ends of the religious spectrum are in effect "bullies" when they are "in your face" people.

We will discover, if we read on, that bullying people is not a successful approach to an organized society. It only benefits the bully. However, we will also learn further on why society does culturally benefit from the bullying. It is not their beliefs that Humanists object to. It is because of their "in your face" behaviors we object to tolerating, regardless of which end of the religious spectrum they might be expressing.

Society does benefit from a bully that is forceful in expressing conflicting information because it does cause others to have to think beyond their narrow vision, thus causing evolutionary change in what we ultimately are willing to believe. Having to respond to the bully modifies what you believe. If we all agree, no change occurs.

Organized humanism supports those whose goal is to assume responsibility for their own lives, regardless of what their personal religious history might be. Humanist religious objections are limited to assuring us that we can live free from those religious Control People who want to take away our ability to think for ourselves, and those that do harm to others in the name of their religion, regardless of what faith they represent.

Fortunately, not all leaders in religion today follow the path of those who would deny you freedom from religion. Many more clergy today use the symbols of their faith solely to help you see beyond your current life, instead of insisting that they are the ones essential to provide you the only path to heaven. Such control by priests trying to keep you in their fold only results in an uncomfortable feeling of guilt, if you were raised in their faith and now you feel you must deny their beliefs because you now realize that many of those teachings have no basis for truth in reality. If you look upon those beliefs as symbols, and not facts, you can reinterpret them so that they maintain valid value for you. Consider what this means further along when I explain where our cultural misconception occurred for those that must believe that Jesus died on a cross, when in fact Jesus actually died on a "T".

The number of people who identify with humanism today is growing algorithmically, while the membership of many more traditional mainstream religions, including Catholicism, is seriously declining.

I was told that even the Catholic Church is now reaching out to millennials, apparently with a vivid reminder that they have the path to heaven, Personally, though, I have trouble seeing how anyone would feel spiritual sitting next to either of the two mummified Popes, each lying in a glass casket, as they do in the sanctuary of Saint Peter's Basilica in the Vatican toady. I was told that those Popes have been "Sainted." Therefore, many Catholics I saw sitting around them did not seem to share my concern. That is an interesting way to make the point that the Church is the path to heaven, I must admit that it did get my attention. That may also be why the Church has been working diligently to make John-Paul II a "Saint" so that he can be added for the public to view, because he was personally known by·People still alive today. I have even been within 20 feet of him while he visited the community in which I live. He should therefore dramatically increase public attention toward their goal. I must admit, it is a novel approach. It may work for others, but I would personally feel more spiritual sitting at the edge of a lake with my wife watching a beautiful sunset on a warm summer evening.

Further along we will learn of the religious teaching of the former Episcopal Bishop John Selby Spong, whose view of Christianity best expresses Christian humanism. He feels our current mainstream cultural religious beliefs are dying, or at least should. Society has moved on. What we are seeing today is a cultural shift in religion. For those who have been captured in a strict religious tradition in their early childhood and are being controlled by strong close relationships with others that limit their exposure to any conflicting belief, those churches may still be sustainable. But within mainstream religions we see decline in membership. Even the Catholic Church is concerned with the decline in membership of millennials and younger. Which is why they hope their mummified Popes speak to them.

If all Christian churches taught their faith from Bishop Spong's view, even mainstream religion could survive and possibly grow. The difference introduced by Bishop Spong is that he adds Christian symbols to humanism truth. Otherwise, mainstream Christianity churches could die out as our culture matures.

The Epicurean philosophy we know today as "humanism" now seems to have enough strength to become an acceptable meme of its own, available for future generations to come, when hopefully the philosophy of humanism will have become an accepted view for all people in the world, available to everyone to consider in the future. Regardless in what religious context it may be expressed. The goal of humanism is for all people to actualize their own existence, regardless of the path that they find acceptable for them to get there.

Religion attempting to control our society will diminish as people rise to higher levels of Maslow's hierarchy of needs, and as society provides more alternatives for filling the security and low social need levels. As our culture matures the meme of religion will modify and those that adapt to fill the needs of their parishioners and to keep them relevant will survive while those slow to change will wither and must merge or evaporate. Those millennials and those younger will determine religions future, while humanism continues to grow.

Chapter Four

Why was I Born?

Does a flower blooming in an uninhabited wood have no value? Has its life no purpose? Fulfilling its own destiny, in addition to pollinating its posterity, may be its only purpose, but for that flower, being the best that it can be is enough for its own life to have meaning.

Through the Hubble telescope astronomers have now already discovered hundreds of thousands of galaxies, each with millions of stars. Carl Sagan, a popular Humanist astronomer, once said to me, "In the known universe there are at least 300,000 planets, each of which is capable of sustaining life similar to that here on Earth." Therefore, he asserted, "It is rather vain of us to assume humans are the highest form of life in the universe." If there are higher forms of life, is our goal as humans to evolve into that form? That may be true, but what implications does not be the highest form of life have for why we are living our own life here on Earth today? It was Sagan's statement that raised the question for me, "*Why Was I Born?*" I decided to dedicate my life to finding out the answer to that question.

I discussed my concern for Sagan's statement about our possibly being the highest form of life with Donald Johansson, the Humanist paleoanthropologist who discovered "Lucy," the four-million-year old ape linking humans to our ancestors (the evolutionary link which connects human existence to the natural evolutionary chain of life extending from the level of the amoeba to that of the ape). Johansson claimed that Lucy proves human existence to be an accident—known in science as "an anomaly." Much like the arm on a Saguaro Cactus is caused by a break in its surface which allows the inner fluid to ooze forming an arm on the side of the main stem, human existence appears to have occurred due to a breakdown in normal genetic evolution.

Responding to my comments about Sagan's observation, Johansson pointed out that the statistical odds of such an anomaly occurring again are about one in two million. In a known population of only 300,000 planets, a second occurrence would be quite rare. Therefore, we humans may be the highest form of life in the universe. If humans are the highest life form in the universe, does that provide "special meaning" for our own lives? Perhaps it would.

At some time in their lives, many people wonder why they exist. In our early formative stage, others have attempted to answer that question for us. We accept their notions, at least initially, especially if they are our parents' views, and these experiences permanently influence our beliefs. Most of us then perpetuate those answers by passing them down to our children. After all, the purpose of our own existence is a difficult question to answer all by ourselves. Unfortunately, most of these answers are not very well founded. We are riddled with inconsistencies in our understanding of our world; and any evidence-based knowledge of why we are here on Earth does not exist today. The evidence suggests that there may not be a reason.

There are many questions about our world that science has yet to answer. For instance, when asked if "God" exists, some have quoted today's Humanist "Einstein," Stephen Hawking, who stated that, in viewing the basic forces of the universe in a unified theory, there is a gap that so far has only been explained as the Presence of nature. Even though Hawking does not think so, some believe that this force is God.

Even though Hawking may not have been religious in the traditional sense, he did share an awe of nature, Hawking's view does not imply a concept of an intelligent god micromanaging the universe in some supernatural fashion that some people still insist upon. Hawking merely claims that, so far, we cannot understand some forces in the universe. We cannot base a useful existence on Earth through guidance from such an impersonal god—other than to assume that we are supposed to live our lives in harmony with nature. We should already know that. Failure to live in harmony with nature is dangerous to our health.

But why am I here?

In *Spirituality Without Faith*, (The *Humanist*, January 2002), Thomas Clark reports that current science shows us that the universe is expanding but does not have enough mass to collapse into another "Big Bang." He claims that ultimately all matter will turn to dust; the universe will become black and cold. Science shows that, apparently, our ultimate destiny is to become space dust—which does not make the notion of immortality very appealing. Perhaps it is not very realistic?

In the next article of that edition of The *Humanist*, entitled "Whence Comes Death," Joshua Mitteldorf discusses why humans die. We know that our bodies develop from a single cell that subdivides according to a unique genetic plan, creating all parts of our body. And, beyond that, at least every seven years, most cells in the body have replaced themselves. Apparently, there is no biological reason why we could not exist forever—or at least until our sun stops shining.

Mitteldorf points out that our physical aging deterioration is due to nature's evolution of the gene pool. As individuals we become irrelevant after our childbearing days. Therefore, our genes contain a self-destruct mechanism to extinguish our individual existence to keep the gene pool evolving. If every human lived on Earth forever, the gene pool would never change. Apparently, the purpose of human life is tied to the survival of the species, and not the individual. The ultimate purpose, or meaning, for our own existence remains unanswered. The truth is there might not be one.

Some people do not accept science as relevant to their view of life. Some assert, "Humans are merely living out God's plan." Yes, this notion answers the question simply and definitely—but it makes humans into puppets. For many that notion is naive. If the script for our life is already written, why bother to live? Likewise, some believe in reincarnation, where we live successive lives until we ultimately become perfect. Unfounded as such a belief is, one can understand why those who find their lives inadequate would welcome a chance to come back and try again. Unfortunately, few, if any, of these theories can survive informed intellectual scrutiny. Many people are simply unwilling to live their lives based upon such unrealistic or trite premises. So surely there must be a better answer.

When we consider ourselves against the vastness of time and the universe, our individual existence becomes insignificant. Why would any god even want to micromanage a tentative and all too short-lived speck on Earth? What would be the point? Such views of life can only be accepted by "blind faith." Why should we do that?

Yet each of us has "faith" in something, even if it is only in the power of nature to respond to our actions. Such is the case when we correctly plant a seed. We have faith that nature will cause it to grow.

My action was to plant the seed. Other than realizing that the seed has evolved from earlier plants' existence, we do not really know why the seed grows, even though science can tell us how it grows. What happens after planting the seed is beyond my control, although I may continue to influence the result by watering the plant. However, nature may not really care whether that seed lives or dies. After all, it has plenty of others. Nature only provides the opportunity. No one really knows "Why," although some Control People may claim that they do. We are reasonably sure the flower will grow based upon "faith," because we have observed others growing before. That form of faith is acceptable. "Blind faith," based only upon authorities, we should only accept tentatively until a more reasonable answer appears for us. There is a big difference when you add the word "blind." Not all truths based upon faith are the same level of truth. When there is any doubt, Humanists will accept any belief only tentatively.

We soon learn that, as individuals, we are part of something that is bigger and more powerful than we are. The problem is that our ultimate relationship with our universe eludes us. Many more people today are content to believe that nature does not have to be fully understood for us to accept nature as being all that exists, Humanists are among them. Most Humanists are willing to accept that such belief leaves many unanswered questions. Nature appears to be all that is available for us to interpret, and thereby understand, our own existence. Science is still expanding, and we are still learning. Humanists can acknowledge that we really do not have to know the answers to all questions for our own lives to have meaning.

However, some people expect more immediate completed answers and left with few alternatives, they frequently fill in the gaps of verifiable knowledge with historically accepted religious answers from more primitive times, or they may even create answers of their own. Once any answer is accepted, no one likes to have their own answers challenged. Each of us feels that our own answer is "right" and, therefore, enough for ourselves. Thus, for some people requiring their "truth" to be based upon fact becomes irrelevant. These people frequently accept a myth as their own personal truth. Once accepted, they will defend it until their death, even if science has proven such belief to be false.

Uniformed people still exist, and the masses today are ignorant on almost any given subject. We are all ignorant before we learn. You must work at being stupid by denying valid evidence that differs from views you prefer to believe. Since that is a simpler path, some prefer to be stupid. Fortunately, most today do not. They may just not have enough motivation or opportunity to learn. It is one thing to be uniformed; we all are on some subjects. To be provided the opportunity to learn, and to reject it only because it conflicts with a belief you prefer, even after you have been exposed to valid evidence to the contrary, verges on being stupid. You are not one of those people or you would have already handed this essay to a younger person or stuffed it somewhere to haunt you until you finally realized that there may be more to learn.

The difference for Humanists is that we see no valid evidence that the powers of the universe that are superior to us as humans have any intent to control us as individuals. We find no evidence that there is a "supernatural" God. Nor do we find evidence that there is any life beyond our life here on Earth today. If all of that is true, then does that change how we will live our own life that differs from our ancient cultural traditions? You bet it does! It allows us as individuals to be free to make the very most of our own existence in the little time we have.

How do we do that? Read on.

Chapter Five

What is "truth" for me?

At the root of our ability to accept any belief for ourselves is how we determine what is true for ourselves. Obviously, we cannot test every fact before accepting it as true for our own use—at least temporarily. For many of our beliefs, each of us will accept the opinion of people we trust, especially when those beliefs are not, at this moment, particularly important to us.

Early in our lives we rely upon our parents, older siblings, teachers, pastors, and caregivers for the answers to our questions. This is especially true when we are given answers to questions we did not ask, such as the foundation for our religious views. We accept these answers for emotional reasons. At that moment, the truth was irrelevant.

As we mature, at least for those who are braver, some will test selected beliefs. But even the brave will continue to accept some answers from others where they have no immediate personal concern for the answers. Allowing authority figures to provide our answers is easier, and most people follow the path of least resistance. However, for those who are less prone to blindly accept the answers of others, they must be able to obtain the same results for themselves by testing at least some of their beliefs before then accepting them as their "truth."

What distinguishes Humanists from many other philosophies of life is the means Humanists use to find acceptable truths. Some say that we have four distinct means of ascertaining our own truth.

Socrates' Approach to Discerning Truth

The first of these may be seen in the way we test the question of guilt or innocence in criminal trials through a Socratic method of debate. Two attorneys taking opposing positions test the veracity of the available evidence, and from this effort a decision maker in the form a judge or jury determines what they believe to be the truth. This is the best system we have for protecting the rights of an innocent defendant, but the system is hardly perfect.

Even though Socrates may have found this to be the best means ascertaining what is true for him, Humanists would never accept this as a valid means of determining their own truths upon which they would be willing to base their very existence on Earth.

Relying Upon Authorities to Establish our Truths .

The second means of establishing our truths is evidenced by how most people are willing to rely upon authorities to establish what is true for them. Humanists may accept an authority tentatively to meet a current need but would not rely upon them without question. To the degree that a proposition has importance in their lives Humanists may accept their Authorities' opinion until a better answer appears, but they will retain the right to doubt, and they will continually test the veracity of that belief.

A Humanist is apt to be a skeptic. Most Humanists cannot accept anyone's opinion, or any written word, as an ultimate truth upon which they would be willing to base their entire existence. At best, their authority's claims might be accepted tentatively. Humanists feel that all ideas and beliefs should be subject to continual testing against what each person has validated to be true, and that which is observable to them in our world. If they conflict, a Humanist will doubt that authority and will not rely upon their view. Most authorities are eventually proven not to be the absolute truth. They are only the best current interpretation or analysis of that person then available to them, because our knowledge continually expands. Thus, accepting the opinion of another person, or placing faith in any text as an immutable truth, is very difficult for a Humanist.

Let us examine further an example I used earlier: There is no valid evidence that the Bible is the "divine word of God." Only Control People have told you so. Among the Dead Sea Scrolls were found forty-one copies of one book of the Bible, and they are all different. Which version did God inspire? Or was that book of the Bible simply the best idea of a concerned person who was writing in a more primitive culture, and each person who copied the original book felt free to add their own thoughts to the effort of ancient humans to interpret life with the best information they then had available? Is the person who told you to believe every word of the Bible because it is "the word of God" merely trying to control you "for your own good"? Or are you simply that person's sheep? How do you determine what is true for yourself?

Logic is the Basis for Testable Truth for most Humanists .

Logic is a third technique for determining truth. Humanists are most apt to apply logic by applying their prior knowledge to any situation to ascertain the truth of a new proposition. Those who need to validate the truth of what they are told by their Authorities must be able to logically deduce the resulting truth by thinking through each step from truths that they already have validated to arrive at a reasonable (and even then, only tentative) acceptance of any new proposition. Our knowledge is continually subject to change with new information. Therefore, our acceptance of our truths also changes as our knowledge grows. That is why you must have an open mind to even read this book. This book will challenge your thinking, but the result of that is that it will provide you with sufficient information for you to be able to build bridges over the scotomas that currently block you seeing anything that conflicts with a prior belief. Thus, to gain the most from this book you must constantly remind yourself to keep an open mind. Remember, you can always go back to a previous belief if where you are going in our discussion you do disagree with. You are always in control of yourself.

Science Demands Validation to be Accepted as True .

However, not all truths are discernible by deduction. The fourth means for ascertaining truths that Humanists find most reliable are those arrived at through the scientific method, with much information acquired through inductive reasoning. In science the researcher starts by observing or considering certain phenomena or events, establishing a hypothesis of what caused that occurrence, then testing the hypothesis to determine if it holds up as a plausible explanation of the phenomena. To be regarded as a valid theory, other scientists must be able to duplicate the results. Even then, the hypothesis is accepted only tentatively, and other scientists will continually test the theory, attempting to discredit or to improve upon it as more evidence comes to light. A Humanist is most apt to accept this means of establishing what they will believe as reliably true. However, even these truths are always tentative.

Science is built on the principle of testing beliefs. For every observation of phenomena, scientists propose a hypothesis as an explanation. To be accepted as true by scientists, others must be able to test the theory by duplicating the result. If others can do so, the hypothesis is tentatively accepted as true until another answer emerges as a new hypothesis, usually based on a deeper level of explanation for the origins of those facts. This way, the process of our developing the "truth" we currently accept evolves to a deeper, more informed level of belief.

Albert Einstein's *Theory of Relativity* was first published in 1915. It was only recently accepted by science as a fact, instead of a theory, in 2017, over one hundred years later.

For some, accepting childhood authorities in established religious faith beliefs may be enough for the rest of their lives. Others, especially those capable of living on higher psychological need levels, may become skeptical. They may feel that more proof is necessary for something to be acceptable. Like scientists, many skeptics recognize there are no absolute truths. All beliefs should be accepted tentatively. A notion may be accepted as tentatively true by everyone because it serves us for the moment, even though we may recognize that belief may not be relied upon as an indisputable "truth."

Many scientists apply the same standard to accepting their religious views that they apply to accepting observations of our physical world. Many others accept their religious views as a matter of social or family convenience and are, therefore, not troubled with testing the truth of their personal religious views. Truth may be irrelevant for them. Like an object of art, they simply like it, so truth has no relevance for their religious views. The distinction for acceptability for a Humanist is whether they retained control for themselves.

Many people are unable to accept any truth merely on "blind faith" that their Authority is right, or by "wishing" that something be true is tantamount to knowing that it is. Some people need to know for sure before accepting an important belief as an immutable truth. Humanists tend to be among them. To accept something as "true" most Humanists must be able to test the facts for themselves. If they cannot prove it, they will not rely upon it. An untested belief is simply a wish that a skeptic recognizes may only be accepted tentatively. It does not matter to skeptics if the belief is a scientific theory or their religious beliefs. Humanists are willing to acknowledge that we cannot live forever. As truth unfolds through discovery and search— generally Using the scientific method— our beliefs, including our own religious views should also grow and continually adapt to the changing world in which we live.

If you were raised on what, prior to your arrival, was a deserted island you would not have Authorities telling you what you should believe. Most people in that situation would naturally acquire the philosophy of humanism.

This is because when you view life without the influence of any outside Authorities you only have nature as a guide.

Humanism does not require faith for our own lives to have purpose, and for us to be able to live a good life. In fact, Humanists feel that the absence of a faith component gives greater meaning to their ethical values. One problem for a Humanist is that requiring blind faith to guide your life means that somebody else is controlling your existence. It is worth repeating what distinguishes Humanists from most of our cultural society is that Humanists assume their own responsibility for themselves, and they want primary control over their own lives. They are unwilling to give anyone else absolute control of their life, except they will give momentary control to someone they trust in order for them to solve an immediate need.

Humanists acknowledge that their reasons for accepting the values regulating their lives are simply because such behavior is the right thing to do, and produces the best results for them. They do not depend upon a divine declaration that we must follow, lest we suffer the consequences. A Humanist's behavior is not motivated because of fear of retribution that some Control Person has imposed upon us.

Humanism does not intend to challenge anyone else's faith, but Humanists do affirm that people can live a good life based exclusively upon current empirical knowledge without a need for ascertaining our own truths by having to rely upon "blind faith," or to base our life on Earth in the search for a life after death that has no valid supporting evidence. All we really know for sure is that it may not exist.

There may be an afterlife, but since we have no valid evidence of its existence, Humanists simply do not consider it a factor of concern for their own lives. We do not care if you believe in Santa Claus, if you still need or want to do so, but we prefer to simply view Santa as a culturally imposed wish to create excitement for our children. Santa is simply a myth told to children in our society before their age of reason to make our Christmas tradition meaningful and exciting for them. Some parents also use the myth to control their own children's behavior at Christmas time. I do not mean to imply that continuing that tradition is wrong, but only to make this point: similarly, the notion of a life after death is imposed upon adults by Control People, who have been accepted as Authorities, based exclusively on "blind faith." There is no other basis of truth for the notion that something exists for us as an individual after our death other than our wish that it is true. That is not enough reason for most Humanists to accept that an afterlife is a valid reason for influencing our behavior. We do believe that the only form of immortality that we are certain really does exist, is the extent to which the world is a better place because we were here. That belief we know is true.

Many people believe that their religion must be based upon "the truth" to be acceptable for themselves. Religion culturally fills a very important segment of the needs of many people, especially those living primarily on lower need levels. Their participation has little to do with the historic traditions or the myth, or story that unifies its members. Truth may not be relevant for them. For many, they are merely fulfilling their security and lower social needs.

Each religion, and the philosophy of humanism, contains an ethic, or set of moral values, because they are necessary to sustain any organized society. For each tradition theirs is claimed to be "the truth." Unfortunately, most faiths claim theirs to be the only truth as a means of control over their own members. For our organized society each religion is a self-contained system that allows large numbers of people to safely live together by providing mutual Support that is necessary for each of us. Religion fills a definite cultural need. Each church, temple, synagogue or mosque has a purpose in that it fulfills in the daily life of its own members that goes beyond their faith belief. Therefore, each religion serves important needs in the lives of their members that have little to do with the truth of the myth uniting them. That is why many Humanists can comfortably participate. And there are Humanists within any religious tradition; most simply do not know the philosophy exists. So, see if you are a Humanist. That could be why you are reading this essay.

Even if there were no "truth" in the underlying myth of any religion, there is only tradition, that should not be cause for a person to simply reject their own religious symbols, unless they adopt something that becomes even more important to them as their view of the world grows through their education. It requires education for a person to be capable of replacing their childhood symbols, and filling that person's needs, because these symbols have emotional values that have been very important in the life of that person.

Therefore, it takes real effort for many in our society to even arrive at the philosophy of humanism. Many feel that they would be rejecting their deeply felt lifetime beliefs. They do not realize that they can place their religious views on top of the philosophy of humanism. It is not an either/or decision. It is simply starting from the point of view of taking charge of your own life.

It would be wrong, and contrary to the ethic of Humanistic behavior, to condemn religion based on truth because the church as an organized institution does fill a very valid cultural and personal need for many people that has nothing to do with the truth of its central myth. The Humanist philosophy does not currently address the needs of those who fill their needs on the high security/mid- social level with their own religion.

Most Humanists would agree, however, that if the knowledge that the myth that is central to our traditional religions is not based on fact, it would change how that religion controls our own lives. Our control must then be based solely upon reason, not on a primitive truth we now know may not exist.

Humanists who are members of any faith will normally feel that members should not be controlled by guilt or fear, or by the promise of an afterlife that is available only for those who believe in the limited view of a Control Person. Humanists are motivated to act only by reasons that they are willing to accept, and they will retain control over their own lives.

As said before, even though Humanists are found within most religions, most Humanists find it is impossible to accept a particular religious doctrine or authority as an immutable truth based purely on "blind faith," or by accepting any authority, without it being based upon facts they independently find to be true. Many Humanists will not do so even tentatively, especially as the sole basis for how they must live their own lives. However, Humanists may accept the Control Person of their religion as their Authority on many aspects of their own life because of the quality of the work of that person, and because of their superior knowledge in an area of thought where the Humanist does not want to expend the effort to duplicate for themselves.

Most Humanists have no concern with whatever another person may wish to accept as their truth -- if that person does not attempt to impose their notions on them. An "in your face" person is offensive, whether that person is an activist religious evangelical fundamentalist, or an activist Atheist who insists you must believe as they do. In some faiths they even believe that if you do not, they have the right to kill you. Some even believe their book of authority, be it the Quran or the Bible, instructs them that it is their duty to do this. Humanists are generally not concerned with attempting to change anyone else's view of life, and normally will not do so unless another person attempts to limit the Humanist's ability to live his or her own life to the fullest as they choose.

That is because humanism as a philosophy is not particularly concerned with any religion since humanism's focus is exclusively on our life here on Earth. Many Humanists are only concerned with the methods imparted by religion that affect how each life is expected to be lived here on Earth today that limits any human of the right or ability to live their own life. Humanists want us all to have the right to accept any belief that we find beneficial for ourselves, or for those for whom we may feel responsible, as well as the right to reject any belief. Any Humanist is free to accept any part of religious traditions that they find comfortable for themselves.

Many Humanists do find they are able to add some parts of our cultural religious traditions as an addition to their philosophy of life. If a Humanist finds a particular religious tradition important for them to address their own concerns that humanism does not answer, or to add a spiritual dimension to their philosophical approach to their life, or they wish the support of their church community, or they feel it beneficial to support the needs of others within their family, or for any other reason, no one should care or criticize. Humanists feel all people can live their lives any way they wish. Humanists do acknowledge that we do not have all the answers to life. Our knowledge is still growing, and no one has all the answers.

We do feel that humanism is a complete philosophy of life. However, humanism does not intend to replace religion for those who wish to reach beyond our philosophy.

The primary common denominator between humanism and religion is that each has a value system. The difference is that Humanists are primarily concerned with how we live our own lives on Earth today. To most Humanists, nothing else really matters. When you view life exclusively from the point of view of how you live it on Earth, you take life itself far more seriously, making your own life as meaningful and significant as you find possible. Humanists do not want to miss living the only life we know for sure we have while worrying about a life after death that may not exist.

Since we have no real evidence other than Authorities for validating many religious beliefs, most Humanists generally would not accept their edicts, let alone the dictates of any Authority speaking for a particular religion, as the primary basis for how they will live their own life. This is especially true for claims that our failure to accept any authority's belief based exclusively on their required "blind faith" would result in eternal damnation. No one knows the answer to such questions unequivocally and absolutely. We can only claim that we do; and such claims have never been proven.

Humanists may well participate within any religious tradition, but most do so primarily for social or family reasons, and each will retain the freedom to doubt. Furthermore, Humanists will usually view their relationship with any religious community as only tentatively filling the gap in their search for answers to those questions we are each capable of raising as we live our daily lives, for which science currently provides no clear answer. Our religions provide the symbols for describing our universe when we have no better means to express it for those who need an answer to the question of "why" that may not otherwise exist. The point for a Humanist is that the question of "Why" itself may not be valid. The "truth" is that there may be no answer to that question.

Chapter Six

Who are Control People?

Our society is built upon the concept of "Control People." We have presidents, governors, parents, teachers, policemen, firemen, clergy, doctors, and lawyers, among many others, who hold their rank in our society by law. Their election, license, or delegation provides their authority. Try and tell a military commander or police officer, or your prison warden, or jailer, that he or she is not a Control Person. Or, that you refuse to obey them. Each has control over some aspects of our existence; some regardless of our wishes, others to the extent that we allow, most others voluntarily. Some are necessary because they control our social system that allows us to live together in harmony.

We allow many others to have control over some aspects of our lives by agreement, including employers, scout leaders, spouses, our personal doctor, lawyers, stockbrokers, and others that increase the value of our lives because of our consent. In addition, we have some who attempt to impose authority over us. Try and tell a bill collector that they have no authority. The point is that many people attempt to assert some power over our lives and behavior. The valid question remains: do you transfer control of your life to them, or do you retain responsibility for your own life by making your own decision to cooperate with their dictates only if you understand that it is in your best interest? If the latter is you, you may be a Humanist and simply did not know it before reading this essay.

To the extent that you agree to follow their dictates but continue to assume the responsibility for your own behavior, that is acceptable to a Humanist. To the extent that you feel compelled to obey without question, you are being controlled. You have allowed yourself to become a puppet. To the extent that you are manipulated by fear, guilt or reward to act beyond your own desires, that is unacceptable for a Humanist because you cease to live your own life. You are not just a puppet, but you are subject to someone else's control that frequently may be against your own best interests. You have become a sheep.

That is why Humanists resist those Control People who insist we must believe or accept anything as true simply by "blind faith," especially if they are only able to support their position based upon a text that they as Control People insist is based upon "the word of God," as their ultimate authority. That would mean that authorities can only be validated by authorities. That reasoning would easily be understood as defying logic by even the average person on the street. If it were not for the mystic creating the cloudy lens through which we view our own religions, you would agree.

It is culturally expected that you believe in your own religion; therefore, many want to believe. That is circuitous logic. The problem for a skeptic is, if we only know something as true because Control People tell us that it is true, how can we validate that Control Person's "truth" based upon evidence that is only validated by Control People? That defies logic. That form of control Humanists find unacceptable.

We may never know when our life will affect the life of another person. A great, great uncle living in Illinois was a skeptic who had significant influence on the life career path of Tony Hileman, a former Executive Director of the American Humanist Association, living in Washington, DC. This is because his relative he never knew published a book in 1899, entitled *The Life Experience of a Skeptic*, where he pointed out: "When they ("Control People") tell you to believe, they are telling you not to think. Because thinking is (creates) doubting. And by doubting, the powers that be that are trying to control you cannot abide."

That one thought changed the path of the life of a relative the writer never got to personally know. Keep in mind the author was writing before the revival of the Epicurean Philosophy in America by John Detrich. For the writer, this thought was a revelation. He reasoned this on his own, and he immortalized his thoughts in print— and Tony pondered what that thought really meant during his formative years. That guided Tony toward his philosophy of life which has made a significant difference in his life, creating a Humanist leader four generations later. The more interesting part of this story is that Tony's sister is a Catholic Nun, and he was raised in a Catholic family. Yet his transition to humanism felt natural for him because he saw through the veil of his religion because of his great, great uncle's message providing a light that spoke to him four generations later. We all have the power to influence others. Some influence creates good for others, because it leads to their fulfilled life. Some causes significant harm, because the Control person created a barrier in the form of a scatoma that blocked some person's growth and kept that person from becoming "fully alive."

That same logical process is true even if the Control Person is our own doctor and our own life is dependent upon his or her judgment. We may be uninformed in that area of concern, but our primary need is to always remain responsible for ourselves. We will feel free to do our independent research to validate what our own doctor is telling us. We generally refuse to give up control of our own existence to another except by our reasoned decision that it is currently in our own best interest, and we retain the right, and the ability, to modify or even to reverse our decisions.

We all must subject ourselves to Control People, to some extent, to support ourselves as we live in our society. Maintaining our society is necessary to support our higher needs because it provides us the opportunity to enjoy the other higher needs in our life. After all, we know from many examples in history that anarchy could reduce our life to a chaotic level of existence no higher than a security level necessary for our own survival.

A problem that Humanists have with any organized structure is when its Control People attempt to abuse their power, especially using such techniques as fear or guilt. You must retain the right to resist. You must be free not to comply, for whatever reason that is important to you, for you to even be able to fulfill your own life and ultimately to make your own life meaningful for yourself, and significant to others. Without that power, and our assuming personal responsibility for our own self, our own life will lack real value for ourselves. We will be living someone else's life.

Certainly, we should not give up our personal freedom for the benefit of sustaining the Control Person. We are no longer controlled by the feudal system that produced kings. Remember that it is only religious Control People that insist that we must tithe. Why is that so? When we give up control, we may then feel compelled to work for someone else's benefit, to serve their needs or wishes, which easily may conflict with your own. Even in our religion we should act only because we agree it is in our own best interests. All life is a balancing act.

An objective in this essay is to cause you to consider what it takes to be able to retain or regain responsibility for your own decisions without allowing yourself to be manipulated by any Control Person. Such control may well reduce the quality of your own life. You may never know. You do have the right to accept any Control Person that you feel is of benefit and acceptable to you, and no Humanist would object if you retained the right to verify their truth. The issue is, will you know the difference?

Chapter Seven

How Should We Live Our Life?
(So, what does this even mean?)

The more relevant question remains: *if all we know is that we exist, how do we establish purpose in our own life?* If our ultimate purpose is only the survival and growth of our species, is our reason for being here only to procreate and then die like some male honeybee, a male ant, or black widow spider? If so, we older folks might as well get about our duty and quit wasting Earth's resources. This is not a very satisfying thought.

We should at least have an answer to the question for ourselves. Human existence may have been an accident, as Donald Johansson suggests. A supernatural god may not be dictating our behavior. Yet this does not mean that while we are here our life should not have value, at least for ourselves. The field of psychology may be the only currently available science that we can employ to increase our understanding of what is ultimately important in our own life.

This is the most important chapter in this book for your own life. Take the time to fully understand what you are reading before you move on, and then refer back to this chapter with subsequent questions or concerns. **Understanding this chapter is the essential key to your every acquiring a fulfilled existence**.

Psychology as a Science

Psychology originated as a science with Sigmund Freud. Freud who assisted the mentally ill to improve their lives by focusing on what was wrong with their behavior. Thus, psychology started as a negative science.

"Behaviorists" represent the second phase of modern psychology. Everyone has heard of Pavlov's dog that associated the ringing of a bell with the delivery of food. His dog would salivate when he rang a bell. This proved that behavior could be conditioned. B. F. Skinner, a Humanist psychologist, built mazes in which he experimented with white rats, showing that they have the capacity to learn. Behaviorism shows that need deprivation causes drive, which results in behavior. By modifying any antecedent stimulus, behavior can be changed. While I was studying behavioral science in Drake's University's Department of Psychology, I was once told "we could toilet train a child in a day using a cattle prod." (The instructor acknowledged that: "Of course, that child would become neurotic for the rest of his or her life, but the child's behavior certainly could be modified." The point of the professor was that all science, as well as all knowledge, can be misused.)

Skinner was a Humanist. I was writing to him as President of the American Humanist Association the month he died. Skinner was working on a book to explain the evolution of psychology from the perspective of Darwin. I am so sorry that he died before it was ready to publish. Edwin Wilson, the first Executive Director of the AHA, sat on a bar stool between BF Skinner and Abraham Maslow during an annual meeting of the Association. They were arguing over their personal interpretations of the meaning of humanism. I would have loved to have been a mouse in the corner listening to their discussion. I have kicked myself several times for not having asked Ed Wilson to write a paper describing their discussion for our Humanist archives, which now exists in the Meadville-Lombard Unitarian Seminary Library in Chicago. It would have been a classic among psychologists.

Maslow's Purpose for our Lives

Humanistic psychology has become the third force of psychology in this field of science, and it has revolutionized our understanding of how we can live our own life to our fullest potential.

Dr. Abraham Maslow, the founder of Humanistic psychology, has articulated a viable scientific theory for finding purpose in each individual life. Maslow grew up in the era of behaviorism. To ascertain why two of his psychology professors were such wonderful people, Maslow could not find a need deprivation that could have caused their wonderful behavior. Suddenly, he realized that maybe the field of psychology had the notion of 'needs" backwards. When need deprivation is present, people become abnormal—until they eventually become sick, like Freud's patients. But when people are totally healthy, Maslow discovered, they lack need deprivation. After giving this problem serious thought, Maslow recognized that there are several very distinctly different levels, or categories, of human needs based upon the driving strength of that need for its satisfaction. Need deprivation strength is not linier, as had previously been accepted.

Maslow then discovered that humans live on multiple psychological levels, and that our behavior, and our individual orientation to life, varies significantly depending upon which level we are then primarily living on at that moment. Our current predominant need level will regulate our momentary existence.

Our objective should be to continue to grow throughout our entire lifetime. Our feeling of success comes from the measure of the trip through life itself. Success is not simply reaching a goal. Success is the feeling that we get from recognizing our own growth as we move toward a goal. By the time that we achieve a goal, a new goal should already have replaced our previous goal as we stretch our lives and make our life as meaningful and significant for ourselves as possible. Our continued growth throughout our lifetime is our objective in life so that we can fulfill our own existence, gaining the highest level of living that we can attain for ourselves. Our goals are momentary and should constantly expand our horizons as we grow for our life to have real value for us. Maslow was the first psychologist to believe that the objective of each of us in life is to achieve our own fulfillment by reaching the highest level of life that we are individually capable of attaining. Maslow recognized that the meaning of our own fulfillment varies on each need level. Most people are content with living on lower need levels. Some people can reach the very highest levels of living. Why the difference?

Maslow's Hierarchy of Needs

Maslow found that needs could be categorized by the strength of the drive level caused by their deficiency; and that needs with greater drive strength prevail. If a person is sufficiently hungry, for example, his or her behavior will address this issue first, deferring a wish to help others, or continuing to listen to classical music. Maslow found that there are six very distinct hierarchical levels of human needs. Furthermore, he discovered that the drive strength of needs on the level below are on the average twice that of the level immediately above, so those needs direct the behavior of the person at that moment to satisfy that person so that they can then entertain their needs on the level above.

Basic Needs

Survival is the primary concern of all living organisms (and all institutions, governments, and organized systems). Hence it follows that the strongest, or primary, needs are those of physiological necessity. Included in these basic needs are the requirement for food, water, air, sex, elimination, warmth, and sleep, among others. If one really must go to the bathroom, nothing else is particularly important for that moment. For purposes of illustration, these "basic needs" may be characterized as those needs with a strength level of one. Many people in some areas of the world can barely rise above this level, even today. Look at the current life during this decade of those in Asia who have been forced from their homes by a deranged dictator.

Security Needs

Once our essential basic needs are sufficiently attended, we naturally "feather our nests" to assure their future satisfaction. We seek shelter to protect us from the elements. We become protective. Maslow classified this next level as "security needs," and found these needs typically have a drive strength level of less than one-half that of basic needs. As we first described in the introduction, some people who have a level of wealth, but have chosen a life that defies society, must spend most of their life living on this level protecting themselves from others for their very survival.

When we feel secure, we will normally not think about the proximity of the closest bathroom. When we are unable to relieve ourselves, however, we certainly will worry about what happens the next time, especially if any barriers to our instant relief are present. A private in the Army having to go to the bathroom while standing at attention in formation learns that lesson very well. It never happens again.

Social Needs

Once secure, we naturally tend to seek friendships and love relationships. We are the able to live on the "social or belonging" need level. We want to belong, to be accepted, and to be loved. We then bring others within our defense mechanisms and allow them to share the satisfaction of our needs with us. Although this is very important to all of us, these social needs have a deficiency strength level of approximately only one fourth that of our basic needs (try explaining that concept to a teenager with hormones), Seventy percent of all American's today are locked on the Social level or below, not even realizing that there are three levels above them.

Ego, Self-Awareness, or Identity Needs

When our own needs, and the needs for those we love—or for whom we then feel responsible—are also safe, and their basic needs are satisfied, we are then free to seek recognition from others. Maslow classified this level as "ego", "self-awareness", or "self-esteem needs," Although ego strength can appear strong, the drive strength of these needs is typically only one-half that of our social needs.

Actualization

Every person's constant goal should be to "actualize" their own existence here on Earth. To feel "fulfilled" Once we are satisfied that we are not only accepted, but appreciated by others, we are then free to identify and integrate ourselves with our environment. We can then recognize and become "in tune" with our own reality. Only then are we psychologically capable of actualizing our own existence.

Maslow felt that people who have actualized become a "whole person." He defined "actualization" needs into fifteen different adjectives. They are truth, goodness, beauty, unity, aliveness, uniqueness, perfection and necessity, completion, self-sufficiency, justice and order, simplicity, richness, effortlessness, playfulness, and meaningfulness. When we are savoring the world around us, we are attempting to fulfill the actualized level of our own needs.

We are only capable of achieving this goal when our basic, security, social, and self-awareness needs are reasonably satisfied. At this level we become concerned with abstract concepts, such as aesthetics, and we improve the environment around ourselves. We begin to become a whole, fulfilled person, at peace with our own self. We then are, for the first time, able to look to fulfill the lives of others solely for their benefit, and not for our own. For the first time we are then capable of reaching beyond ourselves to become Fully Alive.

Up to the point of actualization, Maslow recognized that our needs, to ever-reducing degrees, are deficit or deficiency needs. If we have a deficit, we feel a need to resolve the deficit. The strength of the deficit determines the strength of the drive for our current behavior as we seek to satisfy that need. Since our innate behavior essentially is driven by the need for our own survival, these needs are primary, and therefore the strongest. Maslow said that these needs are "Instinctoid" instinct like needs. In between basic needs through our ego self-awareness needs we gradually improve the quality of our own life. Actualization needs move into the realm of "being" needs. You strive to become the most complete, the "fullest self," a whole person.

Hence the term Maslow used is "self-actualization." All creatures are totally selfish on the lowest levels of living. Our selfish drive strength diminishes at the same rate as all other needs diminish until all selfishness vanishes on the Actualized level. Altruism only starts to appear as we approach actualization.

What happens once we fully actualize our own existence is the most important of Maslow's discoveries. When we actualize our full potential, we momentarily reach a state of total fulfillment. In this state of contentment, we can resonate in harmony with our own environment. For at least that moment we are free of all stress and may then be able to recognize our own sense of peace as a *"peak experience."* Maslow recognized that only about six percent of our current society ever reaches this level. Only one percent achieved a peak experience. One major purpose for an organized society is to create the environment that will allow all who are willing to expend the necessary effort to have the opportunity to reach this level.

When we experience a peak experience we have, at that moment, total insight into our current situation and are totally content. Much like a speed boat plowing through the water that reaches a plane on top of the waves, we function with far less requirement for energy and accelerate with much greater speed and far more depth of understanding because for that moment we can think and understand our own situation with greater clarity. We then momentarily see our own life, and all that's around us, as if we were an observer outside of ourselves looking in without any restraints. More than in any other prior experience in our lives, most people feel truly exhilarated, liberated, and fulfilled during a peak experience.

However, even those who have actualized their own existence must spend most of their lifetime tending to their lower-level needs in order to be able to momentarily live on their highest level of living. We predominantly live on only one level at a time. We start our life on the lowest level, but if we are uninhibited by outside forces, and have the resources available to meet our needs, we can grow naturally through each level. Maslow found that the natural objective and purpose for our own life is for our own continual growth. It is to sustain our life on the highest level we can reach, and ultimately for us to be able to attain a peak experience. Then we will know that we are fully living our own life. From that point we cease to be motivated by our own selfish needs. We can then become Fully Alive.

How do we get beyond our selfish self ?

Maslow discovered that once a person has arrived at a peak experience, some people are then able to make a transition from their own more selfish motivations and are able to direct their further efforts beyond themselves. Some People are then able to accept external motivation that transcends into a cause, or to another person, or even into a lifetime commitment. We may then become fully content in living for the benefit of another person, or for a cause for the greater good of others, possibly even to our own physical detriment. Transcending ourselves allows our own lives to become even more significant and, ultimately, even more meaningful to ourselves. At the point we transcend our own self and, in effect, become "trans- human," we will then feel "Fully Alive" and in tune with everything surrounding us.

Many undergraduate psychology majors insist that Maslow identified only five need levels. Essentially that is Maslow's hierarchy. Later in his career Maslow extrapolated into a sixth level by recognizing some people can fuse their own existence with causes that are beyond themselves.

This sixth, or highest, level opens a new realm for living. A mother becomes one with her son or daughter; an artist becomes lost in their painting to the exclusion of eating and sleeping; a doctor works to save the patient they are serving to the point of a risk for their own needs; and a teacher may lose their own identity and become fully invested in their students. The teacher is absorbed with the growth of their students. A lawyer identifies with the success of their client.

A person currently living on this level has fused the needs of the people they serve, or of a cause or an idea, with themselves, and thereby those external needs may dictate their own needs and wants—even to the exclusion of that person's own personal needs.

A test to determine if a person can live on this level is to analyze how they describe their own efforts. Does their own description of their life's work include a personal reference to themselves? If so, their motives may still be on the ego level. Questions to ask of such people are, "What activities give you the most satisfaction or reward in your life?" "What gives your life the most meaning?" The transpersonal values expressed by people who have transcended beyond their own needs tell us a lot about that person. Once a person can live on this level, the self merges into the cause, which has then become the primary purpose for that person's own existence.

Thereafter, the significance of that person's life becomes all-consuming with the cause for which they feel born to address. They, as a person, become identified, even by others, with the passion that they then serve. Their entire prior life was only a prelude for the life that they now live. One advantage for this person is that most of the rest of their life may be lived on, or above, the actualized level.

Humanist author Isaac Asimov was driven in the last years of his life with his goal to publish his five hundredth book. He was publishing a book about every sixty days before he died. When I wrote to him needing information, or his authority as my successor as President of the American Humanist Association, he always answered. But he wrote back on postcards, not wishing to delay his life's goal. Asimov's wife, Janet Jepson, told me not to feel badly; he did that to everybody, including his family.

Many of Asimov's books were in fields of science, with an in-depth study of a subject. As I mentioned earlier, *Asimov's Guide to Physics and Asimov's Guide to Science are classics.* Asimov's two-volume *Guide to the Bible* takes every chapter of the Bible and puts it in its historic setting so that you can better understand why that Biblical chapter was written. These books are still shown in bookstores today over 40 years after his death. During his lifetime he published 480 books, one third of which were the science fiction works for which he was best known by younger generations.

When a person can pass beyond actualization, they have become a whole person who is no longer consumed with their own needs. Therefore, they can devote their attention exclusively to the needs of others, or their life's tasks. At that point they become altruistic, and their behavior is no longer a result of satisfying their own needs. Their view and motivation are exclusively upon the good that they are doing for others, and for the world in which we live.

To put this into perspective, Maslow drew a diagram of a pyramid showing the levels of needs of human beings. His conclusion was that, instead of linearly, biological and psychological needs vary in strength, producing a drive for their satisfaction that can be quantified on five levels. A stronger level of needs prevails and must be satisfied first.

The goal for each of us is to fulfill our own existence by passing the point of a peak experience and freely contributing our future efforts to achieve our own immortality by leaving our world a better place because we have been here. Maslow's Hierarchy of Needs provides us with the path to maximize our own life to its fullest. When we reach a peak experience, we will know that we are then Fully Alive.

Humans differ from other forms of animal life because of the size of our brains. Because of our larger brains, we can think abstractly. That allows us to mentally picture situations or objects that may not even exist. We can think far beyond ourselves in ways that our dogs or cats are unable to participate. Thus, we conjure up the concept of Gods that may exist, that our pets have no ability of comprehending. We have created the illusion of a life after our own death that has no meaning for any other form of life. We can live on all these levels. Our pets can only get to the mid-social level. Ants can barely rise above the basic level. Amoebas cannot rise above the basic level. Let us look at Maslow's hierarchy of needs as he envisioned it.

			ALTRUISM
0	**Fulfilled Existence**		
Average Relative Strength of Needs			**MOTIVATION**
	Peak Experience		
1/16	**Actualization**		SELFISHNESS
1/8	**Ego**		
1/4	**Social**		
1/2	**Security**		
1	**Basic**		

MASLOW'S HIERARCHY OF NEEDS PYRAMID

Note the relative strength of our needs on each level is approximately one-half that of the preceding level. The strength of our degree of selfishness also reduces for most people as it relates to the primary level at which they are currently living. During a typical day most people will move through several levels depending upon their current endeavors, available resources, the stress and sense of responsibility as they seek resolving goals and, most importantly, their current attitude.

We humans are complex.

The reduced size of each level in this diagram reflects not only the driving strength of each level, but it also represents fairly well the current population living on Earth today. There are many more people living on the basic level than are living on the next level above them. Very few reach the level of actualization. We are still living a relatively primitive existence globally.

The ultimate goal of organized humanism should be to educate the public of the existence of higher levels of living that we each may ultimately reach, to identify and encourage the development of the means for our society to grow, and to encourage those who can provide the paths for our society to grow so that everyone can achieve actualization someday in our future.

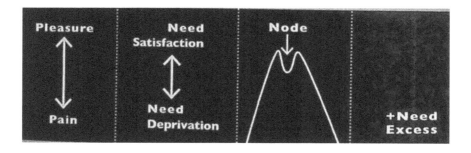

Those with a Fulfilled Existence

Maslow identified people who have actualized their own life as capable of rising above their own self to reach a level of their own fulfilled existence. He realized that these people had a significant change in their values. Maslow labeled the phenomena "being-cognition," or 'B-values," meaning that a person is able to identify the purpose for their own existence with something beyond their self. The "cause" becomes that person's motivation to exist. They become indistinguishable from their cause. In the end, fully actualized people not only have become a whole person with a meaningful purpose for their own self, but they have become significant to others and are then able to measure the value of their own lives in terms of the good they create.

Individuals can transcend themselves at any level of the hierarchy of needs. However, unless a person has actualized themselves, their motivation remains primarily selfish. Only a person who is totally fulfilled lacks a personal unselfish motive. Below the sixth level, degrees of selfishness are the primary influence of our behavior.

Ideally, people will earn their living doing whatever fulfills their own actualization and transcendent needs. For those able to do so, their mission in life provides a sense of purpose; thus, we may be capable of supporting all our needs in life with work that fulfills our passion. Teachers, ministers, artists, doctors, even some lawyers, and many other occupations may experience a sense of wellbeing and fulfillment as a result of supporting all their needs through their professional experience.

Maslow's Methods of Research

Wishing to interview in depth higher functioning people to better understand how they achieve fulfillment for themselves, and to understand the effect that peak experiences have in people's lives, Maslow first needed to know which of the people he was randomly interviewing, were capable of actualizing their own existence. He first had to develop tests to find those who were living on the actualized level, in order to separate those people to interview from the masses of volunteers.

His first test was music. Maslow found that a person living on the basic level found only strong and definite music—loud, hard rock or percussion—to be meaningful. Because we start our lives on the basic level, this may explain why our children prefer loud percussion music in the earlier part of their lives. Like all other aspects of life, unfortunately, some never grow out of it.

A person on the social level can easily appreciate popular music. In turn, on the actualized level, a person will be more apt to find subtle orchestrations, such as Beethoven, to be beautiful. A person on the actualized level could also appreciate hard rock, as well as the full range of music, though normally they may prefer more classical or subtle orchestration. However, the person living on the basic or security level will typically never enjoy Beethoven.

For another test Maslow used humor. For a person living on the basic or security level, violence, sex, or some other harsh event must be included to be perceived as humor. On the social level, jokes about people may be perceived as funny. On the actualized level, incongruence could be humorous. Again, the person on the basic level will seldom understand why something incongruent could be funny, while a person on the actualized level could appreciate an "off-color" joke, as well as the greater range of humor. For a person living on the basic, or security level, the perception of abstraction in any form is seriously limited. Using these means of testing will help us differentiate the level of living of those we encounter and, therefore, better understand those with whom we must interact.

Understanding of Needs

Satisfaction of each need is not linear, but rather a bell curve with a dimple, or "node," at the top. Pain can result both from deprivation as well as the excess satisfaction of a need. For instance, one may be thirsty, start drinking water, and feel significantly better until a peak is reached. From there, a little more water will cause a slight descent, until one feels totally satiated for thirst. Drinking more water will result in excess, at which time one will once again begin feeling pain. A person can die from either deprivation or from excess. The same path is true for all needs.

Typical Need Path on a Pleasure-Pain Scale

Homeostasis is the state of balance. Attempting to achieve homeostasis is our body's natural continual effort. The objective for the satisfaction of any need is to remain within the node, or balance point. Our objective in life is living a balanced existence with all our needs reasonably satisfied. If all our needs at any given moment are fully satisfied, we can achieve the unique condition where we are in harmony with our immediate environment. This state, which Maslow labeled a "peak experience," tells us that for that instant we are fully living on the highest level of our own existence. A fully satiated person enjoying a peak experience is resting within the node of all their needs, both physically and psychologically.

When a peak experience occurs, much like a tuning fork, you resonate with your own reality. You are, for that moment, "in tune" with your own universe. It may be subtle and could be missed. Or it may hit you like a brick, especially if it is a first experience. You may experience a euphoric feeling, much like floating in air. While in this state you fully comprehend and are comfortable with all aspects of life around you, even if you might otherwise be stuck in a negative situation. People in jail, even those having just filed for bankruptcy, or in proceedings for a divorce, and those facing their own death, are still capable of achieving this state under the right circumstances. Obviously, it is more difficult if the person's attention is otherwise occupied. However, achieving fulfillment is conditioned by our attitude toward our current situation.

Some of us in our American culture and environment will have felt a peak experience from time to time, perhaps without recognizing what was happening, or understanding its significance. At the moment of a peak experience everything in your world feels right for you. This can be very scary if one has no basis for understanding what is happening. Maslow believed that the typical "born-again experience" of an evangelical fundamentalist is probably a peak experience labeled in religious terms. It is an "ah-ha!" moment. Because most people are unable to articulate their experience in scientific terms, they will look to what they know to explain the phenomenon, and might, thereby, credit their notion of their God for their own sense of wellbeing.

For the person on death row in prison, having a peak experience does not mean that they would approve of their incarceration. However, at that moment, they would at least understand their situation, and then he able to accept the inevitable. They will at least momentarily have much greater insight. A person dying of cancer similarly may have such an experience if they have become resigned to their fate. Hospice services do wonders in helping people accept their own deaths using this principle.

For Maslow, being able to achieve a peak experience is the "apex" of our own personal existence, fully living within our own self. We become a totally "healthy" person, in a psychological sense. In doing so we have at that moment, fulfilled anything and everything that is then relevant. We are for a moment "Fully Alive", and perfectly content. Living continuously on the actualized level with sustained peak experiences would be difficult, if not impossible. However, if we can capture this moment where we no longer have personal needs, we can then transcend beyond ourselves and become in tune with a greater purpose. We then can become a fully functioning person whose life is not only meaningful to ourselves, but even more significant to others. We are then "Fully Alive". Once we find the path it is even easier the next time. We can learn to return routinely.

The Normal Uninhibited Growth Path Through Life

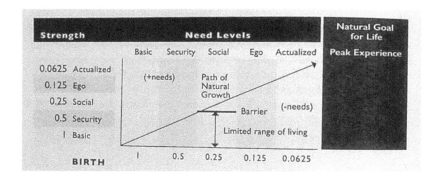

The normal growth path through life starts with the fulfillment of basic needs and, unless blocked by some barrier, ultimately progresses to actualization. Note that the drive strength of needs gets progressively subtler and less of a factor directing our behavior as we ascend the growth path. We grow best on a path that is relatively neutral between positive or attracting needs, and negative or avoidance needs. We naturally ascend the path of least resistance. However, as our drive strength lessens it becomes easier for our cultural society traditions and for the Control People, we encounter in our lives to introduce or impose barriers to our continued natural growth. Some are subtle and may even exceed our own awareness. Thus, we may be unaware we are being controlled. Such barriers can slow or even stop our further growth.

Consider the effect of guilt imposed upon us by parents, or some clergy. Once we encounter a barrier, if its strength exceeds our drive strength for the need we are currently addressing on the need level we are currently living, our natural growth in that area of our endeavors will temporarily cease until the barrier is removed or circumvented. If the barriers become fixated into a scatoma, we may live the remainder of our lives never growing beyond this imposed barrier Many then becoming content within a narrower more limited range of life. Not even knowing that a higher level of living exists. We can become content and feel safe within our narrow range of living. Once a barrier is accepted as bring best for our self, it has become a scatoma. We can then no longer accept anyone challenging that barrier head on. To circumvent our barrier requires building a bridge over or a detour around it. That normally requires non-threatening education developing a new path. Raising our view of life above our childhood scatomas is one of the primary purposes of our college experience.

We might recognize that our needs at the level of a peak experience will be very subtle because there is no drive strength at that moment. Or the euphoric feeling may be intense, because the experience is so new. Or, since there is no strong drive level within us to cause behavior when we reach a peak experience, if we are not paying attention, we may simply feel good and not know why. The experience may be momentary. Because a lower-level need with a stronger drive— we inevitably become hungry, or face a call of nature— will soon take over, and our behavior will change to fulfill this new need because of its higher drive strength. We then may start back up our path for fulfillment unless we hit a barrier that limits our further growth.

Picture how excited you were as a beginner playing the piano when you could first play "chopsticks." That euphoria only lasted until you were challenged by the next more difficult musical lesson. But thereafter you could always still play "chopsticks." Once we have arrived at the level of actualization, being able to again attain a peak experience is similar. If we are not inhibited by barriers or outside forces, we will naturally learn to transcend beyond our current level of living, eventually arriving at the actualized level of living. Our goal should be to continue to grow in our effort to make our own lives meaningful for ourselves and significant for the benefit of others as we seek to fulfill our own existence.

Traveling the Actual Path of Growth Through Lite

Growth does not occur in a straight line. We experience periods of living on a flat plateau while fulfilling the needs on each level as we progress. Moving to each higher level for the first time is dramatic. Like being a seedling on the basic level, and then becoming a plant on the security level, we continue to grow and mature. Realizing that we have arrived on a higher level is as apparent as if you were a rose bud on the social level that blossoms into an *American Beauty Rose* on the ego self-awareness level. On the actualized level, our concerns normally shift to perpetuating the opportunity to bloom for others.

To reach the next level we must be open and accessible for growth, as we age, higher growth can become more difficult because we have acquired more assets or status that requires more protection, and we have established artificial goals that absorb much of our energy. After all, we may have children and then grandchildren who we must protect. Our objective is to stay centered and continually grow. Io accomplish that we must be continually aware of barriers that are placed in our path by others within our culture.

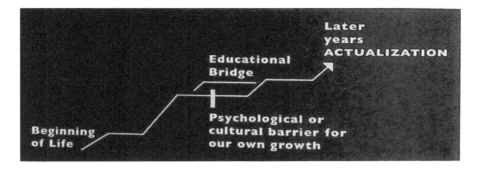

Typical Successful Growth Path Through Life

Typically, our defense mechanisms in the middle age become much stronger and less flexible. We feel we must protect what we have built. On the other hand, as we reach retirement actualizing may become easier, especially as self-imposed goals are no longer as important to us. By that point in our life, we may have reached our personal goals, or they have been replaced with more immediate needs. We may have passed through a mid-life crisis and have finally accepted that we are not immortal, and we may even be willing to accept that we will never be able to get a hole-in-one playing golf.

If we no longer fee] threatened by failure, feel the need to prove anything to anyone else, or feel no longer that we must impress others to get ahead in life, or whatever else has caused stress in our lives, we may then be able to overcome or find better paths bridging the barriers that retarded or blocked our own growth in earlier life. This relaxation from stronger lower needs may finally allow us to reach the highest levels of living life. At that point in our life, we may be able to increase the level of our own significance for the benefit of others.

If we must become 'president" of the Junior League to become momentarily self-satisfied, we can hardly be expected to recognize other opportunities above the ego level. It is laudable to serve as president of such a worthy organization. The distinction is the level of need that motivated our desire to be president. Were we striving to be president for recognition for the satisfaction of our own ego, or did we seek that position for the good that we can provide the world by leading such a worthy organization? The answer reflects the need level upon which we are currently living.

On the ego level and below we can absorb so many problems in daily living that we cannot truly appreciate life. Many of us must reach retirement before we are able to release our commitment to artificial goals, and we can then become free to accept new opportunities and growth in our own lives.

Only if we can overcome our lower barriers in concert with our other current needs getting satisfied are we capable of having the sensation that everything is, for at least that moment, 'right" in our lives. At the point of actualization, we will be free of our own limitations. We may then be able to transcend our own selfish needs, allowing ourselves to magnify the good that we can accomplish in living our life for others.

That should be our goal if we truly wish to fulfill our own existence while we are here on Earth.

Once we have achieved that goal, we will again be able to rise to that level, if at first with effort because we have arrived in unfamiliar territory. Just like the first time we achieve the next higher-level plateau in the hierarchy of needs. With concentrated effort it becomes easier.

Now that you understand your path for growth, you can seek opportunities for living your life on the nest higher level until you have it mastered. You will know that you are able to reach the end of your goal in life when you have a "peak experience". To get the very most out of your life, from there you should concentrate on making a significant difference in the lives of others without regard for how you may benefit. This endeavor can easily become fully consuming. The reward is when you then realize that you can make a real and meaningful difference in our world.

When we find we spend most of our energy seeking to help others, ignoring our own needs to fulfill that objective, you will know that your life has purpose. When that becomes our primary level of living it will soon feel natural, and those needs on our lower levels will diminish in importance. We see this with artists that forget to eat as they produce their art. We see this with physicians that forget to eat while attending to a critical patient. We see this with schoolteachers, who buy necessary supplies for their students despite an income that barely meets their basic needs.

The point is that those who arrive at this level feel exhilarated, their needs have risen above themselves and they now have a purpose that makes them feel fulfilled. Their life truly matters to them, because they see the effect of their lives through those people or projects they then serve. That should be your goal in life, if you want to become "Fully Alive".

The result is what creates your own immortality. The world has become a better place because you have been here. Your immortality becomes permanent to extent what you have accomplished lives on for future generations to come. Just like Tony Hileman's great-great uncle who changed Tony's life so that he could change the world today for so many others, who will go on to improve the lives of others as a result. It multiplies exponentially.

Chapter Eight

Why is achieving Actualization so Difficult?

We live in a world of violence. All life on Earth is prisoner to an environment where the fittest have the greatest opportunity for survival. The first and primary goal of every person, or life of any form—ranging from insects to the artificial life forms of government, politics, business, and institutions—is the same. The primary goal of anything is to survive. Everything else is secondary or lower on our scale of importance. Change threatens existence. To keep a balance, and preserve the status quo, is a constant effort for every form of life or entity. As we do so we affect the lives of others, sometimes negatively. The food chain dictates that weaker life forms sacrifice their own life in order that others higher in the chain survive—but this does not mean that they do so willingly. Those about to be devoured fight for their own existence. You only need to try fishing to understand this principle.

Humans are as much a part of the natural world as any other species. Every person's environment on Earth is often cruel. We each learn to defend ourselves from pain from the day we are born. Our constant quest to live compels us to continually try to improve upon our existing condition in life. Since our own survival is essentially a basic need, we cannot easily do anything else. However, we cannot healthily grow beyond the security level solely on our own. We must interact with our environment and with others within our culture in order to survive. These Outside factors condition our behavior.

It takes the aid of others for us to grow to the next higher level of living our own life.

The many techniques we create from the day we were born to protect ourselves from threats, especially those that are produced by outside forces, may in themselves cause barriers for our own continued growth. All barriers can block our natural progression toward the actualization of our full potential. Continual conscious effort is necessary to circumvent such barriers so that we may continue normal growth along our natural path toward our goal to actualize our own life.

To become truly healthy and able to transcend into a new higher realm of living, the first task requires recognition of where barriers exist. Seldom do we see our own barriers. People feel safer living within known parameters and, therefore, many are content with their current existence. Indeed, removal of barriers may even be threatening. It requires our own energy and more effort and risk than many are willing to endure. Most live without the knowledge that higher, more rewarding opportunities are even available to them. Interaction with other people, while keeping an open attitude that allows us to sample and then possibly accept new information, is essential to provide paths that take us around our own barriers for our own growth.

It is often an all too human tendency to follow the path of least resistance. Growth is not always easy. A few years ago, My Fair Lady made this point. The character, Eliza Doolittle, spent the entire length of the movie (or Broadway play) learning how to grow beyond her earlier life, selling flowers on the street. Many are unwilling to spend the effort and are content to remain within the confines of their reduced existence. They are, thereby, condemned to not ever being able to actualize their own existence. That is truly tragic. She reflected the benefit when she finally realized that she had arrived at the next higher level of her life uninhibited.

We must continually concentrate on finding and then eliminating barriers if we ever wish to become fulfilled, and to be able to actualize our own existence. Barriers occur normally without our knowledge or consent. Some barriers we create for ourselves because of fears we develop as we live life and face our failures. Others are imposed upon us by people motivated for whatever reason to control what we think and feel, and especially what we do. As mentioned previously, there are all kinds of "Control People" who cause us to develop cultural barriers that we meet daily, ranging from parents, to the threat of people in authority such as the police or our schoolteachers. We may even meet those in subtler authority, such as those within our religious faiths who, with all good intention, are trying to teach us their notion of ethical behavior. We may also accept as authorities' people who may be more motivated by their own need than helping us.

Early childhood experiences create some of our biggest barriers to living. As an example, the threat of eternal damnation presented to us in our youth before our age of reason is a big stick that most of us cannot overcome. Regardless of the good intent of clergy conveying such a message, such threats can easily create a barrier that will forever limit most people's range of living, more probably to their detriment. Most Humanists find no valid reason for doing that for any reason.

Some beliefs that become barriers may create scatomas that limit our own view of life, and therefore our very own existence. A "scatoma" is a blind spot in our own view of reality. Scatomas are immutable beliefs for that individual. For something that affects our life we should be the only ones to make those decisions for our own selves.

We all have Control People in our lives that we may never get over. I still am afraid of my first-grade teacher, who told me I could not write legible cursive, and she has been dead for thirty years. To overcome that scatoma may be why I became a lawyer, where I must write all the time. Many barriers create irrational results. Although perhaps she did do me a favor. She meant well. I did get even with her, however. I was the only one left for her when she died, so as her lawyer I buried her, but the fear she caused in my own life did not die with her.

All barriers need to be at once challenged if they are to be easily eliminated. Left alone, irrational beliefs that become barriers can harden from temporary protections to become permanent fixtures.

They may even become defense mechanisms that ultimately take control over that aspect of our lives, thus limiting our range of behavior. In that manner, barriers become a scatoma.

Scatomas

Scatomas work like spam blockers in your computers. They repel any conflicting information to protect a current belief, and they can cause that person to become hostile to any other view of reality. Many times, a person limited by a scatoma can even become violent when they are aggressively challenged about a belief, particularly when that belief is on their security level, which is true with their religious beliefs.

You only need to meet an activist religious fundamentalist or an activist atheist, and then challenge their thinking, to observe their scatoma's effect. Activists on the opposite end of the religious belief spectrum from yourself typically react like how you would react if someone told you that "Your mother or your child is ugly." An "'in-your-face" kind of person, which often includes many activists on either end of the religious spectrum, most people want to avoid. Most often people accept new information regarding their security need level beliefs as a threat. They therefore get violent. You would assume that in your-face people would soon learn that confrontation by an aggressive atheist or fundamentalist simply does not work. So why would you do it?

Formal education may be the best—-possibly the only—means of addressing and ultimately changing these blind spots or challenging such scatomas. Learning new information in a non-threatening environment is the only effective way to provide bridges over our paths around barriers, rather than hitting our beliefs head on where our own scatomas will always resist change. To cause change directly is like hitting a brick wall.

Forcing ourselves to reach a little further with each activity can do wonders to keep barriers from fixating in our own life, as well as in the lives of our children and significant others, whom we have allowed within our own defense mechanisms on our social level.

Some barriers may be physical, such as limitations upon space or time or available diet, while other barriers may be belief systems. Some are caused by ill health, or by our own earlier failures. But more often they are caused by our culture or are imposed upon us by well-meaning people intent on controlling our behavior—for "our own good," of course!

As a seemingly innocent example, the Jewish population historically denied the faithful the right to eat pork because the Bible requires for an animal to be kosher it must chew its cud. Pigs do not do that. Therefore, this restriction continues as tradition. Consequently, a Jewish person eating pork might feel guilty, thus denying themselves pleasure in that food. Like water running downhill, we take the easiest path. The easiest path for any of us is not to take part in any activity that causes stress or discomfort.

Likewise, some within the Catholic faith may still feel it is a sin to eat meat other than fish on Friday (at least during Lent), even though that tradition was largely created to support a declining fish industry. The tradition now takes on an entirely new symbolic meaning for those within the Catholic faith today. This is a good example of how our religious traditions evolve.

These examples are relatively unimportant, and if they have value for an individual, no one else should care. However, some irrational cultural restrictions can be harmful. A Christian Scientist denying a child essential medical care because of their personal religious beliefs may be one example. A recent court decision sentencing two parents to prison for manslaughter for allowing their child to die while they prayed for God to intervene rather than provide their child available medical attention makes the point. Yet it is easy to see how these limitations occur in society. Because all forms of irrational barriers prevail in our culture, finding better paths for living is fertile ground for those wishing to improve our society. Organized humanism should be concerned with that effort.

Alternative Paths to Actualization

Our body is the "temple" of our own lives. It seems foolish not to protect it. The question may be asked, 'If our goal is merely to reach a peak experience, why should we not shortcut the path by using drugs, or possibly alcohol?" Some drugs certainly could cut through all forms of barriers, but is the peak experience achieved with drugs genuine? You would never know. In the 1960s many people experiencing the "New Age" unsuccessfully tried that approach.

The purpose of the barrier was to protect you from something. With drugs, an individual would have blasted right through their personal barriers. The experience could have serious negative psychological side effects—let alone the established fact that the drugs themselves could permanently harm your body. Therefore, drug use is not an acceptable path for actualization.

Fully living each step of one's own life seems to be the only acceptable path for genuine fulfillment of our own existence. There are no shortcuts to a quality of life. Success is the journey, or our measure of the value of the path we have chosen, and not the goal. Once reached, each goal should be replaced with a new one. It is our journey through life that should matter to us, at least while we are here. That is all that has true real value. Possessions accumulated, and titles acquired, ultimately mean little without the quality of life that we have been able to live. Achieving the highest level of living our own life that we are capable of attaining is all that truly matters.

The Home and Garden of Charles Darwin

Chapter Nine

Who or What Created Humans?

How did we really get here? Public belief since recorded history has held the notion that humans were created by God. Some even believed we were created in his own image. This accepted primitive view had never been adequately challenged. In earlier times, challenge of a faith belief generally resulted in excommunication, if not death by being burned at the stake as a heretic.

Charles Darwin's grandfather, Erasmus Darwin (1731-1802) and Jean Baptiste Lamarck proposed a different view from the current Judeo-Christian view that all life occurred spontaneously 4,000; or, in some views, maybe 6,000 years, ago.—but certainly nowhere close to the millions of years ago that we now know to be the reality of today. Some believed that, perhaps simple life forms occurred by God spontaneously, but they were developed into more complex forms by a "vital force" and such species could adapt, and those best suited to their environments had a better chance for survival. Only the fittest survived for the next generation.

In those days people thought fish had fins because a "creator- god" wanted them to swim, and birds had wings because the same creator-God wanted them to fly. Charles Darwin thought all of that was silly. Birds could fly simply because they had wings. They developed wings so that they could forage for food. No one had thought of that before.

Charles Darwin ("Darwin") was born in Shrewsbury, Shropshire, England in 1809. He wanted to study the very origins of life. He was a biologist and geologist who saw in his garden the many differences in the same species of life. He studied worms, pigeons, and even barnacles and confirmed his conclusions while serving as a scientist aboard the ship *The Beagle* on its five-year intended voyage around the world. He could afford to pay for his trip because his mother's father was Josiah Wedgwood, the maker of fine porcelain. Darwin married his cousin, Emma Wedgewood, the granddaughter of the pottery magnate.

On his voyage, Darwin visited the Galápagos Islands. There he discovered animal life of known species that had developed unique characteristics. He reasoned from his observations that in nature there was as a steady state of change from simple to more complex forms of life. He concluded that life evolves much like a tree with a single root and many branches. All species of life have descended over time from common ancestors. That is a much different view of life than the commonly held public belief that "all life was created as a unique species by God," as "the Church" and its predecessors had been declaring for over two thousand years.

The idea there might be another answer than the creation theory of the Church took a lot of courage to show. The very notion that life progressed from simple to more complex forms of existence made God unnecessary in order to explain how humans came to exist. That was a revolutionary idea because it meant all life as it existed today did not have to be uniquely created by God.

Because it was still dangerous in Darwin's day to challenge religion, fearing retribution, Darwin waited until late in his life to make public his now famous book *On the Origin of Species*. That book has had an even greater impact on our view of life than the declaration of Galileo. Galileo proved that Earth was not the center of the Universe, as had been declared by the Church. Galileo wound up excommunicated and banished to his home for the rest of his life. Darwin proved all life has evolved from more primitive life. We do not need a God to be able to explain our existence here on Earth.

It was only in the past century that the Catholic Church finally absolved Galileo, who died in 1642, of heresy and admitted he was correct. Yet the Church continued to dominate what the public believes, and it still tries to do that today. Consider the conflict

between the wishes of women and the Church over birth control, which exists today. Do you suppose this is because the Church wants more members? After all, those born become contributors who tithe to support their Clergy. At the Church's current rate of change, it could be more than a century from now before the Church finally agrees women have the right to use birth control.

Because of the extraordinary level of control the Church still wields, even today, it rules the lives of its members way beyond the public benefit religion otherwise provides. Those that "have faith" and, therefore "believe," are not capable of seeing that. Their belief in the Church is, in itself a scatoma and our even challenging that belief is met hostilely by true believers in the Church. Which pretty well confirms the effect of a scatoma. The Church has exercised unreasonable control over the lives of the public for its own selfish reasons. In one of the worst examples of unbridled Power, Jacques de Molay was slow roasted over hot coals with the combined authority of the Crown and the Church for his "heretical" beliefs in 1314. Therefore, Darwin had every reason for being concerned for his own life. He had just provided an explanation that humans evolved from lower forms of life and were not uniquely created by God "in his image." That tops what his predecessors had said that caused their suffering.

It has since been proven through embryonic history that we evolved from fish through our own DNA. I will bet you never knew that at one point in your own embryonic development, you too had gills. Darwin had proven that all life has evolved from single cell protozoa, like the amoeba, and through evolution nature alone eventually created homo sapiens. God was no longer a necessary element for the creation of humans. It was a quantum leap for Darwin to claim that all Humans are as much a part of the evolution of life as all other forms of life.

The fact that, in one phase of our embryonic development, we each have the gills of our fish heritage proves each embryo restates the evolutionary history of its past, including us humans. Our ancient ancestors were in fact sea creatures.

Since the days of Darwin, scientists have discovered genes. In our lifetime, scientists have mapped the double helix of our DNA structure. We now know that there are dominant and recessive genes; that the male gene and female gene combine to provide the genetic composition of our children. We know today that the role we play in life is for the preservation and the conveyance of our genes to the next generation. That is important for the evolution of our species of life. Our own existence is only temporary so that the gene pool will evolve.

We know today that we, as individuals, become irrelevant after our childbearing days. The gene is what is perpetual, and it is what has a life of its own. Genes are independent of us. We are merely that gene's host for today. If we were able to live forever the gene pool would never change, and higher forms of life would not evolve. Thus, all life must die, including us, but, hopefully, our gene pool lives on.

Chapter Ten

What Does our Age Have to do with our Values?

We are each guided by what we value. Your values are normally not the values of your children. Why would that be true? Values do not vary as much by where in town you live as they do by what the technological level and social issues of the country where you were born at that time in history. Our values were developed in the cultural conditions that existed during our early childhood formative stages. They certainly can be changed by us over time as we educate ourselves, but changing who we are is difficult. In other words, looking at the public at large, a vast majority can be expected to have their current lens through which they view life based upon what was occurring in our society at the time of their formative stage of development.

Thus, our children will normally have a set of values different than our own. You may influence their values as they grow, but unless you understand where their values are rooted so that you speak to them using language tying into their perspective, you have a difficult task. President Trump got himself elected using this strategy. Marketing companies recognize this, so they frame the advertising they create to speak to a specific audience of consumers. They tell us that those of us living today normally have a global perspective conditioning our values that can be categorized as follows:

(*All statistical information is based upon 2017 figures within the United States)

The "Silent Generation"

Consists of those people who were born between 1925 and 1942. 22.4 million people born in this era are still alive in America as this essay was written*. This is also known as "the loyal generation." Most are traditionalists. People of this era were influenced by their parents, who lived through the Great Depression, and their fears of that happening again rubbed off on their children.

Adding to this, World War II required many sacrifices ranging from the lives of family and friends being called to service, to rationing of food and the availability of manufactured products. The Depression and the War certainly caused many uncertainties. The period following "the Great War" provided pride and economic prosperity for most people. Religion and a sense of patriotism produced social order and an emphasis on family which became the prevalent focus in most households. These aspects of our lives were highly valued. People had trust in each other, in their government, and generally in business. There was a great deal of conformity and resistance to change. In addition, there were more limited educational opportunities compared to today.

The people of the Silent Generation are strong users of traditional media and normally read newspapers and/or watch television news daily. They are basically unsophisticated online technology users.

They are not particularly price sensitive, yet they are financially conservative. They are very loyal consumers if quality is perceived. They buy to fill a need rather than for self-indulgence. Therefore, if you are marketing to this age range an emotional approach is normally more successful than a rational or logical approach. When viewing advertising they are more drawn to people than to products. Single images have more impact than a collage. They are negatively hypersensitive to age-related appeals, more receptive to television advertising, but not receptive to digital ads.

They are primarily motivated by the satisfaction of a job well done, and their highest values center on family and community.

The 'Baby Boom Generation"

The post-war generation consists of those born between 1943 and 1964. 74.9 million people born during this period are currently alive. This era created the optimistic generation, where its members centered their lives on "me." They are also known as the "love generation," They are motivated by money, title, and recognition. Success is among their highest values.

Much of this world view was shaped by the mass media culture with the development of television. This was enhanced with the healthy postwar economy and America hegemony. Children were overtly pampered by their parents who had grown up in poverty and sacrifice. There was a great feeling of optimism, and team orientation. The members of this era have an intense desire to affect change. Their parents had more traditional values and understanding their children was more difficult. The change was dramatic.

Baby Boomers are strong users of traditional media such as newspapers, television and radio. They are more receptive to non-traditional/digital media than their parents. The majority are online and have cell phones. They are becoming more confident online technology users.

Baby Boomers value service and low prices, but they will pay more for higher quality or value. They have much less brand loyalty and their purchases are often based on whether a product raises their status or image. They will especially appreciate convenience and customization. For age-related appeals, Baby Boomers are negatively hypersensitive and prefer themselves to be portrayed enjoying active, healthy lifestyles. They are big consumers of travel. Interestingly, they account for over half of packaged goods sales.

Generation X

These people are those born between 1965 and 1980. 61.5 million people from this generation are alive today in America. They are generally skeptical and have been labeled the "Why Me Generation." They are also recognized as the "Latchkey Generation." They are motivated by freedom. Their personal time and keeping balance between their work and personal life is most important.

This generation was influenced because their two working parents forced their self-reliance. Mass media created their culture. They were raised by Day Care. Overall, they show their skepticism, especially of authority. Technology is a part of their daily life. After all, they are the first generation of everyone having cell phones and personal computers. They have an excellent education.

They are consumers of traditional media, television, and newspapers. Calling and texting on smartphone is a great part of their lives. They are proficient online technology users. However, they are disloyal to brands. Due to financial constraints, value is their main determinant.

To attract them, straightforward, honest advertising is important. Product education is part of their buying process. Product features should be prominently displayed and explained. At the mid-point of their careers, most have children. They related to digital advertising formats more than those of earlier generations.

The Millennial Generation

This generation was born in the sixteen years between 1981 and 1997. They are realistic, sometimes referred to as "Generation Y," the 'Echo Boomers," or the "We Generation." In America there are 75.4 million people in this range. They are motivated by work that has meaning. Their highest values are individuality and happiness instead of power and money.

This generation, and those that follow, are rapidly moving away from traditional religion. Over forty percent of those born after 1981 state "none" when asked their religion in polls. The American Humanist Association now has more people in touch through social media today.

They have also now created a Free Thought Caucus among members in Congress for the first time in history. Millennials are far more attracted to the philosophy of humanism than their parents' generation.

Millennials have grown up with relative privilege. Most had highly supportive, encouraging parents. They seek greater diversity and accept differences in people. Technology is naturally integrated into their lives.

They watch more television but have decreasing reliance on newspapers and radio. They are constantly connected to the internet and use multiple online platforms. They are much less persuaded by television advertising, but more persuaded by digital. They are more apt to interact online, and they express themselves more freely. They are more apt to research products online, and they like online shopping.

They are far more brand-loyal, but they want their loyalty rewarded. They will extensively research products before they buy. They will research promotions before they enter a store. They will buy a generic brand or pay more depending on promotions or brand image. They look for "authentic" brands that show reliability, respectfulness, and reality. They search out socially responsible brands to enhance their own self-image and reward the company for providing that product.

Millennials want to be helped, not sold to. They are prone to impulsive shopping decisions. They shop more than other generations. They are likely to interact with brands and to recommend them to their friends with social media.

Generation Z

This generation was born between 1998 and 2009. They are predicted to be the most-connected generation yet. They have never known life without technology. They are the most diverse generation yet. They will have greater purchasing power than all those before them. They will be the most highly educated generation. They are motivated by creativity and entrepreneurialism. They highly value technology, adaptability, and open-mindedness.

They are continuously plugged in online and easily do multitasking on more devices. They do watch television, but usually over the internet. Smartphones are seen by Generation Z as indispensable.

Although functionality is important, products that look good win out. They are more skeptical, less brand-loyal than Millennials and more sensitive to corporate insincerity. They are saving money at a higher rate than young Millennials at their age.

They want brands that let them share their creativity and innovation. For them it is important to create a consistent brand feeling across all brand platforms. They are a big influence on parents' buying decisions. They have a strong interest in food, drinks, social activities, apps, music, and social media.

It has recently been discovered that Tic Tok, which is currently owned by a China company, and therefore controlled by its Communist Party, has been targeting this generation during their formative years, causing the attitude of over a majority of this age group to now be hostile to American values that are shared by our current culture. The suspicion is that this is a test of the tools available to China's leaders to see the influence China can ultimately acquire to change American beliefs.as they continue their drive to become the world's leader by their replacing the role America currently enjoys in the world that it has today.

Generation Alpha

This generation includes all born after 2010 and they predict this cultural generation may reasonably be expected to last until 2025. They are the most globally connected generation. So far, they are predicted to have 35 million in America by the time the first reaches age 40.

Their values will be greatly molded by their Millennial parents. They are more likely to be only children. They are already more digitally integrated. Because their parents had their child at a later age, their parents will age earlier. We know that cultural and racial diversity will be much greater than in earlier generations. The socioeconomic climate will offer marginally more wealth. Families will skew smaller, while life expectancy will continue to lengthen. Ultimately, it is predicted that this will be the wealthiest, most formally educated and techno-centric generation yet. What will really motivate them in the future? Hopefully, not the Chinese.

In Summary

These are the cultural broad shared values, created by the social environment, in which each cultural generation of people has been raised. Obviously, individuals will vary greatly as they have different experiences and institutions that influence their development. Let us next explore how we as individuals affect what our culture provides for us as a set of basic values.

Chapter Eleven

What Controls Do We Have for Our Life?

There is no question that some people could not exist if our government did not aid them. Not all welfare is bad. The problem lies in how our programs are administered. Most people who become dependent on others unknowingly give up living their own life. Life is a growth process. Dependent people often stop growing. They merely exist. Some of our government programs take away participants' sense of self-worth. No one in government seems to notice that they are the cause of a significant portion of our social problems. How do we change that? First, we must have government programs that encourage participants to develop positive attitudes about themselves. To develop a positive attitude, we must encourage people to have goals by showing them how their life can improve with only a little more of their own effort. To be able to take the first step, participants must be able to see an opportunity for their own success. An attitude of positive anticipation must precede any change in their behavior before any real change may ever be carried out.

There is no question that everyone's basic needs must first be satisfied for them to perceive anything beyond those needs. However, our effort to help the recipient of our welfare should not stop there. We must help people whose behavior we wish to change by encouraging them to accept personal goals if we expect different behavior for their future. That may well be beyond the capacity of many who are second or third generation on welfare today. The task of carrying out this goal may exceed our own energy and society's willingness to expend the effort to help them achieve change. However, if opportunities are properly presented to their parents, their children will become aware, and they will be far more susceptible to change that will keep them off of welfare.

Once people are on the path for growth, much like an athlete who feels good every time they perform a little bit better than the last time, most people can recognize a sense of reward which they feel as success. It will increase their self-worth by striving to reach their goals, even after expending only a little more effort. It only takes once getting them on the path, providing them interim goals that are achievable, and then rewarding their interim successes in order to help many people learn the benefits that can be derived from their own efforts. Some will fail, but the effort is worth it for those who achieve their own success. And it will eventually get most people off welfare dependency. We could have social programs that fulfill real needs and improve instead of destroying the quality of the lives of their participants. To be effective we must address the recipients' attitude about themselves.

Contrary to popular belief, success is the journey; not the result of reaching a goal. Once a goal is achieved, a new goal should replace that goal in order that we can continue our own growth path. Marketers continually play on that process by creating our notion of new wants by giving us a positive attitude toward their product, which will soon become our need to acquire. Attitude makes a huge difference in anyone's ability to achieve success. Even with a positive attitude, fulfillment must be earned by each of us if it is to have lasting value. Success breeds greater success. The result of our behavior all starts with our attitude. Your attitude causes your own result, positive or negative.

How Does My Attitude Make a Difference?

The choice is solely up to me whether I open my mind to learning and growth, or whether I close my mind, content within my current world. Attitude, indeed, makes the greatest difference. My current attitude is one of the very few factors in my existence that I personally can control. My attitude is the most critical element in finding the quality of my own life, and the effect that I have on others.

Some authorities declare that there is a "law of attraction" that acts like a magnet pulling our opportunities, or our defeats, out of the mass of stimuli that surrounds us daily. Like fixed ideas we have about certain brands of clothing, or foods, our mental orientation filters acceptance or rejection of all new information as well as our interpretation of the new data acquired from our current experience. We make decisions based upon our bias. Our attitude is the filter that defines how we react to the information that we currently receive.

The attitude we project to others also influences the response we receive from others. Even when we are alone, our own attitude becomes a self-fulfilling prophecy. We get back what we project and our attitude molds how we react to what we then receive. This creates a spiral effect that can either ascend to greater heights and opportunities, or our attitude reinforces negative feelings, causing our descent, which may well lead to a state of unhappiness and chaos. More simply said, a positive happy attitude must precede our actions if we wish to affect our ability to attain positive results.

By changing our reception of all new information, we receive, we modify its effect upon us. Our current attitude will decide the effect new information will have on us. Adopting our current attitude is the primary daily control that we have over our life. By being receptive to new information, we can grow and expand our view of life, and accept change that can enhance our life.

If we do not intentionally choose our own attitude in any given moment, we are then subject only to fate. By keeping an open mind, we are better able to challenge negative information and absorb new beneficial information. If we are indifferent, the information that we next receive may be subject to the attitude we held for the preceding event. Instead of assuming responsibility for our own lives, events will rule us.

We can only live in the present moment. Living in the past may give us a false sense of accomplishment, or a foreboding expectation of failure. That will not only influence our current attitudes and feelings about ourselves, but the result will distort reality. Ultimately living in the past does nothing to improve our future, except to provide us with information in a primitive attempt to protect us from failure or to create wishes we might not be sufficiently motivated to achieve. The past is only a prelude. It can either influence our current attitude or be ignored by us. That is exclusively our own choice. The only aspect of our lives we control is how we perceive and accept the new data or stimulation we continually receive.

Our past experiences may enhance our ability to predict the outcome of our current situation, but the result is not inevitable. If an individual prefers a different result, the only way that they can influence the achievement of that result is by changing how they interpret their current situation. If you think positively toward a goal, you are much more apt to have a positive result.

I like the statements "You are what you think that you are," or "As you think, so you shall become," and "Whether you think you can, or you can't, you're right." Our opinions of ourselves in our current situation will often decide the outcome of our current behavior. It takes fate or luck to cause any other result. We should be unwilling to live our lives relying upon fate. If we truly want to live our own life, we must be the cause of whatever happens next.

What Difference Does a Positive Attitude Make?

Successful people enhance their opportunity to create successful results because successful people believe they will be successful. It all starts with their attitude. They believe in themselves and know that they can achieve what they want to achieve. The opposite view is also true, and even more powerful. With a negative attitude you can easily become your own worst enemy.

If we approach our current situation expecting success and meet a momentary setback because the ball did not hit the basket, or an intervening event caused a different result than expected, we should view that event as a new opportunity to learn and proceed with greater enthusiasm. People who do not take charge of their own attitude will be more apt to curse the cause or their result, blame themselves, and feel badly that they "failed." You can imagine what then happens with their next shot. How we react will decide what happens next. Successful people see loss as momentary and an opportunity to learn so that they can deal with those factors differently next time. It is up to each individual as to how they will react. The only control we have over our life is our current attitude, and that will influence our future behavior.

If we are afraid, we will lose the race, or lose the wrestling match, or miss the shot because we have not practiced, or because we missed it last time, or we weigh too much, or whatever, we have created the environment that will produce that result. Our attitude becomes our own self-fulfilling prophecy.

Does Prayer Help?

Some people pray for a result and then keep doing it with the next problem they face because it appeared to work before. It may well be because they have created a positive attitude toward achieving their objective, and not because God intervened in their life. One resulting aspect of prayer is that it does tune oneself to reality. Those with a religious perspective may say, "God rewards those who believe." In contrast, when they lose or fail, some will not accept their own responsibility by saying, "It was God's will."

Meditation is what is really working. God may have nothing to do with it. After all, it is terribly vain of us to believe that our own "God" will intervene to make a change in our lives that will affect the outcome of our behavior to the detriment of someone else. The implication is that only we are special to our God, and our competitors are not. What we are really doing is affecting our own attitude by focusing on the result we wish to obtain. That is true whether we call it prayer or meditation. No one else is really listening.

There are many ways to become in tune with oneself. Meditation works. It clears all other thoughts out of your mind and focuses on one thought at a time. By focusing on a thought, we open our reception to that thought either negatively or positively, depending upon our attitude at that moment. Psychology explains it is our attitude that orients our lives and influences the result of our behavior by enhancing our expectations, energy, and driving toward a goal, or requiring us to reject it. A current positive attitude allows us to focus upon the goal and to become more receptive to the subtle opportunities that will enhance the result we wish to achieve. The opposite is also true. Consider the effect of the behavior of a parent who feels a lack of their own success and projects that attitude upon their own children. The Parent then wonders why their child has low self-esteem that results in a lack of success and, in some cases, disciplinary problems. A totally different result is achieved for the child whose parents support and believe in their child's own ability to achieve. Your own attitude makes a difference for others.

If we want to achieve only good results, then we should not allow ourselves to think negatively about anything. To test this, we should try thinking only positively for a day and see how we then feel about ourselves and the world around us at the end of the day. Given time it will become a habit that will work wonders. It is important to remember that our attitude means everything, as it influences the results, we achieve through living our own life striving to be the very best that we can achieve.

We are Responsible for Ourselves .
You Cannot Blame Others for Who You Are

To get the most out of our own lives we must assume the exclusive responsibility for ourselves. We can no longer hide behind other people, expecting them to do what is right for us, and still be able to fully actualize our own existence. We will become a reflection of those people, and no longer truly be ourselves. In relying upon others to make our decisions for us, we will never know who we really are. By getting to know yourself, you may be surprised to find that you really like yourself. Life then feels right for you because you know that you are yourself.

Is Your Group Thinking for You?

Psychology recognizes the phenomenon known as "groupthink." This means that by identifying with an organization, the extent we become dependent upon the group, its Control People do their members' thinking for them. Their membership becomes their validation of truth. We see this in political parties, in our high school, every church, especially in the military. This contrasts vividly with those who claim individual autonomy and remain in control of their own lives, like many Humanists would like to think that they do. But they even take part in their group's beliefs.

Many are ardent "Democrats", or "Republicans", or may even be "Independents". Identity becomes more important than policy. Because they belonged to that group, they had not complained when something occurred, they otherwise would have strongly objected to. If challenged, they will claim "the circumstances were different" in order to defend their "group", when in fact the circumstances are identical. The "group identity" is more important than the policy. Be aware; perhaps this includes you. You must retain the ability to think for yourself, and not allow any group to tell you what you must believe, or you are allowing the group to control you, and you will cease to grow in that area of concern. It may feel easier to accept the group's view of reality, but you will no longer be fully living your own life. You must feel that you are always able to freely disagree with your own group, and that you have thought through all avenues addressing the issue yourself independent of your group, for your own life to truly matter.

Chapter Twelve

Live a Happier Life with a Free Mind

Fred Edwords was hired as the Executive Director of the American Humanist Association when I served as its President in the early 1980's, and he has been serving the Association in many capacities ever since. He is a master at conveying his message, as he did in his wonderful article in the first edition of the *Humanist* magazine which now combines the magazine with the membership newsletter of the AHA which it has published since its inception in1941, and since the 1950's titled *Free Mind*. Fred wrote his article as its Guest Editor, with the title of this chapter. I have summarized its content with his permission because it puts in perspective the Epicurean philosophy.

"Happiness is a state of mind". According to Sonja Lyubomirsky, professor of positive psychology at the University of California, Riverside. She defines happiness as **"the experience of joy, contentment, or positive well-being, combined with a sense that one's life is good, meaningful, and worthwhile."** That puts into more realistic focus what Epicurus was saying. It provides the framework for you to consider as you experience your own life daily.

Your answers will differ depending upon which level of Maslow's Hierarchy of Needs you are currently living on as you focus on your current need issues. The reason being that the lower levels have such need deficiency strength that a person living on the security level for instance, means that their immediate needs prevail. You cannot be happy if your life is being threatened. On the security level your immediate needs must be satisfied before you can even sense a feeling of happiness.

Life is essentially a balancing act, but the result starts with whether you have a positive receptive attitude, or one that is negative. Even a positive attitude does not ensure happiness, but it does provide reception to new opportunity that can lead to a happier, more fulfilled life than could ever be achieved from a negative perspective. But if your basic needs are not satisfied, your security level needs are protective, and not receptive to anything that does not provide satisfaction of those needs.

If you look at happiness from the perspective of pleasure, Mr. Edwords says, "the problem is that intense pleasures are fleeting, and longer lasting ones may amount to little more than relaxation. Moreover, a determined effort to maximize pleasure, and minimize pain...can require a lot of unpleasurable work... unsatisfied yearnings are often long, while satisfactions are short. And pleasurable feelings, once experienced are often forgotten." The attitude a person has now will control whether the events will allow the person to receive them happily, or not.

How you perceive your situation will decide how your efforts are received. If your basic and security level needs are satisfied, and you are working to provide for your family, seeing progress toward your goal will give you feelings of happiness. In contrast, if something interferes with your efforts, your reaction will be negative. In America, few people are starving today. Even a homeless person living under a bridge to protect themselves from the rain can feel happy, because they are momentarily safe. Would they be happier if someone offered them a free hotel room for the night? Probably. But when they are back on the street the next night their unhappiness weighs on their night before. When you are living on the security level your security is based upon your view of the future.

People in adverse circumstance that are working for a safer future for their family may have a greater sense of satisfaction with their progress, and are therefore happier, than those who have everything, and therefore no needs, who are trying to decide what they can do.

next. The activity towards a goal is what causes the first person to be happier than the second.

Mr. Edwords uses the example of a house cat in America who is playing with the household mouse at the risk of losing it because the cat is not hungry. There is no challenge based upon the cat's needs. Catching the mouse would defeat the pleasure the cat was looking for. The first may be content, but a cat who is hungry who catches the mouse would be happier. It is their effort resulting in success that produces the second cat's happiness.

In Maslow's terms, when your needs are all in the node you are no longer driven by deficiency so you can fully experience the moment. Freedom from immediate needs allows you to look to the next higher need level to fulfill your existence if you are seeking happiness. Feeling success is experiencing improvement in seeking your next goal, not the result of your reaching your goal. If you want to remain in the happiest state of your being, you should have replaced the first goal with another goal before you reached the first goal. It is the stretching and progress that creates the feeling of happiness.

In our culture, we are not called upon for the efforts of survival that demand the full attention of many in other areas of the world. We do not have the need to forage for food as did the those who first inhabited our lands. Even modern people experiencing homelessness are fed by food pantries, many without charge. As a result, we play games, create art, and join in community activities. To have a fulfilling life we must have constructive activity. Even retired people need goals for their life to have value for them.

If you look upon your current situation you will get a different result depending upon your expectation. We will regard our life as worthwhile if we are engaged in some activity of value, experiencing a suitable amount of enjoyment in our effort. Even if the reason for the effort is to avoid a serious threat, an acceptance that we are soldiering on for some positive result for ourselves, or for others for whom we feel responsible, will provide feelings of success resulting in happy feelings. If we have no goals, we cannot expect to be happy or content. We merely exist.

The primary control that you have beyond selecting the goals you wish to reach, is your expectation of the result. What is your level of tolerance for lessor quality than perfection? If you are a perfectionist, and the result turns out below your standard, you are unhappy. If you lower your standard to one of merely accepting change leading toward that goal, far more results will leave you feeling happy. Putting that in a Practical context, if you are visiting a friend and feeling hungry, the mere fact that they offer any food makes you happy. If you are a gourmet and you expected fine China and caviar and you get a cheeseburger you are not going to enjoy it regardless of what your host says to you. Your expectation is the key to your happiness.

Epicurus said that you should fully experience each moment to get the very most that you can out of life. This means you accept the conditions of where you are at that moment, and fully appreciate what happens without expectations. You need to ***want nothing and need little*** to make the most of each moment. That does not mean that you have not set goals. A goal is the path that you are on. How you react to the obstacles in your path, accepting them, or redirecting your efforts to obtain your goals, is important. Your expectation that there will be barriers keeps you from being frustrated. Incorporating your expectation that your current circumstances will require you to bypass the barriers to continue your path provides your feelings of success. Nearly each play in football is designed to gain a touchdown. Most fail. The players do not walk off the field with the first failure. They try harder the next time. It is continually seeking their goal that is important. The immediate barriers are immaterial. There is always another play in their game plan.

Thomas Edison tried to find a filament that would turn electricity into light over 10,000 times before he tried tungsten that worked. In answer to a question of "how do you feel about so many failures?" said, "well, I now know 10,000 things that will not work." He finally felt success and that was his focus. He did not focus on his failures. He even found value in those. So, he was happy.

We are not in control of what life offers to us, any more than the house guest wanting something to eat. Accepting the reality and attempting to gain the most from the moment will produce happiness. Expectations beyond reality make the imperfections and hustle and bustle of the real-world result in unhappiness. Taking life as it really is and making the most of each moment for what it is, still focused on positive goals, like Edison, results in the journey feeling successful and produces happiness in the effort to get there.

If you have unrealistic expectations over things you cannot control, you cannot expect to be happy very often. You can never totally control another person successfully. Even if that person is your own child. Your goal should be to fully appreciate who they are, guide them when you can, make a difference without discouraging or defeating them so that they quit trying, and then sit back and appreciate whatever happens from their efforts. You will then be happy with the results. Their success will be yours too.

Reaching for the stars starts with taking one step forward at a time. When you hit an obstacle, you might occasionally have to take a step backward, but more often it is a step sideways to get around the obstacle. If you keep going long enough, you will eventually reach your goal, or find another goal along that way you find preferable. My best friend since we were born wanted to go to the Moon. He became the space scientist for NASA responsible for the trajectory of the spaceship from the Earth to the Moon and what the Astronauts did when they got there. NASA dropped their program of allowing scientists to be Astronauts, but he got close. He was on the Moon in the Astronauts activities.

The title of the AHA's newsletter, *"Free Mind,"* should remind humanists that an independent mind free of "others control" allows us to rationally analyze life's situations as they arise, and then manage our personal emotions in ways that foster a positive response. Your expectations, and your reactions all start with your attitude, and these are your exclusive controls for producing your own happiness in any given circumstance.

Chapter Thirteen

Why Do We Have all of The Many Beliefs That We Currently Now Have?

You will find that we have many unfounded beliefs if you search for their truth, or the root for why we even entertain that belief. Most do not matter, and the answer to why we have that belief is not worth the effort to question. However, some universal cultural beliefs can be life controlling, even though they may be false. As an example, we each have our own notion of an afterlife that is acceptable to us.

I certainly have no intentions of challenging anyone else's belief. Only you should do that for yourself. However, it is important for us to understand how notions that form many of our beliefs have been culturally transmitted over thousands of years. Where did this belief come from, when there is no valid evidence that a life after death exists? This belief, can only be accepted by "blind faith."

I am discussing this belief because this example is a universal belief. Everyone has been exposed to this belief. The purpose for a thorough analysis of a specific universal belief is to make the point dramatically so that you might better understand the ultimate effect of any belief that affects your own life. The goal is to motivate each of us to pause and go through a similar analysis before we accept any irrational belief based upon "blind faith" that has any control over our very existence. Not thinking for yourself is dangerous to our very existence. Challenging all "blind faith" beliefs will help each of us make better choices of what we are willing to each accept as our own truth so that we will take charge of our own lives, and not let ourselves be anyone else's puppet. We certainly should not want to live our own life like a sheep.

Why we have the belief of a life after death is not an easy question for us to find acceptable answers. Not because there are not multiple plausible theories to explain this belief. The problem is there are too many. Most answers lack depth of thought. Most people start from the premise that one must exist because everyone believes it does. Therefore, it is easier not to question whether that notion is true. It seems to be a subject that everybody has written about from the perspective to justify the belief. There are, however, very few who approach the question from a skeptical perspective. That seemed to me to be the most productive way to start. That is probably because that is the way that lawyers are trained to look at life, and the problems we address daily in our society.

What I have found so far, to provide an overview of a few theories as an example of what I consider to be the best answers of why we humans believe in an afterlife, will provide you a large enough range of thinking about this subject so that you can consider what answers you find most acceptable for yourself. The range I found as the most plausible answer can best be summarized in this list:

1. Some claim the belief in an afterlife is simply "**wishful thinking.**" We lived yesterday, we are alive today therefore we expect to be alive tomorrow, even after we are dead. Each of us has a fear of death. It is human nature to fear the unknown. We simply cannot fathom that we will no longer exist, even though most of us understand that we did not exist before we were born in the body where we now exist today. Therefore, we humans are very willing to make this "leap of faith".

2. Others think we have this belief because that it is a way for promoting "**socially desirable behavior**". In other words, it is simply a control device of society conveyed by parents and the priestly class.

3. Some have claimed the belief in life after death has simply evolved from "**ancient people's beliefs**" as their best efforts to explain strange phenomena, such as, dreams. That was a novel, but shallow thought.

4. Some feel that it is the natural result of the fact that we each feel that "**we are more than our own body**". The fact that we have awareness of our environment, because of the size of our brains we can think beyond ourselves. Therefore, we can think independently of our own body. This causes us to feel that we are something separate from and beyond our own physical existence. Therefore, that separate "entity" has a life of its own. That is most probably the most logical reason, but it is easily proven false because in the laboratory today scientists can duplicate the result, proving our belief has nothing to do with an afterlife.

5. An interesting idea of one author I read is that the notion of life after death is the handy work of "**evolution by natural selection**": People who do not feel that death is the end of our life are more apt to be stronger and more aggressive in battle. If you knew that the result of your behavior would be the absolute very end of you, would you be a suicide bomber?

6. Richard Dawkins, the distinguished Oxford professor of biology, agrees that afterlife beliefs are products of natural selection; but not natural selection that is working on genes or any other biological entities such as those that were identified by Darwin. Instead, Dawkins says that afterlife beliefs are products of natural selection of the evolution of ideas. It is the natural selection of our brains holding on to specific ideas out of the myriad of ideas that we are continually exposed to, rather than the natural selection of our genes which perpetuates our species. However, they both work the same way. Those selected for our retention are what Dawkins has labeled as "**memes**". This was a word

he invented. He defined a meme as any coded information with the power to influence its own replication. Just like genes are our biological replicators contributing to our very existence, memes. They are the replicators of our ideas that are manifest in the existence of what we each believe. They may have little relevance to reality.

Let's explore in a little more detail these separate views. Here are some of the more in-depth explanations that I found merits our further thought.

Wishful Thinking

In exploring the first view, that of wishful thinking, according to some scholars, and many bar stool philosophers, for them religion is all about comfort and consolation. To put it a bit more bluntly to describe their position in order to distinguish their views from those that follow: for them, to quote the most vocal one, "such beliefs are mollycoddling illusions, especially when it comes to afterlife beliefs". He said that belief in life after death is "exhibit A" in the case as to why the belief in an afterlife is a by-product of wishful thinking. For them, the reason for a belief in life after death is because it may eliminate, or at least weaken, the fear of personal extinction, or the overwhelming sadness we experience when any loved one dies. One more intelligently added that it is magnified because many of us have the sense that a life of finite duration would be meaningless if our own life could not continue.

For those who espouse this position, most people hold the religious beliefs that they do simply because they were taught those beliefs as children by their parents and this notion is shared by their surrounding culture. It is easier to accept the notion because everyone else believes that an afterlife exists, than it is to reject those ideas. That may be true, but the real question then is why did these beliefs become so popular in the first place? And if we can answer that question, why are so many people unwilling to relinquish or change their belief even after they are faced with strong evidence that some beliefs may be false? These are the questions that the people who accept wishful thinking theory fail to answer.

In short, their explanation is that people keep and refuse to relinquish any belief that provides a salve for the pains of life for us as well as the people we care about. I could accept that. However, what I have found is thar it does not work. Belief in life after death does not actually relieve our fear of death. Nor does it effectively avoid the grieving that we all face with the loss of a loved one, Although, as was stated by one philosopher who rose a bit above his bar stool, it is possibly true that our religious beliefs persist not because they provide comfort, but because, once acquired, discarding them produces acute discomfort.

An analogy would be nicotine, drug, or alcohol addiction. Once addicted, cigarettes give little pleasure, but as soon as a person tries to give them up, they experience intense and unpleasant cravings. Therefore, the addiction is kept less by the pleasure it produces than by the displeasure it keeps at bay.

Furthermore, millions of people have lived in fear of Hell or eternal damnation or other frightening postmortem possibilities for their entire life. The idea that an eternity of suffering might await oneself is one of the most unpleasant ideas devised by human minds. As noted previously, Darwin called it a "damnable doctrine". In other words, rather than relieving people's fears of death, some afterlife beliefs often create fears that people would not otherwise have. Therefore, wishful thinking as a theory might be part of the reason but it certainly cannot be the whole story.

Organized religion provides social cohesion or "Social Glue."

The second concept in this list of why people have such beliefs, one author called "social glue". The idea is that our religious beliefs are the cement that holds societies together. Regardless of the truth of the doctrine as a primary reason for a belief in a life after death, there is little question that religion provides social solidarity and a sense of community by providing common beliefs and values, thereby motivating people to be moral. The comforting side of afterlife beliefs is that they are designed to encourage socially beneficial behavior, whereas discomforting beliefs are designed to discourage socially harmful behavior. There is a lot of "Santa Claus" in that approach.

I would accept that except that not all religious beliefs are socially beneficial, some beliefs can tear groups and nations apart. Look at what is happening with the radical Islam beliefs of today within the Muslim community and their attack on the rest of the world in the name of their religion. In other words, the social glue theory breaks down because it also leads to the notion that it is us against them.

Social Control

Another way of looking at the argument of social glue that is a bit more sophisticated than the barstool philosophers is viewing the concept of social control from the point of reference of those issuing the glue. Here we have a class of people promoting such beliefs as tools for social manipulation. Parents and teachers use them to control the children, husbands use them to control wives and vice versa, slave owners used them to control slaves. The ruling class uses them to control the proletariat, and priests, kings and other leaders use them to control tribes, guilds, and nations. The glue provides the issuer power!

If you apply the same concept to afterlife beliefs that might suggest that people attempt to control other's behavior with the promise of heaven and the threat of hell in exactly the same ways parents attempt to control their children's behavior, telling them if they are good Santa will bring them presents but if they are naughty, he won't.

The belief being conveyed may have nothing to do with the real intent of the person controlling. That may be true even though in many cases the Control Person is doing so out of a firm belief that it is the right thing to do. Bishop John Shelby Spong suggests that there are some clergy who have religious understanding that is significantly deeper than what they are willing to share with their entire congregation because it is their belief that their knowledge is beyond the best interest of the people they serve, and it would result in creating distress. In other words, sharing their true beliefs could destroy their parishioners' current "faith". There is little doubt that the masses may be ignorant on any given subject, however ultimately the best result is to be totally honest. Perhaps that is why many successful clergy stay on the surface during a sermon but offer in depth analysis in more private sessions that are open only to anyone willing to learn more, rather than to threaten their congregation by preaching at the pulpit more than their entire audience can accept, without threatening their existing beliefs.

What those who use this argument are suggesting is that: why we have a belief in a life after death is the motivation of Control People to continue the belief for their control of our society, rather than, at least for some Control People, an expression of their true belief in the validity of the message itself.

This is not to suggest that most of these beliefs are for the purpose of exploitation by the individual carrying the message. Most of those in control probably firmly believe the message. The belief is more universal than the individual. According to those espousing that view, is that it is our culture that creates the belief in life after death and then they defend these beliefs as socially acceptable as a means of keeping social order.

Primitive Science, (or Perpetuation of Ancient Beliefs)

The answer that is prevalent in what writings are available, is that the explanation of such beliefs that have been culturally transmitted through multiple generations is the sincere attempt of earlier people to understand the phenomena of life. In other words, many ideas are fossils of our earlier efforts to explain the world around us. People have all kinds of experiences that would be very hard for pre- scientific people to explain.

For instance, when we lay down to sleep, our bodies stay where we left them, and yet when we dream, we often have the experience of being elsewhere, and doing other things. How might we explain this in the absence of the mature scientific understanding of the world? One explanation would be that part of us leaves our physical body that has an independent existence that can explore strange worlds: quite unlike the world of our waking life. And it doesn't end there. Sometimes we each have vivid emotionally charged dreams in which we meet people who have died. How can we explain this? Well, perhaps the part of us that leaves the body during dreams survives bodily death—and "voila" we now see how such beliefs could emerge from people's honest efforts to explain the things that happen to them. They are simply efforts to explain the facts of our actual experience as we gain knowledge of the world in which we all live.

The problem with that concept is that even though such answers may be comforting, it does not explain why the answer is so readily accepted today, and the belief perpetuates even though many of those kinds of beliefs have been explained away by science analyzing the facts and duplicating the results that produced the beliefs in the first place. Why did the belief not die with the understanding of the explanation of its source?

Evolution

Evolution theory is another recent alternative explanation. Some have tried to apply Darwin's thinking to religious concepts. If our religious beliefs are a direct product of natural selection, just as parts of our body were selected because they take advantage of the individuals having them, takes us into an interesting realm of thinking. In other words, even ideas, such as afterlife beliefs, may be accepted as truths and adapted for our use because they give believers confidence and purpose in life, or because they lower anxiety when a loved one dies. Such beliefs also empower people in combat. They improve our health by reducing stress. Or it could be because they bind groups together and thereby further the interest of the group and its members.

The problem with that as a universal reason is that people's religious beliefs vary so much across cultures and historical traditions. That makes it very difficult to imagine they are all instances of the same form of adaptation. In other words, why do they all not look alike? Even afterlife beliefs within some religions differ. Some are a belief in a disembodiment existence, others reincarnation and still others bodily resurrection. Look at the Jewish faith where all Jews in Israel are buried facing Mt. Moriah so that at the "end of the days" everyone is raised into heaven, and they will be the very first ready to arrive.

Those of the orthodox Jewish faith, at least in the past, have had a belief that heaven is not a place of immediate transition, but requires the second coming of a Messiah. And they are still waiting. That is totally different than most people accepting Christianity find as an acceptable belief today. If it is correct that religious beliefs are not direct products of evolution but are by-products of another more general tendency of the mind caused because of the position of the individual within their respective culture, the Jewish view of the path to heaven should still be the Christian view today. Perhaps accepting immediate entry into heaven might be a major factor in why Christianity became such a successful religion.

One theory of why Christians and Jews differ is that the Christianity of today was the product of Saint Paul. His Jesus may not be the Jewish Jesus that actually lived. That is the position taken by recently retired Episcopal Bishop, John Shelby Spong.

The best explanation for the reason for cultural differences came from E.O. Wilson. As I previously mentioned he was a distinguished professor of biology at Harvard for over 40 years. Dr. Wilson was best known for his research that concluded with the development of the science of sociobiology. His premise is that biology does not end at the point of birth and sociology is the exclusive science of what occurs thereafter. His point is that many of our sociological institutions are biologically determined. For instance, Dr. Wilson claims that spirituality is biologically necessary. Spirituality is essentially tuning our self to resonate with nature. This is a natural phenomenon for everyone, which our religions captured as a central organizing focus. This is Consistent with the social glue theory that religion must attract everyone in order to provide social controls necessary to maintain our ability to successfully live together.

Dr. E.O. Wilson, in a recent book entitled *"The Meaning of Human Existence,"* claims that studies show that in early stages of Homo Sapiens' existence, two forces were built into human nature by selectivity. The first is the selfishness of the individual. This developed because the selfish individual can defeat the altruistic individual one on one, thus contributing to meeting his needs. However, when groups developed to meet the hunting success necessary to sustain life, or the protection of the group from competing tribes, the perpetuation of the group required altruistic behavior of individuals toward each other. Altruistic individuals collectively in the group could defeat the selfish individual. Thus, creating a static dichotomy that exists yet today.

Dr. Wilson claims that this dichotomy between selfishness and altruism contributes to the success of human existence. If selfishness prevailed, we would have anarchy and no cultural growth. If altruism prevailed, we would have no creativity and intellectual growth. For a successful society we must have both. His thesis is that it is the conflict between the individual and the group that resulted from natural selection that has created our quality of life—but it all is because of natural selection.

This might also explain the differences in our religious views. It is because of the development of specific groups, by means of our "group think" that created unique means for being able to identify together for their mutual protection. Since much of Dr. Wilson's research was the result of his study of the cultural colonization of ants, I wondered if ants had any notion of a life hereafter. If that is not a notion the ant understands, and if only humans have that belief, if life after death exists, does it also exist for other forms of life? If I must exist forever, I want my dog to live with me. However,

Science has discovered that our beliefs are the result of the size of our human brains having enlarged to the size where we are now capable of thinking beyond ourselves. Our dogs are not able to do that, so they cannot take part and accept our unfounded beliefs. Only we humans can do that. So, I cannot expect that my dog will be there waiting for me.

Spandrel By-products of the Evolution Theory

What the next level of research has shown is that according to the byproduct approach to evolution, religion is not a product of natural selection. Instead, religion is the result of other **aspects of the mind** that are caused as a by-product of natural selection. This occurs because the brains of humans are now large enough, we now have the ability for abstract thinking. Therefore, we can create new thoughts that exist only in our brains, like unicorns, which do not otherwise exist. That would be consistent with Dr. Wilson's claim that spirituality is biologically determined. We just carry the need to a new dimension. Once religion became a meme religion had a life of its own.

In a conversation I had with Dr. Steven J. Gould, he answered the next question for me. I have personally known Dr. Gould. He was an active Humanist. He was recognized by the Harvard students as their outstanding university professor of the year for most of his career. Dr. Gould calls religious phenomena "**a spandrel**". What that would imply is that the belief in life after death may be an accidental incidental by-product of the capacity for what he calls "**theory of mind**". This is the name he has given to the human ability to construe other people and oneself as independent agents, each having unique beliefs, desires and differing mental states. This ability is found in all normally developing human beings. However, it is absent, or largely absent, in all other animals and this ability is most plausibly a product of natural selection. We humans have arrived and are therefore entitled to take part. Other animals have not yet evolved to that level of comprehension. We can consider the question of life after death. Other animals cannot do that.

Putting that notion together with the human behavioral conflict between individuals and groups described by E.O. Wilson shows why in riot control dealing with mob psychology shows us where the individual loses his or her identity in the mob under certain conditions. The individual's behavior becomes that of the group, like that of the ant, even though there is no group leadership. The group literally takes on an independent mind of its own. People who are members of a mob will do terrible things to others that they would never consider doing if they were separated from the mob. That is why one control technique of a riot is to separate people from the crowd. That is why the military and police use force to separate a mob by encountering the crowd with their shields or water cannons and pushing them in opposite directions to continually reduce the size of the mob. As a National Guard Officer, I have been on riot control duty. I found that really does work. Separate the individual and the individual thinks for themselves. While they are in the group, the will of the group does their thinking.

The reason for a spandrel view is that humans naturally think about physical objects and our minds use distinct mental vocabularies. For instance, we construe physical objects, but not mental states, as having specific dimensions. This perspective makes it easy for us to imagine that minds are something distinct from our bodies. We mentally naturally give our mind an independent location in space as if it has dimensions by translating the way we view the world; with the way we view ourselves as an individual.

However, theory of mind does not force this conclusion, and it certainly does not force the further conclusion that the mind could exist independently of the body or survive bodily death. We do not have to have these conclusions. With education we can correct this thinking. But it does mean that these ideas could come naturally to human beings and easily become memes of their own, especially when we want to believe in them. In other words, those thoughts are easy for us to accept because "they fit the natural contours of our minds". That means the way we are built. Thus, a curious by-product of "theory of mind" is that we are prone to believe, although falsely, that the mind (some call "the soul") is something distinct from the activity of the brain and that, therefore, it is easy for us to extrapolate from the mind's independent location to conjure up the notion that our soul could ascend to heaven, or be reborn into another body, or emerge back into some kind of collective consciousness, or perhaps we could return to life as a cat or a dog. My dog did have a better life than I have had. Maybe I should try that, if there really is a next time?

Memes

The younger generations today use the term "meme" with a different slant than when the word originated by Richard Dawkins was coined naming a corollary showing that many of our beliefs self-replicate in the same manner as our biological genes. Both have an independent life of their own. Both evolve over time to meet their current cultural environment. Consider what a difference his discovery makes in how we view many of our beliefs today. Perhaps Control People started a new cultural definition to misdirect Dawkins threatening theory to support their insistence on "blind faith" beliefs?

So far, we have looked at four traditional non-evolutionary explanations for after-life beliefs that are the most prevalent of the ideas in what little research was not justifying the existence of such beliefs but was in fact trying to analyze the reason for such beliefs. For this discussion they have been labeled them as "wishful thinking", "social glue", "manipulation" or as a "social control tool", and "primitive science": and two evolutionary explanations for after- life beliefs as "addictions", or "spandrel by-products".

However, there is a new third evolutionary explanation that makes much more sense recently named by Richard Dawkins. He coined the descriptive term for his theory a "meme" in the 1980's. For Dawkins, he defined a meme as a unique form of uniting cultural variance. To amplify upon what I have previously said, more precisely: a meme is a thought or an idea that has evolved to a point where it develops a life of its "own." Memes are the social soup of our thoughts or beliefs in which any society exists. Truth and reality have little effect on memes. For Dawkins, **Memes are an unverifiable belief that is shared with others that develop an independent life of their own that sustains them**, literally forever. Memes give the appearance that they have truth to those hosting that belief primarily because others also share that belief. Therefore, as the temporary host of that belief, we pass it on to others, and the belief grows. According to Dawkins, a meme is any form of coded information with the power to influence its own replication.

For Instance, a joke may become a meme. The first four notes of Beethoven's Fifth symphony have become a meme. Catch phrases, urban legends, mannerisms, embarrassing YouTube videos that have gone viral, and irritating catchy tunes, are all memes as well. That means that they each now have a life of their Own.

The central claim of a meme is that, like genes, memes are subject to a form of natural selection. They have become self- replicating. The meme that comes to predominate in a culture are those that, through accident or design, have properties that increase their chances of predominating. Those memes have properties that make them more likely to capture people's attention, Memes are anything self-replicating other than physical objects or living plants or animals. They are ideas, thoughts, beliefs, phrases, visual impressions, behaviors, songs, or concepts that are more likely to stick in people's minds. Because of their nature they are more likely to be passed from brain to brain by word of mouth or by our action. They are anything that can be copied or replicated by others.

Memes are not necessarily selected because we like them; catchy tunes are mimetically successful even though we often strongly dislike them. Try getting rid of the song "It's a Small World, After All" out of your mind after you have ridden the children's ride in the Magic Kingdom of Disney World. It takes many months to get that damm song out of your head, even though you really get to hate it. You can then imagine how hard it would be to get a meme out of your head when you really want to believe it. That is why we have a belief in a life after death, because that is something that we all wish for. Truth and reality have little to do with an accepted meme. The important point to always remember is that the meme exists on its own and truth is irrelevant for that belief.

Memes are not necessarily selected by us because they are useful to us. The smoking tobacco meme has survived for many centuries despite the fact it tends to kill its host; and even though it really does not even provide much pleasure. A meme might be selected because it is useful to us, but it doesn't have to be useful to be selected. It only needs to have attributes that keep it in circulation within a culture. Smoking provided status for children. Once addicted, it was more painful to reject it than to continue smoking.

Appling the memetic approach to religion beliefs as a means to answer the question of why we believe in an afterlife, it is an easy conclusion that our religious beliefs are a product of natural selection derived by cultural evolution, rather than Darwin's biological evolution, and that not all of the religious beliefs that continue to live that are kept in circulation are necessarily beneficial for the individual—especially if they benefit a group of memes. Some could even be at our own expense. Try convincing an Islamic fundamentalist why he or she should not be a suicide bomber by saying that person that there is no life hereafter.

What is found to be relevant is that the Memetic approach does not necessarily displace the other theories about the origins of such beliefs. What it does provide is a useful overall arching framework for integrating whatever grain of truth or purpose is contained in each of these other theories for why a belief exists into one cohesive overall picture. It literally ties everything together for us and shows us how that notion has survived.

To review how this applies with each of the earlier theories of our list of reasons for our belief in an afterlife, their proponents have identified as each of them having psychological or cultural selection pressure acting within a religious tradition. These are:

(1) selection for beliefs that comfort us, or that comfort people we care about.

(2) selection for beliefs that foster social cohesion, or "social glue".

(3) selection for beliefs that help us manipulate another people's behavior for their own good,

(4) selection for beliefs that explain, or at least give us the appearance of explaining, the world around us.

No doubt there are others. These are simply the most obvious that for me make any sense.

That's where our ability to use logic derived through our biological evolution and the natural selection of memetic pressures come into direct conflict with one another and they pull us in different directions.

For instance, we may want to believe something because it is comforting, but we may be unable to do so because it would clash too violently with evidence that we otherwise see.

That suggests that one kind of memetic successful belief would be a belief that promises to provide comfort and consolation which is not too readily falsified in everyday life, because it is culturally accepted. That obviously would include our notions of the forms of life after death that we, as an individual, find acceptable. We want to believe it, we see no evidence of it, so it is difficult to logically accept, but there is also no way to disprove it. Therefore, we accept the meme by "blind faith". Because it is socially unacceptable to challenge any faith, that belief now permanently has a culturally protected life of its own.

In other words, people tend to want to believe that it is true, and we meet little in everyday life that explicitly contradicts it. Not only that, but the belief also makes sense for some of our life experiences. Memes may be the by-products of evolved psychological tendencies of thought. In other words, series of mind transfers to others dealing with related subjects. Those memes that gel best with those tendencies are most likely to catch on and spread. The current term of our grandchildren for that Phenomena is 'to go viral", That meme is protected when it becomes connected to other memes, or beliefs that are already culturally accepted, Therefore, this approach describes the environment to which religious memes, as well as any other memes, best adapt. You do not have to like the meme, or belief, you just cannot get rid of it.

Dawkins popularized the view that natural selection proceeds not in the interest of each species, nor the group, nor even the individual. Darwin showed that natural selection acts only in the best interest of the genes themselves. Selection takes place at the individual level; however, the genes are the true replicators, and it is their competition that drives the evolution of biological design. That is the magic bullet in what Darwin discovered. All life everywhere in the universe exists by the survival of self-duplicating replicators. We are merely the temporary host for the gene. The purpose of life from the perspective of the universe is the survival of genes. As the temporary host, and as an individual, as far as evolution is concerned, we ultimately become irrelevant and so we as an individual die, while our genes live on.

Furthermore, we have found that these replicators often automatically band together in groups to create systems, or machines that carry them and work to favor their continued replication. In other words, we humans, my dog, and the cabbages we eat, exist primarily to protect the replicators. The replicators are the genes that exist within us. Darwin's theory of evolution by natural selection works through genes for our biological existence. Dawkins says that it works the same for memes. What we believe, understand, and more easily find to be true, at least for ourselves, is the self-replicating belief. We are merely the means for passing it on to others.

Memes are a similar unit of replication of thoughts that are stored in human brains that our genes are in every cell in our bodies. Memes are passed on by duplication through other people's brains. Our beliefs, as well as tunes we cannot easily get rid of, ideas, catch- phrases, clothes fashions, ways of making pottery, are all memes. One person creates.

others learn and follow by imitation, and then pass the meme on to still others. In the process the host may add to or refine the meme as the meme transfers from brain to brain. Therefore, it evolves and better adapts to that culture.

The evolution of a meme grows or decays by a simple algorithm, they do not develop linearly. They either rapidly multiply, ultimately developing a more permanent life of their own, or those that have not tagged on to other culturally accepted memes or adapted on their own; rapidly decline and eventually cease to exist. Our brains receive millions of stimulations daily. Only a few of those we store ultimately survive and develop their own existence independent of us as their hosts. When they do develop a life of their own, they jump from brain to brain like a virus. Memetic evolution occurs without regard to its effect on biological genes.

Dan Dennett suggests that any form of evolution is a mindless natural process that, when carried out, must produce a result. He states that the three elements necessary to produce evolution are **heredity, variation, and selection.** Evolution is produced by the gene in a biological sense, or a meme in the sense of a belief, or any thought, which becomes the replicator. Millions of variants are told by millions of people daily. Only a few get passed on by other people. Even fewer make it into meme classics that have an independent life of their own. Scientific papers proliferate, but only a very few get long listings in the citation indexes. Only a few of my brilliant ideas have ever been really listened to let alone appreciated by anyone, probably none have risen to the level of memes. But I keep trying. We can wonder, why do some survive, and others die out?

What makes the most sense Dawkins introduced the term co- adaptive meme complex to explain that memes survive better in combining with other memes in groups that form complex relationships. Thus, gangs of beliefs flourish in one another's presence, each of which might otherwise die on their own. Science fiction may be an example, but so are the fields of mathematics, science and architecture, let alone law and medicine. Computers are creating all sorts of opportunities for memetic transfer. They even have their own form of viruses as a result. During our lifetime these viruses have created a new industry of its own to combat it.

The most successful groups of **memetic complexes** have some memes that serve as **bait** to attract adherents. They also have **hooks** to capture adherents once the group has their attention. Frequently these complexes have memes that act as **threats** for those hosts that chose to leave the group, and **immune system** memes that protect those from that threat that remain within the group. Thus, the group becomes a self-contained system that can exist forever regardless of its relationship to truth or reality. Facts cannot penetrate the system, and truth certainly cannot defeat it. The group system fully protects itself. Therefore, people become afraid of the consequences of their not believing and so they seldom leave the safety of their belief. That is the glue that cements people to their religious faith.

How did we get to where our beliefs are today?

We now know that Donald Johansson's Lucy lived four million years ago, which you might remember is the connecting link of human's branching off from the evolution from the life forms on the level of the amoeba to that of the ape. Our latest evolutionary leap only occurred more recently, somewhere between fifty to one hundred thousand years ago. We know that because other forms of life on the level of humans died off, leaving only us homo sapiens; and the fact that we as humans had a significant change in behavior with this last evolution level of our current existence.

This may be as the result of the evolutionary growth of the size of our brains, which suddenly allowed us the ability to think beyond ourselves. Humans started painting on the walls of their caves preserving their view of their world around them. That had not occurred before. Thus, how life living on Earth behaved suddenly moved to a higher level of living.

Our religious faiths, meaning our abstract answers to our view of the reasons for our life, also evolved. This occurred over thousands of years by creating "hooks" in the form of an attraction belief, such as those promoting our religious beliefs claiming only, they hold the key to heaven, but they will provide the key only for those that accept their belief. Those Control People provided a companion meme in the form of a "threat", such as in the form of "Hell" for those that have been exposed to their belief and then do not accept it. "Forgiveness" for those that return and repent, and "immunity" from "Hell" for those who adhere to the Control Persons beliefs.

The real question is how much "control" can you tolerate and not become a puppet?

This explains why those who were indoctrinated before their age of reason and were protected within that society during their developmental years are normally "hooked" for life, and fear denying that their "blind faith" speaks the truth for them for the rest of their lives, regardless of the amount of their subsequent education. If those beliefs are valid, why have they not naturally evolved and, therefore, become the accepted belief of| everyone today. Do you suppose it could be only because such beliefs are merely a "control device", and not because they are the truth in reality? Note the many cultural religions in the world today, and the significant difference in their beliefs. Each claiming that they are "the true belief."

Do you suppose that they are all man-made? They do fill a necessary role of providing our "social glue" maintaining our society that universally still exists primarily on the high security/ low social levels of existence. We are still living primitively as a society. Rising above this quagmire takes effort, but once you have the ability to view life from a higher perspective you can easily understand the effect of Control People are having on your own life and be far more discerning on the level of control that you will be willing to accept for yourself. If any one of them was "the truth" in reality, why has that belief not become universally accepted by all of us?

Our various religions are a prime example of memes creating their own truth. Recognizing that this is an oversimplification in order to make a point, religions true purpose may be for the protection of the group, or it may be to provide the social glue that sustains our society. Because it is a self-contained system, and because it adapts on its own as our culture matures, the truth of any part is not relevant to its survival, and truth certainly cannot defeat it. Nor would I advocate that it should, because there is currently nothing to replace its role in our society to maintain the glue for those people that have not risen above the social level. Many religions in some forms have become a central part of sustaining our society. But similarly, so has the legal, accounting and medical community. The professions are regulated in our society by law. Most religions are sustained by the belief in an afterlife.

The point of all of this is that we have universal beliefs not because they are related to reality, but because they relate to each other in the same grouping that has gained independent lives of their own. We accept them because they have become a part of us. And the cultural taboo in challenging religion assures its perpetual existence. Religion will change to absorb its detractors. As a culture, we are hooked. To abandon religious beliefs is more painful than to perpetuate them. Thus, they survive despite any factual basis of truth for the belief.

A writer by the name of Aaron Lynch points out that many religious memes are successful when they pass from parent to child because they are cloaked with having "originated from God". If the child thought that what was presented originated by their parent, at least teenagers, would be far more apt to reject it. Therefore, "the group effect" prevails, and this meme contributes to the survival of the group, because it is transferred under the "authority of God". Novel thought. However, perhaps its survival occurs because children accepted the beliefs before their age of reason. Therefore, they cling to the meme, and most are afraid of its threat for the rest of their lives because it is invested with the emotions of our childhood at the time of time of the meme's origination, and our feelings prevail over logic. Thus, whatever the belief, even many scientists working on the subject matter may still take part in their tradition as their insurance policy, even if their logic may conflict.

Imagine what would happen if robots learned memetic transfer of information from one robot computer brain to another robot computer brain without human intervention. Once they have the ability to be totally mobile and self-sufficient, we might have a really serious problem far exceeding the drama portrayed by science fiction writers. I would love to have Isaac Asimov's opinion of the result and its effect on our human future.

However, the meme for life after our death evolved, our human intelligence had a side effect. It allowed us an understanding, unique among all other forms of animals, that one day we are going to wake up and it will be the last time we ever do. Each of us knows that sometimes we are each going to die. In this way the evolution of intelligence created a significant psychological selection pressure for beliefs that would allay our concerns about death. The belief that life will continue after our death, obviously, prospered because it is welcome news to creatures who found themselves in the awkward predicament of having a desire to survive, but are also damned with the cognitive ability to recognize our Own mortality.

Human beings have been burying their dead for many thousands of years before the emergence of large-scale civilization. We also know from archeology that burials of our most ancient ancestors were attended by complex and costly rituals and offerings. This strongly suggests that even our Paleolithic forbearers had some conception of life after death. In other words, afterlife beliefs are way more than tens of thousands of years old.

The next great leap forward in the cultural evolution of our afterlife beliefs came with the development of agriculture. As soon as people started domesticating plants and animals they began to live in much larger and more densely packed groups. Viewed from the point of reference of E.O. Wilson, up to one hundred fifty people, social needs are adequate to keep our society running smoothly. As soon as groups got much bigger, then this social cohesion starts to break down, and the groups ultimately could fall apart unless cultural institutions were put into place to artificially foster the cohesion of the community. Thus, agriculture created a cultural selection pressure for meme's that helped keep social cohesion. Thus, our religions became more formalized.

Those groups that happen to come up with memes fitting all those needs grew and spawned daughter groups. Those that did not create such cultural adaptations did not survive. Memes were necessary to create society, and our afterlife beliefs are a strong participator. They were already present in human belief because they had already been accepted by predecessor cultures. Therefore, the foundation for adopting a new way of viewing such beliefs was already in place.

Agriculture simply intensified and spread such thinking to larger societies. Memes adapt to fit the evolved design of the mind. They also adapt to one another even as they compete with one another. They work much like a virus that adapts to circumvent our medical weapons so that our vaccines and antibiotics become ineffective. Thus, we are unable to stamp out or kill memes. They simply change to fit their circumstances.

The memes that have been adopted by a culture have society as their own protection. Why do you think it is culturally unacceptable to challenge religious beliefs? Doing so is one of our culturally strongest taboos. That notion was promoted by the Priests as the Control People of faith beliefs, but readily accepted by the public because they relied on these beliefs to fill their security needs. Threating someone on the security level often results in violence.

The history of the belief in an afterlife

The earliest recorded ideas about the afterlife show an existence that is nothing in Comparison to our modern concepts today. The "underworld" of the Greeks and Siberians are not a perfect paradise. It was somewhat bleak and an impoverished existence. The same is true of the "Netherworld of the Mesopotamians", and the concept of "Sheol" of early Hebrews as the dwelling place of the dead awaiting the end of days when Jews would arrive in Heaven.

One reason for its success is that Christianity produced an at once accessible heaven that was totally positive and expanded upon the concept of it being infinitely wonderful, and its own definition of hell which is infinitely terrible. Why wait in Sheol when you can go at once to heaven upon your death simply by believing? Some authorities credit the Apostle Paul for creating Christ using the story about the life of a Jew named Jesus that Christians believe today.

Even though the Essenes were daily searching for a Messiah so that Jews could ascend into Heaven at their "end of days", the absence of any mention of Jesus in the Dead Sea Scrolls suggest that our "Christ" today may not have been the actual Jesus of Israel. This is what Bishop John Shelby Spong of the Episcopal Church contends. For Bishop Spong the Christ of today is an accepted expansion upon the life Jesus that lived. Acceptance of Bishop Spong's view makes the Jesus that lived still relevant today. Memetics would say that Christ resulted because of the cultural needs of its time, and it certainly still provides benefit for our society today. That is because Christianity has evolved to meet our current cultural needs. The historic truth of the myth is not nearly as important to most people as is the effect of what the symbols mean to each of us individually, as we each live our own spiritual lives today. Thus, discovering the truth of the actual historical facts cannot destroy the needs within each of us that the religious symbols we use today fulfill. Nor do I believe that they ever should. Traditions that we are willing to accept express for each of us symbols that address our needs that we have no other effective way of fulfilling, whatever our personal needs may be.

Our understanding of the facts supporting our religious views has been changed over the course of history. The Dead Sea Scrolls have clearly proven that. They were written from 250 BCE until 67 CE, so history has not touched them. The comparison of the words being written at that time with our cultural beliefs today is vivid. They prove that our current cultural beliefs of that era have been seriously molded over time by well-meaning Control People. This evolution can at once be seen in the conflict of faiths today, especially with the armed conflicts between differing religions and their proponents upping the ante to attract adherence and to continue some form of control over their members as we see with the Taliban, or with ISIS.

As a less violent example, over time heaven has gotten better and better while hell is now worse as our faith beliefs have evolved. This is in effect an example of a memetic arms race of faith beliefs, comparable to the arms race we have seen in biological evolution, to keep pace with our advancing culture and science.

The advantage for memetics, as described by Richard Dawkins, is that for a belief to prosper it does not need to be helpful to the believer. It only needs to be helpful to itself. This insight of Dawkins may prompt us to ask important new questions about the nature of all our beliefs. Turning from any accepted belief causes some initial discomfort, much like the withdrawal symptoms from smoking. Once a person no longer smokes, the quality of their life might expand, and hopefully they become ardent proponents of the 11th commandment, "Thou shall not smoke".

However, it is the fear of negative effects of an addiction that drives most people, even knowing that it is harming their body to feel that they must continue to smoke. Even for those now conflicted their behavior will normally not change on its own. Frequently it takes some form of intervention to even get the person's attention. However, as a result their children who have seen the effect upon their parents, may themselves never touch a cigarette. It is painful for any of us to abandon any meme that we have accepted as a part of ourselves.

How do memes work?

A meme that all of us know has existed for over 700 years is the poem, "Ring around the Rosy. Pocket full of posies. Ashes, ashes, we all fall down." Why do we teach our children about a plague in England that killed tens of thousands of people in the 1300's? Why does this poem have a life of its own? Why is it that little children like it? Is it because it is short, easy to say, and has an action step in it? Perhaps. But why do we still perpetuate it? The point is that adults do not teach it to our children. It lives because kids teach it to other kids. Therefore, it does have a life of its own. And truth cannot kill it. We adults do not have to take part in it to continue to exist. The children are innocent of its meaning, but they undoubtedly do like the rhythm and the action step. Little children think it is funny. That has been enough to perpetuate the poem for seven centuries from brain to brain only being transferred to others by children before their age of reason; and we adults cannot stop it. That is truly a good example of a meme and how it continues to exist today.

Most Humanists were raised in a traditional religious background. Some still keep their childhood church affiliation for family or social reasons. No one should object if they wish to do that. Humanism is all about each person having the freedom to live their own life to the fullest however they choose to carry out that. Others have abandoned their childhood faith they viewed as controlling or inhibiting at the very least. Some have no religion. Others have found a new home that is less threatening. Many have become Unitarians.

In the Catholic Church, many people have been excommunicated, as their religion's response to their denial of a belief the Church accepts. That can be threatening for some, or simply ignored as irrelevant by those who are stronger in their own self-confidence. We are frequently told that most of those people who rise above the grip of Catholicism feel relief from a great weight, much like a person passing through withdrawal from an addiction, when they are finally feel free to live their own life as they chose, instead of being controlled.

The point is the transition from your own religious heritage can be a traumatic event. For those that arrive at a point where they experience freedom that allows them to now feel in control of their own lives, everyone has said the transition was more than worth doing. Each of us must do the very best that we can to make the very most out of our life while we are here, in whatever feels right for them. Hopefully it does not require the trauma of rejecting their childhood beliefs to get there. Having done that there is pain in some form involved. Fortunately for me my parents did not object, and the distance from my early faith to my life today was not far apart. Someone leaving the control of some faiths has significant issues to face including rejection from those important to them.

There are many ways for each of us to enlarge our beliefs to keep our symbols by making them relevant in a new context. For instance, as a child their god concept may be fear related to be perceived. In the period where you are able to think for yourself, but before you are normally able to think abstractly, a parental God concept is normally more appropriate. An educated person will normally find an abstract god concept makes More sense. It allows them a use for the term rather than the emotions they might suffer were they to reject God since they have their childhood emotions invested in the use of the term.

When I was four years old my fear was caused because my mother told me that Jesus could see everything I was doing. That was really scary: If "Big Brother" is really watching me, where could I be safe? That changed my entire perspective of religion for the rest of my life.

As we age and our life centers on the social level a father god concept may be more acceptable. On the actualized level an abstract concept may be more acceptable. During our growth, changing the meaning of our symbols keeps them relevant for us without having to reject them. Your view of religion can mature with you so that the symbols you have learned continue to add value in your life—as long as you retain control of your beliefs and keep them meaningful for yourself without your symbols controlling who you are. There is a difference.

The effect of a belief in life after our death

This is just one belief. All our beliefs can be tested in the same manner. Consider this example before you declare any belief to be the absolute truth on any subject. Many arrive at the point where they would not even want a life after their death if it did exist, because it would diminish the quality of this life. They say, "What would be the point?" This life is enough in and of itself. That was what Dr. Janet Jepson was saying. Perpetual existence would make this life meaningless and take away the meaning of our own life we are living today. To quote the Reverend Martin Luther King, those with that view are "Free at Last", and they cherish that freedom.

Instead of saying there is no life after death and causing conflict with those that believe otherwise, you could redefine life after death to mean that the work you have done during this life that lives on after you is your own immortality after your death. Then you have placed a more mature definition on an ages old concept to keep it relevant for you in a way that does not cause conflict with those that have not grown beyond their childhood beliefs. I am not suggesting that you be dishonest if they want to discuss what that means. However, you do not have to deny their beliefs in the process, until they have the ability and desire to grow through non-threatening education for themselves. If they ask, that tells you that they have opened the door for them to learn.

Thus, Humanists do not expend their energy searching for a ticket to the afterlife find that frees them from that burden so that the effect of their life upon others is, in itself; the only form of immortality that they know for sure exists. Humanists typically believe that their own life is significant only to the extent the world is better because they have been here. There are no facts that exist which will confirm either side in order to ascertain "the truth". Logic causes the conclusion that a physical life after our death simply does not exist. Every bit of physical evidence that supports those anxious to believe a life after our death is real has been duplicated and explained by scientists.

A similar analysis applies to almost all other beliefs that we each have where we must tentatively accept beliefs without testing the relationship of that belief with what we have previously found to be an acceptable truth. That process also applies to most of what we each simply accept daily as reasonably being true in order that we can move forward to address issues of greater concern. A better approach might be to consider approaching most of what we are told from a skeptical point of view, using what works best for us tentatively now, but being fully aware that you are not relying upon the same information for future decisions.

As we look at each situation, we might prefer to judge what gets us closer to a reasonable goal without hurting anyone or doing anything that conflicts with what we feel is right or best for all people who are affected. Otherwise, we face paralyzing our advancing forward for fear of not always being right. The ethical approach may be the best approach in the long run since it generally produces the least conflict and enhances the best result for the most people. See my personal ethical philosophy in the appendix as an example for you to consider.

Humanists create a stronger ethical value system for themselves, because it is the right thing for them to do. It is what will work best for them. My example may not be true for you. Since everyone creates their own values, our own are much stronger and more closely followed by a Humanist than those imposed upon us by Control People.

As an example, the notion of Confession and repentance with clerical forgiveness is unacceptable to many Humanists. Most feel that the goal of those who are confessing is solely to appease God. Most Humanist cannot live that way. Humanists accept being responsible for themselves as primarily necessary to keep their belief system. For others, the belief confession frees them from guilt may be essential since that belief was imposed upon them as children and it is now accepted as a valued part of themself. But, if you are responsible for yourself, you have to accept the responsibility for your own actions. You cannot simply be forgiven, and the impact of your actions negated. You have to learn from your own mistakes.

The difference lies in your point of reference from which we view our religious tradition; and for someone raised in an authoritarian environment their lens is cloudy and they cannot see the advantage of being free at last. However, attacking other's traditions is not appropriate humanist behavior. When we examine the definitions of our symbols, they can be made to make more sense. These religious traditions are merely symbols we use to address valid human concerns. The need to address guilt is valid for everyone. Confession is merely one approach. It is easily accepted by a Catholic and adds value to their life. A Humanist takes pride from accepting responsibility for them self. Neither is wrong. They are merely different ways of solving the same problem.

Chapter Fourteen

Myths of Faith, The Role of Religion, Varies Within Our Culture

I pointed out that E. O. Wilson has made a strong case for why religion is the social glue for the Western world, and that this book is written from that perspective. But to be fair to academics, before proceeding, I need to point out that not all cultures are bound together with the same glue in the same way. This is more of an academic issue beyond this book's reach. But to make that point understandable, China does not have a similar dependence upon religion filling the security and low social levels of their society. They do have multiple religions available. For example, most Humanists could make good Chinese Buddhists. However, the typical Chinese family uses their own religion primarily only for special events, but not regularly throughout the year. Sort of like, those Christians that show up for Christmas and Easter and look at themselves as "good Christians," but their religious "faith" does not guide their behavior.

The social glue prevalent in China is "saving face" with those you trust, or with those who trust you. Losing face is a cultural sin of the worst kind. That is the social glue upon which their legal system is dependent. The American Bar Association sent me to China to study their legal system. They had only been graduating lawyers for ten years at that time. I discovered that the Chief Justice of the Chinese Supreme Court was a railroad engineer. He knew nothing about the law and could not have cared less. He spoke for the Communist Party. Lawyers in China often work from the perspective that public image is their reason for causing change.

The public accepts that saving face with those that trust them preserves the normal peace in a country that is five times the American population, in an area two-thirds America's size. Of course, fear of a police force that is larger than its military of two million soldiers also helps keep the peace.

You do not see much crime because those caught even in what we would consider minor crimes you may never hear from again. You are incarcerated or worse until you prove that you are innocent. Seems to work for them, even though it would not stand up to our Constitution, which thankfully protects your rights. But for those of us whose social glue is religion, let us examine Christianity a little closer for now.

Christian Faith

An important consideration for all of us is the degree to which we rely on truth, and reality, as the basis for acceptance of our ultimate beliefs in life. Where we draw the line between truth and faith is one of the most important decisions that we have the power to make for ourselves. Faith is acceptable, and it is an important consideration in what we find that we will rely upon, if it is based upon what we can verify or logically deduce from our other beliefs. Or we recognize that we are accepting something only temporarily to meet an immediate need. The reason is we cannot know everything. We have to act on faith in those areas where we have not devoted the time or energy to have studied and researched the facts behind some beliefs, we are willing to accept for us to be able to live our daily lives. Without some faith, we would not be able to sustain ourselves. As an example, I have mentioned before that I have faith the seed I plant will grow, which is verified when it sprouts. The reason that faith is valid is because it follows logically from my prior experience.

Blind faith is where people limit their ability to grow personally because it is where they allow others to take control of their lives. Blind faith means you rely only upon chance and wishful thinking that the person you are relying upon is right. For many who do not get the result they were hoping for, they delude themselves by thinking the result was God's wish, so it is my wish too." That is the kind of thinking we should have given up in our childhood. Yet most people accept their blind faith because of the Control People they have allowed in their lives; normally before their age of being able to reason for themselves, or because of their introduction by parents or people they trust. Does that sound like it may include you? Because that path is familiar, it becomes preferable for many, and they never grow beyond that point. They limit their own ability to fully live their own life.

Abraham Maslow shows us why that creates a serious problem if we want to get the very most out of our own life. Blind faith thinking can cause a barrier, in the form of a scatoma that only significant education can overcome. Your problem then is whether you seek that education, or whether you accept a life that limits your ability to grow. One goal of this book is to start you on a growth path to provide sufficient education for you to see the difference it could make for you if you allow yourself to continue to grow for you to be able to actualize your own life.

Religion is the perfect example, because it fills an important role in the lives of most people. As I will say many times, so that you will realize how it can limit your existence, religion does that by filling the security and low social level of most people's needs, as described by Maslow's Hierarchy of Needs—at least for those that have not passed the ego self-awareness level. Many are dependent upon their religion for their foundation of support in their endeavors beyond the security level. That is because religion for many people confirms who they are. Thus, religion is currently a necessary element in our society.

I am not challenging religion per se. I am challenging only those who cease to control their own lives. The valid question is whether we rely upon our religion because of the current good it provides, or are we taking part in our religion because of habit, or because of fear of the alternatives—or guilt for not obeying—if it is imposed upon us by Control People? Are you controlled by fear of retaliation upon your demise, of spending eternity in hell, or fear of not doing what God expects of us? That can be all-consuming.

No one wants to "burn in hell for eternity." To think otherwise would be stupid. But did you ever think that there is absolutely no proof such a place exists? There is plenty of evidence that those beliefs are more likely a mere control device to sustain power over you. Since those seeds were planted early in your life, before you could think yourself, and since they were given to you, or at least reaffirmed, by those upon whom you were totally dependent, like your parents, you probably have never questioned their validity. The acceptance of those beliefs became an integral part of who you are today. For those being controlled, they have become puppets, and they are merely living the life of a sheep. Look around yourself and answer: who are you letting pull your strings?

Fundamentalists, those who take the Bible literally as their guide, are easily led yet most have little understood of their Bible, even though they read it diligently. They are conditioned to accept it as the "word of God," so they never look upon it logically. Let us explore that subject in a little more depth to make my point.

The Bible is the fundamental document for much of our Western population today. Jesus was a Jew. He had no intention of being anything else. It was those who followed Jesus that made him into the Christ of Christianity. There were many versions of the life of Jesus in the early days of Christianity following his crucifixion, each expressing significantly different views. Our Bible of today is that which survived Constantine's Council of Nicaea in 325 CE. Its acceptance was the result of the most organized Control People. That resulted in the Catholic's version because they had a universality, other beliefs lacked. The majority ruled the day. The word "Catholic" means "universal" so they controlled a large number of those attending.

But let us look at some of the facts conveyed in the first four Chapters of the New Testament, called the "Gospels," that express the life of Jesus. Keep in mind there were other Gospels proposed that did not make the cut in the Nicaea Council. But for our current purpose, let us consider only these four different views and compare those with our beliefs today. Then, let us sneak a peek at reality as an example, to get an idea of how our cultural views may differ from truth. By seeing a small example, perhaps we can then realize how most of our beliefs have little relationship to truth. Those beliefs may allow you to live a good life, so why do we care? The real point is that if you are focused only on what is within your comfort zone, you will never know what you are missing that would offer even more opportunity to get the very most out of your life. Let us stretch your thinking a bit.

Most people in America today are content to live on the social level tasting periodically the ego self-awareness level of Maslow's Hierarchy of Needs, for their own validation—but never realizing the level of a fulfilled existence above, which includes the actualized level, even exists. Even more important, having reached that level, they could then reach beyond and become Fully Alive to really do some good in our world today, resulting in their own immortality in a form that we know really does exist.

Leaving our world, a better place because you have been here, gives your life real permanent value, not merely having lived a fun life when very few really care whether, or not, you lived after you are gone. Try making a real and permanent difference in the lives of others, most of whom will never know you. That will give you an inner peace beyond most people's imagination today. Later I will give you an example of my grandson. A decision he made as a freshman in college resulted in permanent good for over 30,000 people living in a faraway land of Uganda who do not remember him and will never know his name, but many people are alive today because of his decision. So, he now has a form of immortality we know is real. Put that in the back of your mind as a goal for you too. Let us see how to get there. Read on.

First let us explore in a little more depth than you have before, the faith of Christianity. For the meaning of Jesus' life to survive, he had to be more than a mere prophet; there were many others with that claim. The story of his resurrection turned the life of Jesus into

Christ. The real question is this: did his resurrection really happen? We were not there, and there really is little evidence to consider. Could this only be a belief of blind faith?

Why I ask this is because of a valid concern of how the belief that Jesus was resurrected can overcome the fact that from 250 BC until 67 CE the Essenes, living in Qumran only 12 air miles from Jerusalem, did not make note of that event. The Essenes were searching daily for over 300 years for a Messiah to come. They believed a Messiah's coming was necessary as the precursor for the "End of Days," when all Jews would ascend at once into Heaven. They were all hopeful it would be next week. Yet, they did not recognize Jesus as a Messiah. Why not? Even more important, they did not record his resurrection. That is an event you would think might have gotten noticed by someone. If it is true, it would have had to be noticed for us to know about it. Otherwise, how could we know of it today? Anyone who has seen that would tell everyone. It is hard to believe only 12 miles away no one ever heard of it. If they had they would have been written about it. They were desperately searching daily for a Messiah.

The Essenes were expecting that a significant event was about to occur, and they were writing daily on their scrolls throughout the entire life of Jesus. Their scrolls were preserved in caves between 67-69 CE and not found until 1947, so history has not touched them. Yet they missed reporting such an important event as someone rising from the dead? Since it had never really happened before it would have been hard to ignore. Does that make any sense? Or was the resurrection story merely a means of well-meaning people writing, 40 years after Jesus death, in their effort to make his life noticed by the Jewish community, because they wanted Jesus fulfilling the prophecies of the Old Testament so that his life would be as important to the Jews as it was to the writer. Of course, St. Paul making him "the son of God" also adds a lot to also provide his credibility. No one should question God. But are those only a means of marketing Jesus by followers who desperately wanted his acceptance by the general Jewish population? It is more than highly doubtful that a resurrection even happened.

There is pretty good evidence that it was St. Paul who created the Christ immortalizing the life of Jesus. He had been a tax collector, not such an exciting life. Preaching about the life of Jesus gave him a life where others supported his needs. Telling Jews that if they believed in Jesus, they did not have to wait to the end of days to get to heaven. Accepting Jesus gave them a ticket for immediate access. It was a pretty good marketing tool. No wonder why others were willing to house, feed and clothe him.

Another issue we need to consider is just how those chroniclers of the New Testament got the information about which they wrote. And then there is also the question of why we have two divisions of the Bible in the first place? Could they not have left the Old Testament to the Jewish faith, and Christianity simply have created their own book? Or, perhaps those writing about Jesus could have merely written as a new chapter for the Old Testament? Or did the New Testament happen because tying their New Testament to the Old Testament is significant proof that Jesus was only trying to be a Jew, and it was just that his life was meant to convey a new message? Most scholars would agree that writing about Jesus in a New Testament added credibility by connecting him to the Old Testament, as the historic Jewish Bible. It was supposed to make Jesus relevant to Jews. Instead, it launched a new faith. Bishop Spong takes that a step further. He points out that the major events of the life of Jesus in the New Testament line up precisely with the major events in the Old Testament.

Keep in mind, nothing was written for 40 years after Jesus' death. Therefore, those writing the chapters of the New Testament could not have personally known Jesus. They could only report what others had passed on for information. Have you ever tried the game of sitting in a circle of more than a dozen people, and starting a complex message at one end, everyone telling the story that they just heard to the next person, and then seeing what the final story sounds like? If the story is more than three sentences long, you will not recognize it when it reaches the last person. True, those writings took the names of the first four Gospels from those who did know Jesus, but if those four disciples really did write those Chapters, why do they so significantly differ? For those who answer that question by claiming that God inspired those chapters, you would think that at least God would have been consistent.

Let us look at some of those examples to make my point. Mathew says Jesus was an aristocrat, descended from David, in the lineage to become King. Perhaps that was guided by the Jewish belief that there would be two Messiahs: a kingly Messiah, and a priestly Messiah. Some say the story of Jesus throwing out the Temple Money Changers was to prove that Jesus was both. He was from the lineage of David, and he had power equal to the priests. That is an interesting thought, isn't it? Luke agrees in part with Mathew, but that Gospel reduces Jesus to a lesser class.

Mark carries that further and shows Jesus as a descendant of a poor carpenter. If you visit Nazareth today, you can see caves dug in the ground where people lived that archeologists claim was the way all people lived in that community 2,000 years ago. Probably so. If you look around while standing in Nazareth today, you see very few trees in the area from which wood housing could be built. Without wood it is hard to be a carpenter. Perhaps Joseph was a rock- smith? Yet Mathew suggests that Jesus lived in a house. If you visit Capernaum, where Peter came from, it is easy to see Peter probably did live in the stone block home they are rebuilding today on its ancient foundation.

If you visit Israel today, tell me how you think anyone is going to be able to take any woman about to deliver a baby the 120 miles from Nazareth to today's Bethlehem before more modern transportation. It could not happen as portrayed. The current Bethlehem is six miles south of Jerusalem. Nazareth is over 100 miles north. Even if you had a donkey for Mary to ride, you could not make the trip in ten days. Such a rough trip could easily have caused delivery in route. Perhaps there was a Bethlehem of those days within a day's journey, as many of the smaller ancient communities in that area no longer exist today.

But even though Jesus' birth that far away does not make sense, and the attempt to justify it saying a tax had to be paid in the community of your ancestor, lacks any credibility. That excuse had to be written by some zealous person trying to justify their message.

Nevertheless, the experience of visiting today's Bethlehem is very interesting. The place they claim today where Jesus was born is a cave. No doubt it existed 2,000 years ago. Hardly the image we have of a wooden stable. I have been to the cave twice. It sits under a Greek Orthodox Church built by the Crusaders. A newer Catholic Church sits perpendicular to the Greek Orthodox Church with a connecting hallway, but it sits over 100 feet from the cave. The cave is possibly twenty to twenty-five feet long, eight to ten feet high, and maybe twelve feet across. It interested me that the first time I visited the cave a star on the floor where they claimed the manger sat was in a pit to the left of the cave's back entrance. Twenty-five years later the star was on the right side as you entered. Someone must have told the Orthodox priests what a pit in a stable was for.

The point is they did not have a wooden stable where they claim today that Jesus was born. Wood was scarce. They only have spindly cypress trees or olive trees. No one would cut down an olive tree for the wood; the olives were far more valuable. You would have to cut down all the cypress trees you could see on the horizon just to make one home. I am inclined to believe our religious beliefs today have little to do with facts. I chuckle to myself when I see a wooden stable scene at Christmas time.

Many of our cultural traditions have little to do with reality. We adopt them for emotional reasons that may have no relationship with truth or reality.

Other than people like the Essenes in Qumran who were writing daily, most people of that day could not read or write. so, preserving the actual life of Jesus in writing, by people who knew him, did not happen. At that time no one who knew Jesus bothered writing his history, because they either were unable to write, or they did not think it necessary because they "knew" that "the end of days," when everyone would go to heaven, was just around the corner. So what reason was for them to write it? Their thinking was a bit primitive.

It was close to forty years after the death of Jesus before the first Gospel of Mark was written. The Gospels of Matthew and Luke were written around 80 CE, ten years later. The Gospel of John was twenty years after that. Being the last Gospel, it differed dramatically from the others. Which one was right? or are any of the Gospels, right? The early believers were doing their best to make Jesus relevant to a Jewish audience. They were written in Greek. What few, if any, of their authorities that existed were written in Aramaic. The Old Testament was written in Hebrew.

Later, we will discuss the work of Episcopal Priest, John Shelby Spong, recently retired as the Bishop of Newark, who tells us that the whole point of the writers of the New Testament was to make Jesus relevant for Jews. Probably so. It is later than those writing the Gospels that those who followed Jesus drew a line in the sand creating a separate religion. Many think that St. Paul created the Christ by declaring that Jesus was the "Son of God." He never knew Jesus.

Let us take a moment to look in a little more depth at what the Gospels are really saying, before we merely accept them as "God's word", or the truth about a time in our religious history which supports our own faith today. We need to know what we are talking about before we use the Gospels as our reason for rejecting any other view of life. When you read all four together, the only thing they agree upon is that a man they called Jesus existed.

We recognized that there was good reason for creating a New Testament and placing it with the Old Testament, because it provided those of the Christian faith their best means to elevate Jesus and to show he fulfilled the prophecies of the Old Testament. They needed to do that to show Jesus as the Messiah that the Jewish Bible predicted. The Christians could have used other means of separating themselves from conquest, or from their Jewish past, but was not their goal, creating the New Testament cemented their message. To add frosting on the cake, his resurrection made Jesus the Christ. Just think of the power over your life the notion of an afterlife gives the priests.

Keep in mind that until the development of the printing press in 1400, the Priests were among the few that could read, write, or even have access to the Bible. The Gospels were written for the elite. Religion was the apex of government. God's power, presented through priests, anointed the Kings. The power to rule came from God and the Priests were God's representative. They had the power, and they were primarily the Only ones that could read what God said. So, up to the Renaissance, the masses had no other competing claim to the truth except what the Church dictated. Let us explore what God said in a little more depth.

Matthew, talking about Jesus tells us, "His blood be upon us and upon our children." That biblical statement is what has justified to Christians their killing Jews for two thousand years. Did God really want "his people" killed? Once Matthew's message was published, Priests had a perfect message for Jews, and it spread quickly through Roman civilization. It has dominated the Western world now for two thousand years. Add to that the cultural protection that it is a taboo, and it is even now still socially unacceptable to question anyone's religion, and you have perpetual existence.

If the Church had to defend itself, using any means for measuring truth in terms of reality, could it survive? I do not know. I do know, however, that it fills an important and necessary role for a segment of society by filling the security and low social need level of most Americans today. According to E. O. Wilson, it is our "Social glue." 1 see no public benefit in attacking religion itself. I do see benefit for helping people better recognize when they are being controlled, so that they can make their own judgement of when being controlled is acceptable, and when they need to remain in control of their own lives. That, I believe, is essential for their being able to fulfill their own existence. You cannot actualize your own life if you are blocked by fear, guilt, or control mechanisms embedded in you on the security and social levels before your age of reason that then block your view of reality. Until you build a bridge around your scatoma you will never be able to rise significantly above the social level of living your life.

You are blocked on your current level by "blind faith beliefs" that dominate, blocking any view beyond.

To read the Gospels you would think, from their perspective, that the writers knew Jesus personally. Has it ever occurred to you when you read in Matthew or Luke about Christ's temptation in the wilderness, that Jesus was alone in the wilderness, and nowhere is he quoted saying anything about it? So, where did the Gospel writers get their information? As another example, the writers of the Gospels quote Jesus' prayer in Gethsemane right after they say he left Peter, James, and John "a stone's throw away." If he was alone, how does the writer know what he said? He died before he got to talk to anyone about it. When Jesus returned from praying, he found the disciples asleep and was arrested and then crucified without his talking to anyone. Yet we are given every detail. How does that happen? You might say it is God's word, but then 1 ask again, which Gospel did God write, since they all differ?

The Gospels tell us of the disciples fleeing after his arrest. But all four Gospels give a different version of what had occurred. How does any gospel writer really know what happened? Who told them? Yet they speak of what the Roman soldiers, Pilate, and Simon Peter did, or said. Where did they get that information? As 1 said before, Jesus' birth is confusing. Even going back to Jesus' youth, the Gospels do not agree. Yet we have a singular, consistent version that is accepted as our cultural tradition by most Christians today. Visiting Israel challenges so many of our deep-felt beliefs.

Before 1 talked about Jesus' birthplace. Now let us look at Calvary. In America we have the notion that calvary is a grassy hill, and that Jesus carried the cross. Neither is true. When you are in Jerusalem and look around yourself, there are no grassy hillsides. You are on the edge of a desert. What is reality is that there is a rock that stands about 15 feet high with a relatively flat top about 50 feet across, that at the time of his crucifixion was just outside the wall of Jerusalem. The rock today is also under a Greek Orthodox Church and the wall of the ancient city now surrounds that area. This rock has three post holes on top. I have put my hand in these post holes. The priests of that church will tell you that the rock is called "Golgotha," which means "Skull," describing its shape. They do not use the term "Calvary." Jesus did not carry the cross because the posts were permanent. Jesus carried the cross member because that is how they placed him on top of the permanent post. Jesus died on a "T," not a cross.

The reason for the Romans having their crucifixions at Jerusalem on top of that rock is because it only took one soldier to protect those being crucified from being released by someone, because anyone trying to rescue them would get speared by the soldier before they could get to the top. In addition, it was not kosher to kill someone within the walls of the city. The rock was adjacent, but it lay on the outside of the city wall. Yet it was close enough that those within the wall could see the person being crucified. That added value because seeing someone getting crucified controlled their behavior. It makes perfect sense when you see it.

What does not make sense is the Tomb below Golgotha that the priests want you to pay to see. The tomb they proudly display would only hold one body. No one would give up an expensive mausoleum that only holds one body to someone they did not personally know. Even the large round stone laying nearby had no possible relationship to that tomb. It made no sense when you saw it, but people were prostrating themselves on a marble slab nearby because they were told that is where they prepared Jesus' body. Talk about a tourist trap. The public is quite gullible on almost any given subject.

The first time I was there, after I questioned the truth in what the Orthodox priests were saying, our guide said she agreed. She then took us down several flights of stairs to a sub-basement area where there was a cave carved out of the wall, which had a dozen or more niches carved into the interior wall. The Jewish practice of the day was to create such caves in rock, and to place the body in one of the niches and seal it with mud for a year, then open it and remove the bones after the body decayed. They placed the bones in an ossuary, and then the family who owned that cave could then use the same niche for the next person. That made far more sense for how Jesus was buried, and the place we visited might well have been his actual tomb. When you go there, ask to see that tomb site. It makes the story much more believable for you.

The real point in this Chapter is for you to realize that the stories that you have been told since your early childhood are merely stories. Their truth is irrelevant. They are symbols that you were normally given before your age of reason that provide you with an abstract 'faith" for you to rely upon. Your reason for participating in your faith group, church, synagogue, temple, or mosque, is essentially to fill your security and low social needs. They do this by giving you a sense of belonging, and they fill your lower social level by providing a support group that you find acceptable. It establishes for you who you are.

The central myth is not what is important to you. The religious society with which you participate is what is important to you. It is the cultural society, not the myth, which regulates your behavior. The myth only provides you with the value system you collectively use so that you can live a civilized life in society today.

You belong to a small group that knows you. So, you behave as you are expected to behave. It works much like the sense of identification you get from your High School experience. You root for your team because "You know that they are the best." Or at least you wish that they were. But you do belong to that group, and belonging does regulate your behavior. The primary difference is that religious identification for most people extends for a lifetime. Truth is irrelevant for those feelings of identification. The fact that your religious myth may not be true does not really matter. As we will discuss in more detail later, belonging to that smaller society is your social glue that holds our society together in the Western world yet today.

The point of this chapter should now have made clear to you that where you draw the line in the sand of accepting what you are willing to believe by blind faith is important. Raising blind faith to the level of becoming the sole basis of truth guiding your life may be culturally acceptable, because everyone else does that too. But it can, if not corrected before it develops into a scatoma, block you from further growth.

When you start to believe something is true because you want it to be, or because someone you trusted told you it was true, stop yourself and think. You could be creating a barrier for your further growth. The best path for growth is to acknowledge that your acceptance of any belief is only tentative. If the belief is important for you it needs to be continually tested. The best path is to remain skeptical of new ideas — or of other people who tell you what you should believe — without processing that information based upon what you have previously proven to yourself to be true. Even then, test the validity with all available facts. Then if it is still something you wish to accept, keep an open mind so that additional information you acquire in the future will be able to modify your belief. Always remember, there are no absolute facts beyond the fact that someday you too will die. In the meantime, your goal should be to continually grow, and to gain the very most that you can from this life. It is the only one we know for sure really does exist.

As you become able to live primarily on the higher levels of Maslow's hierarchy, you may grow beyond the need to participate in organized religion because you spend little time on the security or social level. Typically, this occurs for those who can live above the ego level. But most of our society will never get there. According to Maslow, in his day, less than six percent of American society has ever actualized their own life. Fewer still live above their Peak Experience. I would be surprised if they exceeded one percent. Perhaps, a more advanced culture in the future will no longer need that social glue. But we are a long way from that today. Our society is still quite primitive.

Chapter Fifteen
What Happens Next?

Because Humanists do not believe life's value is created by achieving an immortal soul's existence, which in all probability does not exist, they feel that everyone should live their own life fully in the present. Humanists feel we should all make the most of each day while we are living on Earth—and certainly not sacrifice this life for a ticket to an afterlife that may not exist. If there is an afterlife, living a proper life should entitle everyone to whatever rewards are then available. Control People have no valid right to condition our behavior with threats of damnation, or to claim only they have the ticket for our immortality. Even if we wish to believe in an afterlife, and are seeking our ticket, we still should not miss our opportunity to live this life, to the fullest extent that we can achieve.

There may be a life after death, but since we have no valid evidence it exists, Humanists simply ignore that belief and feel a great sense of relief not having to consider that as a possibility. It makes this life far more meaningful for them. Science shows us that the notion of the separation of the body and the soul is not well-founded. If we believe in an afterlife, we only have hope based upon 'blind faith." Therefore, why would we want to sacrifice our lives on Earth with only the hope that a life in the hereafter exists, especially if it requires our denial of the opportunity to live our own life to the fullest here today? Limiting our ability to live this life, conditioned only by Control People, with no other supporting evidence other than their claim of authority, leaves us with no way to validate their claim other than to accept their authority by "blind faith."

That makes no logical sense, even if it is something that we all might really want to believe. We find that our lives are richer, and are far more valuable, when we believe no life exists after our death.

Belief in an afterlife often happens because of conditioning that occurs before our age of reason, creating an intense desire to belong within a specific faith community, and embracing the prescribed conditions for being accepted within that faith community which ultimately become our faith belief. It occurs for emotional reasons. Facts and truth will have little influence on most people 's faith beliefs.

As an example, wanting to become a suicide bomber really makes no logical sense, except to the bomber. To a Humanist, that person is sick. To deceive such a person, causing them to act against their own best interest of living life on Earth to the fullest extent possible, with a promise of 'vestal virgins in heaven," is ludicrous, and a fraud on the in dividual believer, especially if there is no heaven hereafter. Even if there is life hereafter, why would any God worthy of your acceptance make such unreasonable demands of killing its own creations? Such thinking can only be created by a Control Person. If the result of such behavior is valid, why are the Control Persons not the ones to do it?

Striving to maximize our limited opportunity to live on Earth can cause significant internal conflict. There are people in control position claiming authority that use very powerful control devices, such as insisting that heaven is restricted to only those who 'believe" in their particular faith. Not only is that notion absurd, but why would anyone want to associate with a God that makes such unreasonable demands, particularly when it results in most people in the world being denied eternal life who otherwise live a quality life on Earth? Such a belief seriously affects those who feel they must now spend their limited time and resources on Earth in search of a ticket for which each faith belief claims to be the only source. While it hardly makes sense, if that notion becomes a scatoma in childhood, intelligent people will be afraid to follow any other path.

The requirement that you must 'have faith" is what empowers many religious Control People. As we previously discussed, such a faith requirement by a Control Person is 'blind" because there is no validating evidence supporting most of their claims, especially when they claim to hold the only ticket to heaven. Most Humanists find that unacceptable,

Some Control People still today use fear and guilt as primary tools. It does not matter if it is your parents, the schoolteacher, policeman, fireman, clergy, your doctor or anyone else that feels they must control the current situation, meaning they have a need to control you. A test for how you should respond is to ask: "What is their motive?" If you conclude their motive may be valid, perhaps you should listen.

Most Humanists accept that those with the belief of a life hereafter have every right to their own notion of truth—except for those who insist that it becomes their religious duty to see that others follow their same prescription to obtain their ticket. Then it becomes offensive, indeed, this thinking causes wars.

Our society is still living on the lower levels of Maslow's hierarchy; and we continue to have crusaders even today. Some religions even claim it is acceptable to God to kill those who do not accept their particular belief. Why would any God make such an unreasonable demand? Ignorance abounds in our societies. The point is that although many aspects of our life may be threatening, even to our own existence, religion unfortunately has been one of the prime sources of such threat and has been since the cultural organization of human civilization created religion as our "Social glue."

Ancient civilizations often made human sacrifices. Even as late as the 1400's the Mayans of Mexico and Central America used human sacrifices to their gods to keep the survivors safe. The Cuna Indians on the San Blas Islands off Panama killed white men if they remained on their islands after dark as late as 1917. Human life was not sacred even for their society when they felt threatened.

Some cultures still do this today in the name of their own god, but in a more organized and less personal manner. We do this today in the form of wars. Many wars are still being driven by religious conflict, even today. In many respects, our existence on Earth as human beings is still quite primitive. Science has advanced far beyond where our civilization can effectively absorb it. Therefore, we are currently at risk of our own annihilation. And our lives are at risk of a nuclear annihilation of all human life on Earth that could be brought about by religion. We will have shot ourselves in the head because of our own primitive beliefs.

The Effect of Our own Religious Affiliation

Our own response to any religion with which we identify becomes basic to the value system for our life. Our beliefs have a significant effect on our behavior and the quality of our life. Thus, an educated member of the Islamic faith may be capable of their own self-destruction without even questioning what it means for their own self. The behavior is expected of them, and their belonging is a security level need that is lower and much stronger than their ego level needs. On that level you may act, but you do not necessarily have to think for yourself when group think takes over your life. Thus, we have intelligent suicide bombers today.

Many people experience trauma in struggling to move out of the cultural limitations of their early childhood acquired before their age of reason. Many experience guilt, fear, or estrangement from society's mainstream for challenging their own religious traditions. They may especially experience it from their own parents—even after their parents may be deceased—particularly when they challenge beliefs instilled in them by their parents before their age where they have the ability to reason for themselves. Logic and higher levels of thinking do not prevail over emotional beliefs.

Because it is the first duty of any living person or institution is to preserve itself, religions place many cultural barriers on growth to keep their own adherents from escaping. Christians and Jews even today may use negative labels for people who have differing beliefs. After all, who wants to be called a "heathen," "heretic" or "Sinner"? You learn in grade school that calling another person a bad name gets results.

Although most Humanists consider themselves free of such cultural religious barriers, each will still have some. Life is not simple. Ultimately, difficult as it may have been to earn freedom from the limitations of our cultural traditions, most Humanists find that focusing exclusively on this life—rather than being concerned with seeking an afterlife—is far more exhilarating, and more than suffices. Simply looking beyond our childhood faith beliefs by living only in the present avoids the sense of guilt we might otherwise experience by denying our parents' beliefs we were initially taught. We look only toward the future. Consider for a moment why we have children. It may be because they are the very best means for us to extend the meaning of our own lives. They may be the best, but certainly not the only, means for us to obtain our own immortality.

The Measure of our Own Life

For most Humanists, our reason for existing is measured only by how we live this life today. Even if there is anything beyond this life, our effect on the people that follow us should be our own means of measuring the quality of our own life. **Immortality**, accepted by most Humanists, **is the difference we have made in this world because we have been here.** Because of the quality of the life we have lived, we should thereby have more than an equal claim for whatever rewards may follow this life, if any exist. Most Humanists are content knowing their good work on earth, and their effect on the people who survive them, is a sufficient form of their own immortality. There need be nothing more for a Humanist's life to have value. Especially if, because of what they have created, improved, or changed, they have improved the quality of life for people who may not have even been born before they died.

Recognizing that we can be deceived by how our mind works is important in order to better understand how our opportunities to experience life can become seriously limited. Everyone is oriented to life based upon their own perceptions. Our experiences condition the way new information is received. In psychology, conditioned orientation (our own attitude or expectation for the receipt of new stimuli) is called a "preparatory set." A preparatory set establishes the framework for how new information is received by us. The same stimuli may be totally accepted by one person and totally rejected by another, depending upon their own pre-existing orientation.

Scatomas

Now that you realize their seriousness, it merits taking this time to think though what a Scatoma really means for you, based upon what you have already learned. So, let us discuss in more detail scatomas one more time. It is important that you address your own scatomas if you are to grow around your own barriers, because once a stimulus, notion, or position is accepted to the exclusion of all others, we then become fixed in our own belief. Scatomas block our growth. We then feel that this is the only belief that is acceptable because that is the means a scatoma uses to protect itself. Remember that when a notion becomes valued to the exclusion of all other information, and it becomes a "scatoma." they act similarly to a computer spam blocker. Because they block any information contrary to our present belief, whether it is beneficial or detrimental, from even being seen by you. Scatomas are the point at which our ability to accept any contrary notion ceases, our minds become closed, and further dialogue is useless. We are thereafter conditioned to be blind to reality on that particular issue, literally for the rest of our lives. Our own scatomas become our own reality— regardless of whether that belief is right or wrong.

Not all scatomas are bad. The one that surrounds the person we love is necessary to protect our marriage. We do need scatomas in some areas because they do help us filter information so that we can receive useful consistent data and reject the vast number of useless bits of information constantly bombarding us. However, they also harm us by denying us any further acceptance of the truth in that area of concern. That is why you need to learn how to build bridges over your scotomas so that you can continue to grow in those areas where you wish to explore to find paths for your own life fulfillment – so that you truly can become Fully Alive.

You now know that when we internalize or accept notions as true for ourselves, they can become highly valued even when they are inconsistent with our own best interests, or even if they may be recognized by the rest of the world as totally false when compared to reality. A good example is those who still believe today that the world is flat; and if we travel far enough, we will fall off. Most people are bound up by scotomas that make the world in which they live more limited, but it makes them feel safe for themselves. Many people with very limiting scotomas may ensure that those whom they love, or for whom they feel responsible, are also bound up in their same, safe little world. The notion that they might step out of their own hard shell and live even a little beyond is too scary for many to face. Therefore, we might even need to look to the next generation if we want to make a more permanent difference in our world today.

We all have some scotomas because our life-long task is processing the vast number of stimuli we constantly receive so that we may select those beliefs beneficial to our own survival and reject those that could be harmful. Once we select a life-mate, for example, no other person should thereafter be as important. That scotoma is beneficial to maintain a healthy marriage. It also causes us to accept their faults because we can no longer see them. (unless you are my wife). Hopefully, now that we know what we are looking for, we can learn to recognize the difference between good scotomas that guide us in a positive direction, and those that block our further growth. Maintaining a positive attitude, and an open mind, is essential to sustain our growth. Continually growing should be our lifetime goal. We next need to learn how to build our own bridges.

The problem we now understand is that we cannot see our own scotomas. That is because they block any inconsistent information from even being seen by us since their primary purpose is to protect us from unnecessary information. We now know that the best way for us to know we are dealing with a scatoma is when we become emotional, or defensive when we encounter a contrary belief. That is our best evidence of our scatoma. You now know that you cannot challenge a scatoma head on or your negative reaction only gets worse. You also realize that to even move forward in any direction you want to consider in order to improve the quality of your life, the only way to get there is to build a bridge over, or a detour around. your own scatoma. You now know that you can only accomplish that through non-threatening education. That certainly is one major benefit of a college education. It may be a reason that you are reading this book.

To advance the quality of our own life is to always be aware of the benefit and the restriction provided by our current beliefs can block us so that we cannot see beyond them, we know that we have a scatoma that is limiting our ability to grow. Our primary objective should always be to grow. Since seventy percent of all Americans today cannot rise above the social level to even see the three levels above because they cannot bridge their own scatoma, we have to consider that we really may be one of those. Since their scatoma cannot be hit head on, telling the person you want to help to "get over it", or that they are wrong, only increases the strength of their threatened scatoma. The same works for you when you have a negative attitude toward anything.

If you are trying to help someone else, you have to approach the person you wish to help change slowly and indirectly, by providing them with new information that helps them see the path around their current belief. It is easier to see alternatives for others than for yourself. That is a major b e n e f i t for y o u reading this book, and why you now have the information you now have that you have never had before.

This book has caused you to think about the contrast with your current beliefs. If you still do not want to accept that Jesus did not die on a cross, go back and reread that chapter as you are now dealing with a scatoma. Or go to Israel and see for yourself in order for your beliefs to grow. I have been there three times, and each is a significant growth experience. Going to China and seeing the dramatic difference in the life of their people from that of America was more than eye opening for me in many ways that have taken me beyond the safety I felt before in my previous view of my life. In other words, it was clearly a life changing experience for me. Think about what you might do.to advance your own life.

Since our goal is to continue growing, by identifying and eliminating negative barriers before they become scatomas, and for us to accept new information that advances our life, it is a constant endeavor. The healthy approach is to not allow such psychological tools to become permanent barriers for our growth. By recognizing how our experiences can combine to create unfounded expectations, we can reduce many of the barriers we encounter to our own growth. Maintaining a positive attitude for getting something of value from all opportunities from any new experience will make a big difference in our ability to grow. Growth should be a lifetime goal to enhance the value of our own lives. We do this best when we keep an open mind, always seeking new information and ways of looking at whatever we see and are doing. Always try a new path whenever there is an opportunity to do so. That way we grow.

We can help our own children grow by continually exposing them to new experiences that keep their beliefs from becoming fixed. Ask them questions that lead them to think new thoughts rather than you telling them what they should believe.

How Should my Own Beliefs Grow?

A person trained from early childhood with any belief will have value and emotions invested in that belief. If asked to accept a contrary notion, people will respond emotionally. That is because the feeling you experience at the moment of accepting a belief typically becomes associated with the belief from the time it is first acquired. It will continue to be associated with that belief for the rest of your life, unless intentionally modified by subsequent education. This is particularly true with those beliefs acquired at an early age, before you had developed the ability to reason for yourself. That is why most people's religious views are so powerful, and why it is very difficult for them to change them in later life even if they want to change. If you want to test how scatomas work' try and tell another person, why their deep-felt beliefs are phony and see how violently they react to you. Their behavior shows how their scatoma easily blocks any other conflicting view. That is exactly why the only way to grow beyond a scatoma is through non-threatening education.

Because the emotions you experience with a belief when it is first accepted are typically forever a part of your belief. Therefore, our religious heritage has such a powerful effect on us. That explains why facts are not relevant to our continued endorsement of that view. If you have been raised in a faith, you cannot simply ignore your own religious beliefs without suffering an adverse psychological effect. As an adult, to leave behind childhood beliefs that were reinforced weekly requires significant education. Such a change could take a lifetime. Therefore, most people find no reason to change. That is unfortunate. We should continue to grow in all of our endeavors throughout our lifetime. That does not mean giving up your religion. It does mean that your religion needs to grow with you.

Our emotional connection with our own family is the result of the same mental and emotional process. However, we should seek opportunities for all processes to grow to keep them fresh and meaningful. If you practice learning how to change your mind or your attitude for anything new, that effort will soon be looked upon as fun. It will minimize the effect of your scatoma and help you grow. Your ability to grow in new ways will soon become your goal.

Because we naturally associate any belief with the emotions present when they originated, and because we cannot easily take any aspect of our lives out of its context, alternatives to our own scatomas are not only unacceptable, but can be threatening—even to the point where people are willing to risk their lives to defend their current notion of what they believe is right if they are challenged head on.

We know from when the phenomenon occurs today, when otherwise intelligent people become suicide bombers in the name of their religious belief, that their act has nothing to do with truth. A logical argument cannot defeat an emotional belief. Significant non-threatening education is required to cause behavioral change. In the Middle East today there is insufficient time for their public's education. The result is that we are at war today in the Middle East because of their scatomas.

The mature way of accommodating childhood beliefs in the adult world is to continually redefine each concept, or belief, to keep your belief currently relevant. People cling to their own beliefs. However, even our religious beliefs should mature just like any other notion influencing our lives. A 'fear God" concept is normal in childhood, a "Father God" concept is more believable for a High School student, but by the time we become adults a more mature abstract way of defining God is far more effective. Yet some still believe their fear God as an adult. Why? It is because their mind closed in their childhood. As a result, they ceased to learn from their own life experiences.

As said several times before, in order to put this in proper perspective, what we are saying is the same mental process is how you dealt with the myth of Santa Claus for yourself as a child. That belief is accepted by all children raised in the American tradition of a Christian family. However, this only lasts for a few years because, eventually, Santa Claus is undermined by reality. Each child is devastated. How they respond next is important. Those who do not substitute the good of giving to others for their childish notion of Santa as "their gift giver" feel disappointed. Those able to develop a healthy change of perception, looking at Santa from their parents' perspective, may continue to celebrate Santa with Christmas as their symbol of giving for the rest of their life. How we address and are affected by our own religious views are exactly the same.

Our objective in life should be for us to continue to grow. If our beliefs evolve healthily, to the extent that we can live within our full range of needs through continued growth and development, that will put us on a path where we can eventually be able to achieve a peak experience. Our goal should be for our individual life to continually become richer, more fulfilled, and more satisfying. Although the specific goals that fulfill our individual lives will be unique, fully understanding the universal process for human growth makes the journey easier.

Chapter Sixteen
What About Religion?

People living life primarily on the social level, or below, live on fertile ground for religion. Organized religious institutions provide a Mini cultural, mutual support system that becomes vital for many people, especially for those living on the high security/mid-social need level. For our society that is a major purpose for a church. Many people belong solely for social support reasons. Their participation has little to do with the theology or myth of their particular faith. Those are merely the threads that bind their members together. Their Church becomes their security and, for many, their primary social support system.

Although all religions have members living on all of Maslow's hierarchy of need levels, and Humanists can be found in all faiths, humanism is not seeking to become a substitute for religion. Humanism does not have the structure to fulfill the security and social needs for religious church members who look upon their church experience primarily for supplying those needs. It is easy for most living in our society to become identified and accepted within the social structure of any church. People living primarily on a high security/up to mid-social level easily fit in their faith, which then becomes intricately woven into the fabric of life of members while providing them a social structure. Their current religious faith often is how they identify themselves. In addition, their church easily resolves questions of how they should live life with answers that add value to the lives of those who are content to live within a structured society. For those not hurting anyone else, if they are content living within their current level of needs for the rest of their life, why would anyone want to disrupt that person's life? No one should. Humanism alone cannot fill those needs.

Humanists that have abandoned their own childhood religion, and not replaced it, have filled their security and social needs in some other manner. Or they simply ignore these needs because they spend very little of their life living on those levels. Others fill these needs on their own with other relationships, which may include participation within a church or faith. Or they become Unitarians. Unitarians have no faith component. Identification with others who reinforce your beliefs is important.

All people have strong social needs that cause them to feel that they must "belong" somewhere. As proof, consider the attitude expressed by high school or college students, or even many graduates, toward "their own team." They might not have the skill to play football themselves. But it is 'their team," and they aggressively share their opinions of what went wrong in last week's game. Look at the attitude of an American Marine, especially if you knew that person before their enlisting. Their assured attitude can be felt merely by their physical presence. Consider your own attitude regarding a descriptive identification of yourself, such as being "an American" when you are in another country. We all have a need to belong somewhere. This is a security level need. Acceptance by any structure establishes or confirms our personal identity, which may be satisfied within social organizations. To that extent the identification fulfills a security level need.

Many people have few other opportunities immediately available to them for filling these needs. Religious organizations readily fill those needs. They are recognized as the primary social support systems for much of our society. That is how they provide their "Social glue." Even though they each have their own collective myth or view of certain historical events as a unifying symbolic message, their myth is not the reason church members participate. Membership in their own religion is for many a necessary support system, one that goes back to the origins of human society that humanism, by itself, does not fulfill for anyone who has not reached the high ego/low actualized level of life as described by Maslow.

For many living primarily on lower need levels, no other institutional structure in our society so effectively meets fulfilling these needs.

Churches will always be viewed by these people in our society as necessary, if not essential. Humanism is not an acceptable alternative view of life for people living primarily on the social level, nor is our philosophy of any comfort for people who wish for answers and not questions as they face the world in which we live today. Therefore, challenging another person's religion for any reason is not appropriate behavior for a Humanist.

Recognizing that most people in our society are relatively content where they are in their own life, and then telling them there may be more that they are missing in life, only serves to cause unwanted discontent if we do not provide them a path for fulfillment at the same time. Where we as Humanists should concentrate our effort is to ensure that the children of those, we might feel compelled to influence, and all other children, be able to at least realize there are higher levels of living that they can achieve. They should be shown a path that would allow them to achieve these levels. Maslow does that. That has nothing to do with anyone's religious faith. We do owe it to the next generation, at the very least, to educate them to see beyond themselves, to be motivated, and to fulfill their own potential. Each child should be encouraged to seek fulfillment of their own life. Maslow called this "Self-actualization." Humanists can help by educating the public about its existence.

Does Everyone Need Religion?

As previously mentioned, Humanist Harvard professor, E. O. Wilson points out that all people have a "basic spiritual need" which ties us to nature and our own reality. Therefore, religion claims a spiritual Posture as central to its existence. Wilson's point is that even those who have fulfilled their security and social needs through other means, may no longer feel the need for organized religion, still have a spiritual need. There are few organized institutions other than religion where this need can be met by the public with others' help. There are some Far Eastern cultural techniques that provide those results better than any techniques we currently have. Yoga may be as close as we come to the result of their principal techniques. some Humanists can satisfy their spiritual need watching a beautiful sunset or feeling a peak experience while being in tune with their natural surroundings. Many people need more than that. They cannot get there on their own, possibly because their daily routine captures their attention. They need supporting leadership to get there. Their religion fulfills that purpose for them.

Rabbi Sherwin Wine was the spiritual leader of the Birmingham Temple in Detroit. He created the *Society for Humanistic Judaism* to meet these needs for, and yet remain within, the Jewish cultural tradition and symbolism. When I expressed to Rabbi Wine that we Humanists do not offer a religious tradition or myth, he claimed "Humanists have the world's best religious epic, given to us by Charles Darwin in his identification of the evolution of life. And it is not a myth; it is a fact that has been proven." He further stated 'there is no better expression for adding meaning to our own lives. It is why we exist. The *Society for Humanistic Judaism,* using Jewish symbols and traditions, and the *Unitarian Universalist Church,* for people who come from Christian or more liberal forms of Judaism traditions, are both concerned with these issues. They provide alternatives that remain within our society's cultural religious traditions, as the means to fill security/social needs, and they offer low social support. What they all provide is a spiritual opportunity that points people beyond themselves. This is very effective for people who view life from the Humanistic perspective. More than one-half the membership of the Unitarian Universalist Church are Humanists. Many Humanists arrived there, like I did, from a Christian or Jewish family.

Even though some Humanists can fill all their own needs within the philosophy of humanism, and some Humanists are associating in a church setting to fill these needs, organized humanism is not concerned with replacing religion and should not be looked upon as a threat by anyone in the religious community—unless they are fanatical religious Control People abusing their flock using fear and guilt as their control devices. I think organized humanism has every right to educate their public that what they are doing is abuse of those they serve. Humanists will attack those that deny anyone their right to fully live their own life while they are here on Earth by using fear or guilt as a means of control.

If a person needs more than a philosophy of how to live a full life here on Earth, members of any religion can place their own faith on top of humanism's philosophic view of life. Humanists are most concerned with not missing this one opportunity for each of us to live this life to the fullest extent that is possible while we are here on Earth today. Religious concerns are easily placed on top of our philosophy by those who find value for themselves in doing so.

In fact, this is a part of the thinking today of religious leaders like Episcopal Bishop John Shelby Spong, who has adopted a Humanistic view of reality—using only provable historical religious facts—within his own faith community. Such a technique may become a major part of organized religions of the future, and ultimately could sustain the church when our cultural society finally reaches higher need levels of living that might otherwise cause their membership to decline.

As I have stated, religions are made up of "memes," which are self-replicating beliefs that pass from person to person that do not necessarily have any relationship to truth or reality beyond themselves. Many are learned before our age of reason and become the symbols that we use to answer serious questions we have that science so far has not addressed. Or if it has, those answers have not been accepted by us. Our beliefs provide the "Social glue" that allows us to successfully sustain our society. We do not have to kill religion just because the historic facts of their myth may not be true.

Many people fill their security and low-social level of needs through their religion. On our security level they provide us with purpose and provide an outside force that we can influence for our own protection.

The notion of life after our death arises from that perspective. On the social level it gives us an identification with others in our mutual support network that adds to our security because we then "belong" with likeminded people who reinforce our belief system. In other words, there is no other system in our organized society that fills those needs so effectively. Without religion our society could descend into anarchy. Therefore, until society reaches levels of living for most people above the social level, we all need to support those religious faiths that benefit but do not harm people.

Memes adjust to absorb any cultural challenge. Perhaps organized humanism can help elevate those religions whose control is currently based upon fear and guilt. One means could be by recognizing what Bishop Spong is saying, and to make their religious symbols relevant but not harmful to the people they purport to serve. They would then serve their members instead of primarily those Control People who currently might abuse them. Hopefully most do not. But some obviously do.

Chapter Seventeen

What is God's Answer?

Human beings for thousands of years have been identifying forces in nature that exceed our current ability to comprehend or understand. Such forces have historically been called "God." Many early peoples felt that the sun or elements of the weather, or even the sea, were gods. People prayed or sacrificed to such gods for their own safety.

Prior to Abraham many gods were acceptable. However, when religion required accepting only one God, the use of the term became more complex. As science explained away mysteries that had once been associated with more primitive "gods," the definition became more abstract. We are still doing this today. **"God" is a universal term used by most people for identifying whatever is beyond our own personal knowledge that we, as an individual, fear or revere**. For some, God is the word they use to identify the forces of nature that allows our universe to exist and to support life that they currently do not understand.

We each have our own definition of "God." There could be serious disagreement in any congregation if all members were required to accept the same god concept. Try asking any congregation to explain what the term "God' means, and you will have a serious argument, unless the members are so tightly controlled by their Control People that they are not able to think for themselves. Most merely accept Group Think answers. For Others who are not so deeply controlled, many clergy explain "God" by expressing generalities, or adjectives that are universal or non-threatening, because they describe the effects of God rather than defining what the term "God" actually means. That avoids conflict.

Claiming, for example, that 'God is the Creator" says very little but implies a lot. The concept of creator could be synonymous with God being nature. Obviously, if nature were your definition, the statement that (God is the Creator" would be true—if the universe has not always existed, which we now believe it is most likely that it has. Creation could be limited to meaning our individual lives when using the term "creator' to avoid the logical dilemma of 'What created God?' The notion that God is the creator, however, does not imply a caring god, nor does it explain the existence of evil. Nor does this sort of God explain anything about our purpose in life, other than that we were created and are to live this life on Earth. Besides raising the question of whether there was intelligent thought behind our being here today, that definition of God has little utility.

The real issue is whether you must provide God with "Supernatural" characteristics to make your own God meaningful for you. When you do that, no Humanist would agree with you. You will have made yourself into a puppet. The notion of theism, instead of deism, is a recent addition in our more contemporary religions that Humanists look upon as a control device, and we see no valid proof such an entity exists, nor any valid reason why it should. It takes the responsibility for your life away from you and gives it to Control People. Why would you want to do that?

The Validity of "Why" Questions

Aristotle expanded the study of philosophy and introduced the notion that a central philosophic question is "Why something occurs." Our current religious views have evolved from that perspective. We now have a cultural dichotomy. Science tells us "how", religion claims to tell us "why." Humanism accepts that there may not be a reason "why" we live. All that we know for sure is that our life exists. We also know that we are part of nature. However, since "why" is a central question in most religions, we cannot simply ignore the question.

Most Humanists realize that we do not need to ask "why." We can accept that there may not be a "why". Instead, we are content to only seek the answer of how" things in our universe occur. Those questions are within the realm of science and therefore within acceptable knowledge. They are testable to ascertain truth. Humanists see no reason to seek solutions beyond our current science. We easily accept that "why" may not be a valid question because there are not currently available facts to support truthful answers for all 'why" questions. Perhaps the answer to a "why" question regarding our own existence lies only within what each of us is willing to believe in ourselves.

If one believes that there was an intelligent independent cause for life, a grand designer perhaps that we might call 'God," we might conclude there may be a divine purpose for our individual lives. However, if a person believes that Darwin was correct, and that all forms of life have evolved into more complex species through natural selection, it is more logical to accept that we are here simply as a part of that process. We exist as the result of the current state of evolution. From that perspective, there does not have to be a reason for our existence in nature. You might ask: "Why does this particular ant exist?" only to realize the absurdity of that question. That is why science suggests that asking why we exist is probably an invalid question. For a Humanist, we must create our own "Why" if that is an important question for ourselves. Some may adopt religious answers for convenience. Most Humanists simply ignore the question.

Because Humanists, based upon science, can accept that we human beings are merely a part of the natural evolution of life, and that how we came to exist was merely by chance. That theory makes more logical sense than the notion that there was an unknown prime mover. Who or what created the prime mover? If you can say the universe has always existed, then nature could have always existed. There would be no need for a prime mover or creator God. If you accept as true, that such a God has always existed, such a creator God cannot be a logical concept unless you say that God and nature are one and the same.

The fact that Humanists believe science is the closest we can currently come to truth; we are apt to have different conclusions than many of our currently accepted historic religious traditions.

There need not be a reason that we exist today. We are simply a part of the evolution process. How our genes will evolve in the future is exciting to consider, but impossible to predict. Our genes see no reason to share their goals with us, if they have any. Science says the process is random but conditioned by those traits that adapt better to our current environment.

Those who are willing to accept the hypothesis that God created us by design, by accepting this notion on "blind faith," can conjure up all sorts of reasons to interpret their God's plan. You can only come to that conclusion by "blind faith," which is akin to wishful thinking. Others, however, recognize that facts, tested and proven by science, support a more obvious truth that is far more believable without requiring "faith" in an esoteric something that logic simply cannot support.

The statement that there is a "creator God" ultimately expresses the postulate that powers exist in the universe that are superior to us. That should be obvious. People saying that "God is the creator" may only be describing nature. Most people would not pray to nature. With a nature view of life, we could still pray, or meditate, to tune ourselves to our own reality. However, the notion of expecting an instant response from nature would not fulfill the needs of those who find prayer necessary for themselves. Their 'God" must be more than the forces that created our universe for their comfort. Most Humanists see no valid reason to do that.

Chapter Eighteen

What About Those Who Claim to be Atheists?

As we previously discussed, Abraham Maslow points out that people's current God concept varies depending upon which level they are predominately living. Religion's most important role in our culture is to fill the needs of people on the security and low social levels. Many are dependent upon religion to fill those needs so that they have the courage and stability either to attempt to tentatively advance beyond them, or to comfortably live on those levels.

On the basic level people typically have a "fear God" concept so that God can be recognized. On the security level a "provider God" becomes more appropriate. On the social level many develop a "Father God" view of God. On the ego self-awareness level, a "creator God" may be deemed more appropriate. By the time people arrive at the actualized level normally their God concept has become abstract. It is then possible for them to identify their 'God" as a synonym for nature, or their 'Ultimate Concern," or whatever they fear or revere. If that occurs, and your concept of God is abstract, how can you be an Atheist? Atheism only works with a lower social level or below of belief for what the word "god" means to you.

Thus, Atheists denying your right to use the term "God" is simply wrong. What Atheists are really objecting to is the existence of a more primitive concept, or a 'supernatural God," where God is attempting to control your life. Objecting to that "God", most rational people would agree with them. Instead of Atheists saying, 'No God exists," if they changed their message to say, 'No supernatural God exists," most

Humanists and many clergy would agree with them, and the public would not find their belief so offensive. Their problem is that they must have a primitive concept of a God on the social level or below to deny God's existence. How can they deny the existence of nature?

The term "Atheist" has such a negative cultural effect upon the public today because it is a direct attack on the cultural meme of religion itself.

Therefore, a better means of conveying an Atheist real message would be to cease using that word and, when asked their religion, prefer to be identified as 'none". That response today is becoming predominant with the younger generation who find little value in identifying their beliefs. That would free Atheists to direct their very valid attack on the definition of God, instead of holding themselves out as a lightning rod for public attack when claiming to be an "Atheist". Perhaps for many claiming to be Atheists, their real motivation is the personal recognition they receive for themselves as a contrarian instead of it representing their search for truth? They are proud of their lack of faith beliefs. Humanists are proud that their beliefs are not "blind".

Except for those who are determined to deny someone else's beliefs or are still fighting their own earlier childhood god concept that has not matured, the term 'God" does have utility for most people. That word denotes something very personal and, culturally, it is used to express what we cannot discern, or that which we deeply revere or fear.

The more appropriate approach for those who do not find value in the God concept, and yet still feel compelled to challenge anyone else's right to use the term, should restrict their challenge to the more primitive definitions of the meaning of the term "God", or, even better, to attack supernaturalism.

Since their objection is more appropriately addressed to those who require supernatural qualities in the definition of God, most mainstream theologians today would agree with Atheists who claim that theism (providing God with supernatural characteristics) is no longer relevant, but most of these theologians all still accept deism as valid. The difference is that a deistic God may have created the universe, including us, but does not thereafter intervene in manipulating the universe or attempting to control our daily lives. The deist God could be the "Grand Designer"; that is consistent with those who accept an abstract concept for God, such as nature. Or the term "God" could simply be an abstract word for whatever it is that we fear or revere that we have no other way to express.

Most of American Founding Fathers were "Deist", but certainly not "Theist". Theism was not predominant yet. Thomas Jefferson even cut out what he found as the offensive parts of the Bible and made his own version of the Bible. Those that think America was founded on religion are simply wrong. Many of our early citizens came to our shores to get out from under the oppression of European religion. Our Constitution was based on the concept of providing us "freedom from religion". Our Constitution was not intended to allow religion to prevail against us by allowing people with faith beliefs using our government as their tool for imposing their beliefs upon those wishing to be free from religion. Out Founding Father's families came to America to get out from under the oppression of European religion.

For these theologians who accept deism, we all live by the rules of nature. Nature does not make our free-throw for us, resulting in the other team losing. From any intelligent perspective, no God worth accepting would do that. Humanists do not find any valid need for supernaturalism, and there is no way to get there except based upon "blind faith." Humanists are not willing to be "blind" and cannot get there.

The more important issue is that Atheists gain little by denying another's right to use the term "God" in any way that they wish. For many other people the term 'God" has great emotional security value because they have no better way to express their concerns, or to explain their awe of the universe, or to receive answers to the unknown.

There are forces in the universe that are greater than us. If that is their use of the term 'God," then why object?

Because churches exist primarily on the high security/mid- social level, God is typically a security level belief for many people. Attacking anything on the social or security level more frequently results in a violent response. All people will violently defend an attack on their social or security level. Non-threatening education is the best, and probably the only, means of challenging beliefs on those levels. If the Atheist's goal is to reform another person's beliefs, they should challenge supernatural definitions and not challenge a word that validly may have an actualized level definition. To even attempt to do that makes the Atheist position absurd.

Throughout the ages, wars have been caused because everyone knows "that their own beliefs are true". Therefore, most fervently believe that everyone else's conflicting beliefs must be "false". There may be "no truth" regarding any faith belief. Truth may only exist "in the eye of the beholder".

Christians and Jews still fight today over whether Christ was the Promised Messiah. Muslims and Christians fight over whether Mohammad was a later prophet sent by God. Muslims and Jews still fight over whose lineage represents the rightful descendants of Abraham to be sacrificed at the altar. Who really are "God's chosen people"?

Muslims believe they are descendants of Ishmael, who was Abraham's first born. He was born out of wedlock by Abraham's servant Hagar, and they are upset over Hagar and Ishmael's rejection from Abraham's tribe and being sent into the wilderness to fend for themselves by Sarah after Abraham died—and apparently, they will never forgive Jews, and their descendants. The Jews, and therefore the Christians, believe they are descendants of Isaac, who was Sarah's first born of her marriage with Abraham, because God believes in the sanctity of marriage. Which lineage was chosen by God? What would happen to their excuse for war if both realized that "God really does not care"?

Yet there still is dissension and discord even among members of all major religious faiths. For example, even among those of the Islamic faith there is significant disagreement over who represents God. Does that person have to be a lineal descendant of Mohammad (Shiites), who value the spiritual experience, or can that person be elected by the people who are more focused on the scripture, the Quran, and other writings (Sunni)? Those are relatively small details. However, they lead people in the Mideast to kill each other to defend their own truth. The Iraq Constitution is a test of compromise over three radically differing views within the same Islamic faith.

In America, evangelical Christians challenge all other Christians. Each has based their position on their view of historic facts that makes their interpretation the only valid truth, at least for themselves. What if both are wrong? Why can't we all accept that we have our own beliefs, and everyone else is entitled to have their own?

Similarly, The Dead Sea Scrolls have proven to scholars that the historic "facts" upon which many in our culture have based their "faith" must be false. Yet, even when confronted with this knowledge, most will continue to believe what they have always believed, and they will defend their position to their death. Why is that so? The answer may be seen in our previous discussion. Psychology has shown us how our minds work.' Once we have a sufficient answer to any concern, we typically develop a scatoma that blocks any challenge to that belief. Our own truth becomes our own reality regardless of what may be true for everyone else. Only through non-threatening education can we change that view.

Humanism and Atheism

Humanism is certainly not atheistic, although many Atheists may also be Humanists. **Humanism, as a philosophy of life, could possibly be categorized as "agnostic" because the use of the term God is not relevant to humanism**. All humans should recognize that some forces of nature in the universe are superior to their own existence—whatever term they use to describe them is up to each person. Atheists simply cannot accept using the term "God" in any form. Atheism expresses only what the proponent is against. It only means that they are generally opposed to the use of the term "God" for any purpose. However, that stance does not say what the individual expressing their distaste for using the word 'God" in form actually does believe. We know what they do not believe. The more important question is what do they believe?

Filling that need is why many Atheists identify with humanism. Humanism is a positive philosophy of life without any faith component, let alone a requirement of accepting truths based upon 'blind faith". Most Humanists recognize that it is not necessary to adopt any religion for a person to have a full, ethical, and successful life here on Earth.

Humanists Reserve the Right to Keep Beliefs Meaningful for Themselves

Some people identify themselves as Humanists, but also subscribe to a personal belief. Many participate in some form of religion. For some people that aspect of their life goes beyond the Humanist philosophy for social or cultural reasons, such as family tradition. For others, their beliefs established before their age of reason have meaningful emotional value for them. Since it is for emotional reasons, humanism simply does not address those needs. These people have personal needs that humanism cannot fulfill. Humanism is not concerned with these issues, nor does organized humanism take any position on the subject other than to say it is "un-humanistic" behavior for anyone to intentionally attack another person's beliefs for any reason except to defend themselves, and those for whom they are responsible, from personal attack.

Humanists seldom attack another person's beliefs, because humanism advocates personal freedom for everyone to embrace life to its fullest as they so choose. The best that Humanists can offer is education that allows a person's religious views to more realistically mature. We feel that we must do that in our positive effort to help people understand the value of fully living their own life while they are on Earth today. And for their lives not to be controlled by others rather than exclusively by themselves.

Except for Supernatural Beliefs

As previously stated, where all Humanists may validly object is when "supernatural" requirements are necessary as a prerequisite to use the term "God." All Humanists object to a 'Supernatural" characteristic for God, because at that point there is no discernible test for reality, truth, or veracity. There remains only subjective belief, based upon "blind faith." Humanists find no valid reason to base our lives merely on "blind faith" for anything. That would risk reducing the measure of truth to the level of absurdity. We may not fully understand nature now, but that does not mean humans never will. Any supernatural belief becomes unnecessary. Humanists do not feel that they must have an answer to every question to be able to live a good life. Some questions have no answer.

As for "Blind Faith"

More important for a Humanist is that living your life based upon "blind faith" really means that some Control Person has taken control of your life. You have allowed yourself to become their puppet. You are now a sheep, and they are your shepherd. Why do you feel it necessary to give up control of your own life? Doing so makes no intelligent sense to a Humanist. In fact, most Humanists will want to get far away from you. Like a cold, it might be contagious.

No Humanist can accept that. The problem for a Humanist is that it does not require thinking. It is perceived as simplistic, and that makes no sense to a Humanist. That is because they feel that something central to your own existence deserves to be fully understood and verifiable if you are going to dedicate your life based upon that belief.

There are many additional aspects of understanding the subject of God that go beyond the parameters of this discussion. We know for a fact that we are currently unable to fully comprehend nature. The important point is that our approach to understanding those forces beyond ourselves is currently deeply personal. No one so far has discovered the "truth" to life, and the use of the term "God" has no clear definition.

Because of a lack of education, or exposure to different alternatives or other viewpoints for life, or for whatever other reason that is important for them, some people feel compelled to answer certain of their questions of life with myth or lore. Challenging their faith would leave them without an alternative belief system. Therefore, real harm, and very little value, is found in an unsolicited challenge to another's deeply felt beliefs. Most Humanists would simply avoid the subject.

The result of gratuitously attacking another's deeply felt beliefs may cause irreparable harm, not only to the believer, but also to the attacker. Such behavior generally will not make anyone feel better. So why would you even want to do it? Most Humanists can recognize the effect such behavior would have upon others and would not intentionally do so. An ethical Humanist normally does not intentionally harm others.

Maslow acknowledged that all humans are subject to cultural and psychological restraints. As we have learned, once a notion is acceptable to a person, it can easily be developed into a limiting scatoma. We can become blind to the effect of our negative behavior toward others, just like we block any information challenging our deeply felt beliefs.

Try telling those who are still fighting their parents' God concept that "atheism is irrelevant." Their concept of God is limited to a narrow range, and because of this barrier, they must expend energy defending their position because they are still fighting the 'God" concept of their childhood. One would think they could have found an easier way to emancipate themselves from their parents that is less harmful to others. Many even feel justified offending others' beliefs in their zeal.

Their God concept simply did not mature as they grew, forcing them to now waste their limited energy, much like Don Quixote did fighting windmills.

Many Atheists are unaware, or do not care, that what they are objecting to is their own limited definition of 'God," and not the legitimate current cultural practice of calling whatever forces are beyond us that we currently do not understand, but still revere or fear, as a 'God", having nothing to do with supernaturalism. Atheists can validly object to the notion of supernaturalism, which they wrongfully assume is necessary for the use of the term "God". However, they fail to make the distinction. Because they find no utility in the use of the term, their belief is that the word simply should not exist. Most people disagree.

A more constructive approach for an Atheist would be to challenge the definition and the conclusions reached by a person compelled to use the term 'God" if the Atheist really wants to engage in meaningful dialogue. That would at least change the playing field, requiring the religious community to have to defend "supernaturalism", a position many people within the faith community would soon recognize as absurd. The most Atheist can prove is that we do not have valid answers for everything today. But that does not mean that we never will. Humanists are willing to wait for an answer.

Most Humanists simply do not worry about such concerns. I intentionally stuck my foot in my mouth and asked Stephen Hawking's colleague, Steven Weinberg, who is a Humanist Nobel Laureate in theoretical physics, about his view of God. He responded, "Why would I even worry about such things?" Such effort is trivial and of little value for many agnostic Humanists.

Where Humanist Differ from Atheists

Most Atheists can accept humanism as a valid life view, but many Humanists do not accept atheism as adding relevance to life. Why offend others with a negative belief when humanism has so many positive arguments to make that support this life? Education is the only valid, socially acceptable approach for changing others' opinions.

Negatively challenging another's belief system is not acceptable for most Humanists.

In fact, such behavior offends many Humanists and makes it difficult for them to even want to associate or be identified with activist Atheists. As a result, many mainstream Humanists do not become active in organized Humanist events. "In your face" kind of people are offensive, and many Humanists intentionally avoid them. Most Humanists simply do not worry about the subject, and many do not want their time wasted being confronted by those who do want to emphasize their hostility toward "God" when humanism could be doing so much better in the world without that unnecessary distraction.

Some Atheists proudly waive their banner bragging about their negative view of life as if it were a 'badge of honor," instead of a reflection of their limited view of life. That behavior is unfortunate for many mainstream Humanists because we really do not want to even be in the same room with them. People with that very limited view of reality are as much of a nuisance for mainstream Humanists as the far right is for those who are mainstream in the Republican Party. Both may become "in your face" kinds of people, and that is as offensive to mainstream Humanists as farting in your church pew is to a Christian.

If Atheist like the positive side of what the Humanist philosophy means for adding value to their lives, then among other Humanists they should act like a Humanist and be respectful of the beliefs and feelings of others and leave their 'in your face" behavior at home to only share with others who also think negatively. They should put on their best behavior among Humanists, who generally feel that everyone is entitled to whatever beliefs add value in their own lives.

This is the only life that we know for certain we will ever have. However, it is not our duty to educate people who do not want our education. Most Humanists feel obligated to be respectful of others' feelings because we feel that everyone should be free to believe whatever enhances their own existence, if it does not hurt anyone else.

Therefore, for those who do not accept that responsibility for themselves in their personal behavior, all moderate or liberal Humanists would ask is that they not reflect that behavior that is disrespectful of the God of others in the name of humanism, or at Humanist events. However, most Humanists would not object if they do so within organized Atheists events, which they can do in addition to, but outside of the bounds of, being an Atheist Humanist.

That is so that they are also respectful of moderate and liberal Humanists that believe insulting other peoples' beliefs is simply un-Humanistic behavior, and everyone should not want those moderate or liberal Humanists to be uncomfortable attending organized Humanists events. I imagine most Atheists would recognize that, as a Humanist, you would not go into the Vatican shouting, "There is no God, so get over it." There is an appropriate time and place for everything. Although an activist Atheist might stand outside the Vatican with a banner claiming their belief, they should not expect Humanist organizations to participate, nor to sanction or support such events.

Chapter Nineteen

What is the Role of Religion?

Religion came into existence as our human solution to providing social control of a community of people too large to maintain the social control that was possible when everyone in a community knew everyone else. Retired Harvard professor, E.O. Wilson observed that, somewhere around 150 people, society control starts to break down. Therefore, larger communities needed a common value system, and a structure for encouraging or enforcing the members of the community to adhere to those rules. Those who violated them with force were met with police force. Those that merely ignored those rules were challenged by priests and shunned by participants.

E.O. Wilson also pointed out that a bully can dominate any other person to gain satisfaction of their needs. However, an altruistic crowd or a group of people supporting each other can control a bully. The dichotomy caused by the existence of both is what causes our society to grow. The dominant person initiates social change. The organized social structure modifies the conflict between the new and the previously existing order to allow integration of change within our society. Therefore, our society grows and adapts.

As previously mentioned, E.O. Wilson also stated that everyone has some spiritual need. That is, a biological need to connect with nature. Sociobiology is the study linking the field of biology with sociology. According to Wilson biology does not end at birth, with the study of everything that occurs in our lives thereafter moving exclusively into the field of sociology. Wilson finds that many of our institutions, including that human need for connecting with nature we call "spirituality," are biologically determined. Spirituality in the form of reverence for life is biologically necessary for everyone.

All healthy people have a natural spiritual awe of our universe. People may label their reverence for life however they wish. The need for spirituality is a human characteristic. The need of each of us for a sense of spirituality is what grounds religion as it integrates with reality. However, our need for spirituality is not the exclusive province of religion. How it is recognized is an issue everyone is biologically compelled to reconcile for themselves. Spirituality is an emotional feeling of being connected to nature and our own reality. It is a very important need for us to be connected to our own roots and reality. That is why religions early on attempted to capture it for themselves, and why many people even today accept that the realm of spirituality is their religion's domain.

Fortunately, they are wrong. Spirituality is innate with all of us. I believe that arriving at spiritual feelings while watching a sunset, walking in a wooded area, sitting on a mountain looking over the world in front of you, or on a beach when the sun sets beyond the horizon, or watching your newborn child, breathing deeply and enjoying your own life, is the very best form of spirituality. It is then that you are in tune with your world and may even be sharing in a "peak experience."

Realizing that it does little good to challenge another's beliefs, Humanists can accept that each person is entitled to live his or her own life as they choose—at least until they attempt to limit the rights, or to challenge the beliefs, of others. The religious far right and the atheist far left are both in the wrong when they use an "in your face" approach to proselytize their own "faith" belief, although the religious right is far more aggressive when they attempt to use the law as a tool of their faith. Not only is the historical factual basis for each of their beliefs wrong. but their conclusion is not an accurate interpretation of the facts that do exist. Their approach only results in encouraging greater resistance in those people whom both "faiths" hope to change.

The only valid way to change another's belief is to provide a nonthreatening opportunity for the introduction of evidence so that a person's view of life may grow through their learning new information. To change another person's deeply felt beliefs, we must help them build a new bridge over their scatoma for change if it is to have lasting value for them. Only non-threatening education can change a person's view of their own truth, by adding that new information to their preexisting structure of beliefs. To be effective, people must be receptive to another idea they may have previously not considered, at least from the point of reference that is now being presented. Our attitude must be open and receptive for new ideas to take root. New ideas can only ultimately be accepted if they are properly presented in a non-threatening manner. This is how college freshmen, there to learn, grasp a view of life that enlarges their perspective. It also is the reason that many religions have colleges that keep their sheep in their fold.

A Current View of Religion

We are now ready to summarize the previous information to make it relevant today. Our own life is viewed through the lenses we use. Humanism is only one lens. There are multiple valid views of life. John Shelby Spong was a retired Bishop of the Episcopal Diocese of Newark, New Jersey. Bishop Spong believed that theism is dying, and should be replaced with a deistic, more relevant view of God. He found no need for supernaturalism. Neither do Humanists. Bishop Spong extended the thinking of the earlier Unitarian Universalist minister Henry Nelson Wieman, who developed theocentric naturalism and the empirical method in American theology of the 1970s. Wieman viewed his God as the "life force." (Whatever created "life") Bishop Spong incorporates that concept into the Christian tradition.

Bishop Spong stated that Jesus was merely a human being who died just like all the rest of us human beings. He pointed out that it was later theologians who added the notion of Jesus' resurrection. Historic facts support that is true. The apostle Paul created the Christ, which is our Christian tradition today, thanks to Constantine's Nicene

Conference in 325 AD. Evidence today, including the Dead Sea Scrolls, tell us a different story than our current religious traditions.

The Dead Sea Scrolls were written from 250 BC through 67 AD only twelve air miles from Jerusalem. You would think an historic event like a resurrection might be something they would write about. Especially since the Essenes were busy writing them daily throughout the life of Jesus and thirty years after his crucifixion. You would think that an event like that would be noticed. That is good evidence it did not happen. It is now a "faith belief." The living Jesus was a different person. The apostle Paul did not personally know Jesus, but he certainly made his teachings marketable.

St. Paul was formerly a tax collector, not near the quality of life of being an apostle of Jesus where the public served his every need. He told the Jews that instead of their having to wait for "the end of days" in order for them to get accepted into Heaven, belief in Jesus got you in the next day. His message caught on, and Jesus became the Christ.

Bishop Spong told us that Jesus was merely a living Jew who had a unique message. Bishop Spong said that the story of Jesus we see today was told by writers more than 40 years after his death. Because the life of Jesus was so profound for the gospel writers, they felt that they needed to tell their story in the context of the current Jewish Old Testament, writing to make Jesus a relevant Jew worth celebrating. Bishop Spong uniquely placed the New Testament over the Old Testament, and a view of Jesus emerges different than that of our current Christian traditions. The major events in the life of Jesus corresponds with the celebration of primary Jewish traditions.

According to Bishop Spong the purpose for Jesus's life was to teach us how to live our life here on Earth to the fullest. Jesus' message was for us to live a good, moral, and meaningful life to the highest level of actualization we can achieve while we are living here on Earth. For Bishop Spong, Jesus was only concerned with our life here on Earth.

It was later Christianity that changed the message by adding myths that went beyond the life of the Jesus who lived. Followed to a logical conclusion, Bishop Spong's view of the life of the Jesus who existed makes Jesus into a Humanist. For people who have strong attachment to their early Christian symbols, who claim to be Humanists, that view of Christianity can make their own religious experience far more meaningful. It is certainly closer to historical facts, if such facts have any importance for you.

Remember, fact has no real bearing on the symbols we may choose to use. Similar to a painting we like, our symbols mean so much more to us than the canvas on which they are painted. Symbols are adopted by us because we have no other better means of describing or expressing our own *ultimate concerns*. Since we have few words in the English language to use to address those issues today, religiously we speak in a symbolic language. According to E.

O. Wilson, we all have spiritual needs to address, and many of us do so with the symbolic language that we learned before our age of reason. Because our spiritual need is associated with the emotions that we had at the time of accepting those symbols, those emotions also become a permanent part of ourselves. Thus, for most people, the religion that they have accepted before their age of reason fills those needs, and the path of least resistance keeps them within the bounds of their own symbols for their lifetime. They continue for many even after they realize that they really are a Humanist.

Bishop Spong offers a means of making Christian symbols relevant today for those who are concerned with the truth of their symbols, and who otherwise cannot merely accept their own authorities when the only validation of their truth is by another authority. You do this for emotional reasons that are valid, having nothing to do with reality. Therefore, Bishop Spong gained significant reception in many mainstream Christian churches today during his lifetime. His message is still relevant to many religious people beyond the Episcopal Church. He is relevant for many Humanists. In fact, he was recognized at an Annual Meeting of the American Humanist Association where he accepted an Association award. Bishop Spong finds no conflict with humanism. When asked of his view of humanism, Bishop Spong replied by letter stating:

"I do not see Christianity and secular humanism as enemies reflecting mutually exclusive values. Indeed, I believe the aim of both Christianity and humanism is to seek and encourage the expansion of human life. The differences are found in what each believes is necessary to achieve that goal and the definition of the goal itself. In the struggle to humanize our world I think that Christianity and humanism are allies not enemies.

Secular Humanists have, however, frequently experienced Christianity as narrow, prejudiced, and imperialistic. Christians have experienced secular humanism as anti-religious and anti-Christian. I believe both stereotypes are false.

I look at the 20th century, which in many ways was a secular Humanist century, in which organized religion declined dramatically in influence and in power. Yet in that very century, the emancipation of women occurred, the end of colonial domination of the less developed third world nations was largely ended, the civil rights movement broke the back of segregation, and homosexuals began to overcome the prejudice that has prevented them from achieving full membership and justice in the social order. Each of these is a powerful achievement.

A study of the history of that century also reveals that most of the Christian world, expressed through the leadership of institutional Christianity, resisted each of these changes. These accomplishments were achieved, by and large, through the work of secular Humanist forces. Each of them seems to me, however, to be fully in accord with Christian teaching. Jesus is quoted as saying that his purpose was to give life more abundantly. That is exactly what the death of prejudice and negative stereotypes of minorities, women and homosexuals accomplishes. Mark and Luke quote Jesus as saying: "If you are not against me, you are for me." Secular humanism is not my enemy. It is my ally in the struggle for justice. Indeed, I see secular humanism as the glow of Christianity that remains when the interpreting myths of the past have been abandoned. It is the bloom of the rose that remains long after the rose is severed from its roots. I see a bright future of cooperation—I hope you do too."

Wouldn't it be interesting if all religious traditions eventually evolved to adapt the philosophy of humanism into their religious symbols? Humanism may be expressed through the historic symbols of most faiths. It would be one way for organized religions to continue to exist and always remain relevant as our truths continue to unfold, and the culture of the American public finally reaches beyond the social level.

If a valid purpose of religion is to fill the need for spiritualism as explained by E. O. Wilson, that need could be expressed through humanism without destroying any of religion's symbols.

In addition to many Unitarians Churches, another similar expression of the view of religion from a humanist perspective is that of the American Ethical Union, which expresses Ethical Culture as their foundation. Humanists are unified by the belief that humans must accept responsibility for themselves and accept only facts that can be verified as true. As I previously stated, within the American Humanist Association Judaism has the *Society of Humanistic Judaism*. There is also the Fellowship of Religious Humanists, and the American Humanist Association has the *Humanist Society*. All view the spiritual or "religious" needs of those cultures through the same lens: a view of reality based upon verifiable facts. Each uses an organizational structure fulfilling our cultural tradition through a congregational meeting.

The difference in these organizations, compared to more traditional religions, is that with most religions you are asked to check reason at the door and "accept your beliefs by "blind faith". In the societies listed above, you check "supernaturalism" at the door and come together to build the beliefs you will accept based solely upon reason and your view of what you can validate as truth or meaningful for yourselves because of your emotional early lessons in life, using the means of determining truth we previously discussed. Therefore, those participating are presented issues to consider, but are not given answers their members are expected to accept. Even if they present an answer for the purpose of discussion, there is no rejection if you do not agree.

Humanist celebrants are certified by the Humanist Society to provide celebrations of the rights of passage, from the recognition of a new life to the sanctification of marriage, to celebrations of the meaning of a life upon a person's demise. Humanist Celebrants are recognized as legal officiants by all states in America today. I have been a certified Humanist Celebrant in all 50 states and territories of American but have never used it because Unitarian ministers are available, and they get paid to that. I perform my Humanist services free. I finally got a chance to provide the wedding ceremony for a granddaughter this past year. Only her wedding occurred in Mexico, so I had to first declare that community a territory of America to assure that she is legally married. A Judge in Texas confirmed that they really are married.

Chapter Twenty

This Life May be our Only Opportunity to Exist

Since there is no valid proof a life after our death is available, Humanists simply ignore the issue. Regardless, even if you want to believe a life after our death does exist, because Humanists do not believe that life's value is limited to achieving an immortal soul's existence through a faith, they feel everyone should live their own life fully in the present. Humanists feel we should all make the most of each day while we are living on Earth, and certainly not sacrifice this life for a ticket to an afterlife that may not exist. If there is an afterlife, living a proper life should entitle everyone to whatever rewards are then available. Control People have no valid right to condition our behavior with threats of damnation, or to claim they alone have the ticket for our immortality. Asserting that claim should be valid proof for all that such a claim can only be a control device.

Why would any acceptable God limit an afterlife, if it exists at all, to so few that most of the people on Earth could not participate because they think differently than some Priest? That makes no intelligent sense. Wake up, folks, and recognize that your life is being controlled. Consider who benefits most from that control. Are you a fish that has been hooked? Or a sheep that only follows whoever chooses to lead you? Do you really want to live your life under the limiting control of anyone who dictates your values for you, and then threatens you if you deviate? Even if we wish to believe in an afterlife and are seeking a ticket, we still should not miss our opportunity for fully living this life that we can achieve while we are here, based upon our own determination of what we can verify is true and not merely believing what others define as truth for us.

There may be a life after death, but we have no valid evidence it exists. Science shows us that the notion of the separation of the body and the soul is not well-founded. Scientists have concluded that all reported near-death experiences come from people whose didn't show evidence of death. If we believe in an afterlife, we only have hope based upon blind faith. Therefore, we easily could miss living our life while we are here on Earth guided only with the hope that a life in the hereafter exists, especially if it requires our denial of the opportunity to live a life to the fullest that we can achieve here today?

Limiting our ability to live this life, conditioned only by Control People with no other supporting evidence other than their claim of authority, leaves us with no way to validate their claims other than to accept their authority by "blind faith." That makes no logical sense, even if it is something that we might really want to believe.

Let us look at why we even have that belief in a little more depth. Our belief in an afterlife happens because of conditioning that often occurs before our age of reason, creating an intense desire to belong to a specific faith community and causes our acceptance of a prescribed faith belief. It occurs for emotional reasons. Facts and truth will have little influence on most people's faith beliefs.

An Interesting Experiment

Ask someone to add up a column of figures very quickly as you write each number on the blackboard, saying the sum aloud as fast as you write them down, one number at a time. Starting with the number 1,000, followed by the numbers 20, 1,000, 30, 1,000, 40, and 1,000, the sum at that point is 4,090. If we are then asked to add the number 10, the answer received most often is 5,000, instead of the correct answer of 4,100.

Try this in an audience, and intelligent people will argue with you, insisting that the real answer is 5,000. Try this on your bank teller.

People will get upset that you differ with them. Yet this math problem is not associated with any emotion.

Write each number and pause briefly to give your audience opportunity to say out loud the current sum:

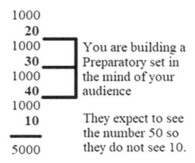

```
1000
  20
1000 ⌉
  30 |  You are building a
1000 |  Preparatory set in
  40 |  the mind of your
1000 ⌋  audience
  10     They expect to see
_____    the number 50 so
5000     they do not see 10.
```

Try this on any group of people. The speed at which you get them to say the answer out loud will determine your success in getting this result. Your objective is to show your audience how their mind works, and what is a "preparatory set."

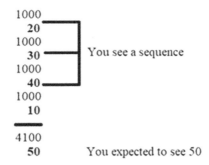

```
1000
  20 ⌉
1000 |
  30 |  You see a sequence
1000 |
  40 ⌋
1000
  10
_____
4100
  50    You expected to see 50
```

The number 10 causes you to have to make a transition from the 3rd column to the 2nd column. Since our brain sees numbers from the outside edges it is easier to exchange the number 50, which you were anticipating, than to make the internal transfer between columns.

Therefore, your brain tells you that the total is 5,000 instead of the correct total of 4,100.

Example of preparatory set

People answer the question incorrectly because a preparatory set was created in adding the figures. We have added 20, 30, and 40 in sequence and, therefore, have an unconscious expectation that the number 50 will be next. Your *"preparatory set"* is the anticipation of the number 50. We do the same thing in many other contexts. People who drive the same route daily have an expectation of what is just around the corner. If whatever they expected changes, they might not see it because of their expectation. The result could be a serious accident. Preparatory sets are all around us.

When, instead of the number 50 that we were expecting, we are asked to add the number 10, we must transfer interior figures from the third to the second column. This is a difficult mental process because people normally process numerical information by bracketing numbers from the outside edges instead of thinking in terms of the middle. Instead of the more difficult mental process of an internal transfer, the mind easily substitutes the number 50 that we were expecting, and since we look upon a column of numbers from the outside numbers, we incorrectly see the number 5,000 in our minds for the sum of 4,090 and 10, which really is 4,100.

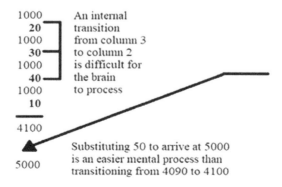

```
1000
  20      An internal
1000      transition
  30      from column 3
1000      to column 2
  40      is difficult for
1000      the brain
  10      to process
 ----
4100
```

Substituting 50 to arrive at 5000 is an easier mental process than transitioning from 4090 to 4100

```
5000
```

Why the Math Problem?

The point of this example is to show you that our own minds can easily deceive us. Because of the way that our brains process information we can deviate from reality. The combination of that frailty with a scotoma acquired in our youth is what empowers Control People who want to maintain control of our life. This is especially true when the subject is our religious beliefs, for which there is no testable evidence. Those beliefs are supported emotionally You cannot merely kill a scotoma. Truth cannot trump our emotions. To rise above a scatoma's control first requires our recognition that it even exists. Then, through nonthreatening education, we must build a bridge around the barrier. You must replace a scotoma to learn and continue to grow. Attempting to do that may be why you are reading this essay. Coming at any belief from a new perspective is the best way to avoid creating a scotoma. This is how the college experience matures us.

How should my own beliefs grow?

This simple math problem is a good example of the effect of preparatory sets and how our own mind can deceive us, and yet this example is not based upon an emotion-laden belief. A person trained from early childhood with any belief will have value and emotions invested in his or her own belief. If asked to accept a contrary notion, people will respond emotionally. That is because the feeling you experience now of accepting a belief typically becomes associated with the belief from the time it is first acquired and will be associated with that belief for the rest of your life, unless intentionally modified by subsequent education.

This is particularly true with those beliefs acquired at an early age, before you developed the ability to reason for yourself. That is why our religious view is so powerful, and why it is very difficult to change those beliefs in later life, even if we want to change. We think we know the truth, so we no longer consider reality. We are hooked and may have become a sheep, and we may never realize what happened to us.

This math example also shows how our scatomas easily block any other conflicting view.

The emotions you experience with a belief when it is first accepted are typically forever a part of your belief. Thus, our religious heritage has a powerful effect on us. Facts are not relevant to our continued endorsement of that view. If you have been raised in a particular faith, you cannot simply ignore your own religious beliefs without suffering an adverse psychological effect, except through continuing non-threatening education that builds a bridge around our scotoma. To leave behind childhood beliefs that were reinforced weekly as an adult requires significant education. Such a change could take a lifetime. Therefore, most people find no reason to change. The fact that you have read this far actually says that you are far more capable of growing beyond your childhood limitations than eighty percent of society, because it also indicates that you are living above the social level. That puts you in the upper twenty percent of people living today. Read on to consider what you can accomplish to assure your own immortality.

Because we naturally associate any belief with the emotions present when they originated, and because we cannot easily take any aspect of our lives out of its context, alternatives to our own scatomas are not only unacceptable; they can be threatening, even to the point where people are willing to risk their lives to defend their current notion that what they believe is right. We know from when the phenomenon occurs today, when otherwise intelligent people become suicide bombers in the name of their religious belief, that their act has nothing to do with truth. A logical argument cannot defeat an emotional belief. Significant non-threatening education is required to cause behavioral change. In the Middle East today there is insufficient time for education. The result is that we are at war on many fronts today because of scatomas.

The mature way of accommodating childhood beliefs in the adult world, consistent with reality, is to continually redefine each concept, or belief, to keep it currently relevant. People cling to their own beliefs. However, even our religious beliefs should mature just like any other notion that influences our lives. A "fear God" concept is normal in childhood, but by the time we become adults a more mature abstract way of defining God is far more effective. Atheists exist because they are fighting a childhood God concept that has not grown with them as they matured. Maslow showed us how we should have developed an abstract definition for our God concept as an adult if we have actualized our own life. If your God is nature, how can you be an Atheist?

The myth of Santa Claus is accepted by children raised in the American tradition. However, this only lasts for a few years because, eventually, Santa Claus is undermined by reality. Each child is devastated. How they respond next is very important. Those who do not substitute the good of giving to others for their childish notion of Santa as "their gift giver" feel disappointed. Those able to develop a healthy change of perception, looking at Santa from their parents' perspective, may continue to celebrate Santa Claus with Christmas as their symbol of giving for the rest of their lives. How we address and are affected by our own religious view is the same.

The objective in life is for us to continue to grow. If our beliefs evolve healthily, to the extent that we can live within our full range of needs through continued growth and development, we should eventually achieve a peak experience. Our goal should be for our individual life to continually become richer, more fulfilled, and more satisfying. Although the specific goals that fulfill our individual lives will be unique, understanding the universal process for human growth makes the journey easier.

.

Chapter Twenty-One
How Do We Face Our own Death?

We can accept that we are here to experience our own journey through this life. By the time our journey is completed, our life will have hopefully been fulfilled. Maslow concluded that when people reach the point of complete actualization, they arrive at a state of mind where even their own death is non-threatening. We no longer need to fear death itself. We only fear how we might die. No one wants a painful death.

For most people elementary school was a great experience during the earliest part of life, preparing us for the next level of our own growth. Few adults feel the need to repeat the experience, although we may still enjoy seeing the benefit of the early school experience in the lives of our children and grandchildren. Though it is a good experience for young children, most people are relieved that elementary school is no longer important for them in their later years. For that part of our life, we adults are now fulfilled. We do not want to go back and start over. (Well, there was this cute little girl in kindergarten. If I could now go back, knowing what I know today, and start over, who knows where I might be today? We all have unsatisfied wishes, don't we?)

Similarly, if we have actualized our own life, having experienced life to its fullest, we will no longer need to fear death. We can then recognize that our own death is inevitable—while it is not sought after, it is also no longer an object of concern, nor is our death a threat. When we need to experience nothing further for our own life to be fulfilled, death can be accepted as a natural conclusion of our life. As our bodies deteriorate our own death may even legitimately be sought. Hospice does wonders to make it painless.

Most Humanists would argue that they should have the same right to determine their own death as they have retained for the primary control of their own life. Medically assisted suicide should be available for those terminally ill and suffering in pain. A Humanist that was a close friend of mine had a brilliant mind. He had served as the International President of Principal Financial Group, creating it an international company because of his leadership. I sat at a dinner table in Hong Kong looking across the bay at a building with "The Principle" in neon on the top of a building. Des Moines was now worldwide. I felt at home – although normally I prefer to have the inners removed from my fish before I eat it. My friend was suffering from dementia, and he realized that the disease was rapidly advancing. In Iowa, our cultural view of life is still driven by religion. Medical assistance for suicide is unavailable. So, he chose to jump off of his 22-story high balcony of his condominium so that his wife would not have to endure caring for him.

Instead, he gave her an even worse memory. She had gone to the grocery store and was driving back to their building garage when the police stopped her car and asked if she was a resident and if she would help them identify a person who was lying on the sidewalk. You can only imagine the shock she received. A more sophisticated society would allow him a more humane way of dying, with medical assistance surrounded by his loving family. We treat our pets better than we treat ourselves in Iowa.

Having reached his elder years, and having fully experienced life, Corliss Lamont, (widely considered the "Dean of Humanism" in the early years of the American Humanist Association) demonstrated death with dignity, peacefully sitting in his backyard in the Hamptons facing the sun, and quietly passed away. Of course, anyone capable of living in the Hamptons probably has had a good life to live. From this perspective, death is as natural as living, and the notion of life after death is not necessary, for our lives to have been fulfilled.

When we no longer spend our life fearing death, maximizing our existence while we are living on Earth, protecting our family and preserving our life's work will be far more relevant and rewarding.

Mel Lipman was a former President of the American Humanist Association during the period of the Association's move from Amherst, New York to its current location of Washington, DC. Mel became a Trustee, serving with me on The Humanist Foundation Board. Mel recently died. He had just gone through quadruple bypass heart surgery and then had a massive stroke. His prognosis was not good, and he seriously suffered. He insisted he wanted no life support, nor any nutrition. Hospice care was provided. He wanted to die comfortably and at peace.

His children reported that he was relatively happy because he felt his life had been fulfilled. His wife had died a few years earlier. His family was grown. He had retired from his practice of law. He had no further mountains to climb, nor commitments that were not already resolved before his heart surgery. Therefore, he had no regrets and he accepted, if not welcomed, his own death.

I thought it interesting, that even among those life-long Humanists there were many expressing grief. Perhaps for the realization that their own time is drawing nigh. Some even thought I was cruel when I expressed that, although it was sad for us to lose a friend and colleague, that he was approaching the end of his life like a true Humanist, and we should not grieve our own loss. That is selfish. Instead, we should at this time celebrate Mel's life. There is plenty of time in the future to lament our own loss.

Once you feel your own life has been fulfilled, death is no longer anything to fear, nor is there any reason to feel threatened when it is apparently near. I acknowledged that of course I was sad for losing a friend, but I was glad he was no longer suffering and was at peace with himself.

Like completing Grade School, which was so important in our childhood, once we feel our life to have been fulfilled, we see no reason for regret. We do not want to start over. Mel's children told us that receiving the Humanist Heritage Award from the Humanist Foundation topped his journey for his life, because it told him that has made a difference for others in our world. That, and the AHA's Humanist of the Year Award for a life of achievement as a Humanist, are proof that his life was significant to others. Nothing more is relevant because, for a Humanist, our **immortality comes from our world being a better place because we have lived.**

I explained that, instead of being sad for our loss, which is selfish, we should rejoice in remembering his life, and what he meant to each of us. Instead of grief, each of us should spend this moment thinking about what Mel's life meant to us, and how he made a difference in our own lives, let alone how his accomplishments during his years of leadership will affect the lives of millions of people, literally forever. That is what our immortality as a Humanist is all about, and it is why I wanted to spend these moments grateful that I knew Mel personally, and that he was my friend.

The only thing that death does is cement our memory of the meaning of that person's life. We are a better person today, because that person was here and shared their life with us. That is the true meaning of our own life.

Chapter Twenty-Two

How Should we Handle Diversity?

Looking at our lives from a strictly humanistic perspective, instead of staying within the safe zone of people just like us, we should seek diversity to enlarge our view of life. We learn so much more from people who are different than we are. Yet so much of our world today limits those opportunities to grow. Prejudice abounds throughout the world because people are far more comfortable surrounded by those who think and act the same as themselves. Many people who differ represent a threat, either as a reminder that our own view of reality may be wrong, or simply because we do not really understand those that are different from us. A normal basic or security level human reaction is to fear the unknown. The serious problem this attitude causes us is that we miss the opportunity to expand our own horizons and to continue our growth in the process. This is especially true with intercultural differences ranging from race to nationality, and to differences in our own religious views.

Dr. Milton Bennett, as Director of the Intercultural Development Research Institute, developed what today is universally called the "Bennett scale" for analyzing where we as individuals are on our ability to benefit from diversity by labeling how we react to those who are different from ourselves. Dr. Bennett tells us that as we mature, we will normally grow from:

1. **Denial of differences**, where we experience our own culture as the only 'real" one. Other cultures are either not noticed at all, or are only understood in an undifferentiated, simplistic manner. On this level people avoid those that

are different from themselves. When challenged, they become aggressive in their attempt to avoid or eliminate the differences. After all, they are the center of their own reality.

2. **Defense against differences,** where one's own culture is the most "evolved" or best way to live. Their thinking is dualistic, it is "us against them" accompanied by overt negative stereotyping. These people openly belittle the differences from their culture and another by denigrating race, gender, beliefs, or any other indicator of difference. They are openly threatened by cultural difference and are more likely to act aggressively against it.

3. **Minimization of differences,** where the experience of similarity outweighs the experience of difference. These people may recognize superficial cultural differences in food and customs, but emphasize human similarity in physical structure, psychological needs, and values. They tend to overestimate their own tolerance while underestimating the effect of their own culture. They may believe that "they think like I do."

4. **Acceptance of differences,** where one's own culture is viewed as one of several equally complex worldviews. These people recognize different ways of living, although they may not agree with, or even like, other ways people live. They are generally eager to learn and to get to know people with other ways of looking at our world. Their ways are just not for them.

5. **Adaptation to differences,** where individuals expand their own world views to accurately understand other cultures and behave in culturally appropriate ways when dealing with people whose views differ from our own. They, in essence, attempt to "walk the walk."

6. **Integration of differences,** where the experience of our own self is expanded to include the movement in and out of different cultural worldviews. Our view of ourselves is no longer central to any culture. Thus, we become fluid within our current environment.

Unfortunately, "In your face" kinds of people, whether they are Muslims Jihadists, Evangelical Christians, or hardened Atheists demonstrate by their aggressive behavior that they have not grown above the second level. A Humanist goal should be to arrive at level five, although many reach level six, where we become fluid with all differences as we strive to gain the very most from everyone we encounter while living our own lives.

Humanistic behavior should be one of tolerance and attempting to understand and benefit from other people's points of view. To the extent that we differ from another person we must first recognize the reasons for our differences, be open in our discussion by tactfully expressing our differences, and then allowing both of us to benefit from that experience. To remain effective in our relationship with that person we must be tolerant of the other person's right to remain different, even if our sincere attempt to educate is ineffective. That is the only way for us to grow and, at the same time, to not lose our relationship with others.

That is the most acceptable behavior for a Humanist.

Chapter Twenty-Three
Why Do We Need Others?

Humans are not self-sufficient. From birth we are dependent upon others. Growing into a fully functioning, healthy person, without support from others is impossible. Knowing that we need others for us to exist healthily, the issue is as follows: *what is the ideal relationship that we should seek with others?*

Martin Buber, a noted Jewish theologian and philosopher, recognized what we gain by accepting another person for who they are, without judgment or attempting to influence them. This relationship is necessary if we are to acquire another's true perspective, to aid us in our struggle to achieve our own full potential. The benefit that results from a healthy relationship—harmonizing with another person without trying to change them is enormous. Buber identified this relationship as the *"I-Thou."*

We know the depth perspective we experience driving down a highway using both eyes, in contrast with driving with one eye closed. Much like the advantage of perceiving three dimensions by using two eyes, complete understanding and acceptance of another person gives us perspective for understanding ourselves. A healthy self-image is derived only through being accepted, and being fully understood, by another person. The feelings achieved from belonging to a community, or being held in high regard by others, are important for our own growth. Therefore, healthy relationships with others become very important and are necessary for our own life to become significant.

Without healthy relationships with others, our self-image becomes protective and is a barrier to achieving fulfillment. We only grow as healthy people through our relationships with others. The better our relationships with others, the healthier we can become. Thus, like digging in the sand, where the more we dig the more sand falls back in the hole, the more in-depth relationships with others we experience, the more we grow.

An episcopal priest once proved to me that we are unable to give enough of ourselves to others. He spent his entire life giving his all, caring for his parishioners and everyone else he encountered, without worrying about any of his own needs. Yet he never went without, even though he could not have anticipated the source of his need's satisfaction. In fact, he has lived an abundant life. He lived the life of Epicurius. The more we offer of ourselves to others, the more fulfillment comes back to us in unpredictable ways. Everyone benefits. Life is far more exciting when we do everything, we can give of ourselves caringly and unselfishly for the benefit of others.

People need close relationships with others throughout life to become truly fulfilled. The recognition of inter-need dependence for need satisfaction, which exists between two or more people that we bring without our own d, is what we identify as "love." The character of love, like all other orientations to life, changes as individuals exist on different need levels. Love on the basic level is felt by those needs that produce stronger emotions, with survival and sex producing the strongest drives. On the social level, the warmth of sharing is evident. On the actualized level, love may be found between soulmates, whose lives are truly integrated together. To be most effective, our love must be shared in an *"I-Thou"* relationship.

A benefit of others as we each seek our own goals.

No person has the innate ability to exceed in all areas of their life. We must rely upon others to fill our areas of weakness. A person once told me that we are each born with ten columns and one hundred marbles. These marbles are distributed differently for each individual. (Marbles are symbolic of our abilities or talents.) If one column has excess marbles, it means that another column may be missing some. One benefit of having a relationship with another person is when your strength augments the other person's weakness. It is especially beneficial if they also can complement your own weakness.

Together you are much stronger than either of you could be alone. The reason for a board of directors in any organization is so that the weakness of the leader does not become the weakness of the institution. A good leader surrounds themselves with people whose skills exceed their own in areas of their own weakness.

The height of our individual columns may be enhanced by the amount of our education, experience, and the culture and environment in which we are living. We may develop columns capable of holding even more than our allocated marbles as we grow. With significant effort may be able to acquire additional marbles. Our growth would be significantly enhanced working with others who have talents that enhance our efforts. The easier solution is to foster relationships that fulfill your needs.

Thus, it is a part of our natural development in life that we each benefit from our relationship with others and our continual effort to grow throughout our lifetime to manage any task, whether it be from a survival point of view, or within our own organization or business. As an added benefit, close relationships may allow us to transition levels of Maslow's hierarchy of needs to achieve actualization more easily by accessing the talents of others, allowing us to bridge barriers that are currently defeating our own growth.

Recognizing where our columns may be weaker, so that we learn to rely upon others where that area may be their strength, is as important for our own safety as it is for our own growth. It is just as important for each of us to recognize our own weaknesses as it is for us to develop our strengths to facilitate actualization of our own lives because, if you do not substitute reliance upon those you trust to protect you from your own weakness, it will become a serious block to your own development, much like a scatoma that creates a barrier to your own vision. The most effective bridge for a weakness in our talents are reliance upon others. The bridge for our own scatomas is education. And we learn best with the assistance of others.

It is true that you can focus on a weakness, and it may be possible to train yourself to overcome your weakness without relying upon others, but the amount of energy it requires detracts from your energy available for your own growth. Think about how much effort is required for you to learn to write your name legibly with your other hand. The multiple hours required for practice could be better spent learning something new.

Thus, we benefit from a healthy relationship with others as we each seek to fulfill our goal of actualizing our own existence. However, the quality of our relationship is dependent upon how we treat the other person. Dale Carnegie wrote in his classic book *How to Win Friends and Influence People* that the first rule is to **never "criticize, condemn or complain."** If we want a healthy relationship with another person, that is the first rule we must always remember. How you phrase everything that you say to another person makes all the difference in how your message is received. What you get back from another person is influenced dramatically by what you project.

One of the first things I did when I started practicing law was to start a breakfast club of others, with only one person from each profession. I wanted to create a fraternity for the business community. Instead of viewing the membership from the point of view of "What is in this club for me," I created the culture of the Club based on a lesson I learned in the military as a Company Commander. I based the club's initial culture on the philosophy of the Episcopal priest who had been the Chaplain assigned to my National Guard Company. His entire life was freely given away to others by asking himself only "what can I contribute to make their life better?" He applied that point of view to everyone he met. He taught me you cannot give yourself away enough. The more you give of yourself, the more comes back in ways that you cannot anticipate. Each club member is expected to contribute to the success of every other member. The result is that one third of my law practice originated from this organization. And my clients now support half of the practice of my twelve-member law firm. We grow much further if we try and give ourselves away at every opportunity, instead of viewing life thinking, "what is in this for me?"

Our differing purposes for life

According to Maslow, all people have the same hierarchical need structure, even though each individual approach satisfying their needs differently. Just how different humans are can best be understood by contrasting our psychological temperament types. Since the time of Aristotle, it has been known that people primarily have four distinct types of personality temperaments. Each type thinks and approaches life from different points of view. Your own temperament type is basic to your existence and will remain the same throughout your entire life. You cannot change it. It is the lens through which you see your own life.

Hippocrates outlined this theory in 370 BCE. There are those of us who live within cultural parameters, providing for others; and those living creatively outside of our societal norms. There are those who comprehend their world and seek lofty goals; and there are those who search for each step to get a foothold necessary to get there. Each provides a different perspective on life.

Each personality type consists of unique standards, or values, which adherents share to some degree with everyone else in the same temperament type. It would be rare, if not impossible, for an individual to fit completely into more than one of these basic psychological types.

Most people do display some secondary characteristics of another type. However, the secondary characteristic serves only as a modifier of each person's primary temperament style of thinking.

Although all people are capable of behavior outside the limitations of their specific temperament style, it is quite difficult. It usually must be specifically learned, much like learning to write your name with the opposite hand. It will not be natural. We each remain our same temperament type for our entire lifetime.

In the early 1950's Kathryn Briggs was a psychologist. Her daughter Isabel Meyers was working in an unrelated field, but when her mother needed her help, together they developed Kathryn's idea of creating a simple test that brought substance to the ancient psychological temperament type theory. Their questionnaire for identifying temperament type was originally called "Briggs-Meyers" psychology. A national testing company bought the rights to market their test. Their marketing director asked, "How am I supposed to ask the public, "Would you really like to know your "BM Type?" She changed the test's name to Meyers-Briggs, and it has been known under that name ever since.

Even though this test is the most used nationally today, it does have its critics. The test results may not be identical if you take the test a second time months later. Nevertheless, the test is popular because the results are beneficial, and non-threatening. My marriage would not have survived had I not learned of this test. It taught me that we do not all process information in the same way, nor do we all think alike. Previously 1 assumed that everyone thought as 1 did, and if they disagreed with me, it was my duty to tell them why they were wrong. My advice was not always a big hit with my wife.

David Keirsey—who authored an excellent book titled *"Please Understand Me II"*—sets forth a more complete, yet still simple, test to ascertain our personal temperament type. His more recent work amplifies Meyers and Briggs' explanation of temperament type theory by pointing out that the basic type of each of us can be modified to a degree with emphasis, or a perspective, for viewing a person's basic type reference of one of the other types. After describing each personality type in detail, Keirsey then shows how differing types interact. When you read his description of your own type you feel like Keirsey is your brother, or next-door neighbor who knows you personally. In a few pages of reading, you not only know yourself, but you also understand your potential areas of conflict and complement your life partner or co-workers. Buying this hook at Barnes and Noble for $17 was worth a semester of college in the education it provided me---and what was in only having to take a very sort test where there was no right or wrong to each question---and then to read six pages that described me better than my own mother could have is life changing.

Psychologists make the point that we are only able to maximize our lives on Earth, and become fully actualized, if we follow a path consistent with our own personality type. Requiring behavior inconsistent with your own type can cause neurosis.

We cannot walk in someone else's shoes. We must create our own path. But to do that, we must first understand ourselves. It is very beneficial, in actualizing ourselves through our relationships with others, to know which personality type we have, and what that means for us. It is even more effective when we can also understand the personality type of those with whom we closely relate.

Idealists

I have identified my own type, as originally defined by Meyers and Briggs, as an *idealist*. This is a very rare type, found in less than ten percent of society. According to Keirsey, I am further identified as an *idealist-idealist*, which he calls a "*counselor*," because I have no other secondary modifying characteristic. I only see myself through an idealist lens. That type is very rare. Less than one percent of our society views the world by processing information in the same manner. Understanding the sixteen differing types described by Keirsey is a significant benefit in understanding others.

Idealists are unable to see themselves. We require recognition from others to find our own self-worth and constantly must seek validation, so we are compelled to spend our lives giving to others to receive recognition of ourselves. Though idealists can solve other people's problems relatively naturally, idealists generally cannot solve their own problems without help from others. Although idealists are incapable of seeing themselves, idealists easily see the big picture for others and can instantly put complex issues in proper perspective for them. However, do not bother an idealist with details, as they must quickly find a solution. Idealists become frustrated when a person must explain a situation by relating each detail.

Rationalists

My wife is the exact psychological opposite of me; she is a *rationalist*. They are even rarer, collectively representing only six percent of society. For rationalists, who can validate themselves from within, imposing the requirement for them to serve others is seriously frustrating. Rationalists will serve others by their own choice, but they do not share the idealist's compelling need to do so to validate themselves. They do so only because it is the right thing to do. This difference causes interesting discussions in our relationship.

My wife must fully understand each step in any process for herself first before she can proceed to the next step. In contrast, I leap to conclusions. I would find her thought process frustrating, but for her it is essential. Truth is her most important consideration. She can only discover the truth by observing every fact. My wife finds the journey more important, and rewarding, than the objective. She gets so absorbed in what she sees on her journey that she may forget where she was going. My mind is already there, but I may not remember the route that I traveled.

How differing types can conflict

We discovered our differences the first time we bought a birthday card for a friend. I immediately found a card containing an appropriate message for the friend, with an acceptable design. I was ready to buy the card and get on with life. My wife, however, was unwilling to buy any card until she examined each one to make sure the one we chose was the very best available. We proceeded to frustrate each other right there in the store in front of others, due solely to our differing personality types. If we had not discovered the Meyers/Briggs theory, our relationship undoubtedly could not have survived. This is serious stuff.

We now have agreed to compromise. If I find a card that I like, I am free to proceed to the register. In the meantime, my wife continues to examine all other cards. If she finds a better card before I have paid, I will purchase her card instead of mine without question. If I had already paid for my card, my wife agreed to leave with me, now feeling that she had at least done her best. We recognize that this solution may not be perfect, but it works for us. At least we no longer embarrass each other in front of others.

On the other hand, we have also enlarged our own experiences by observing the world through each other's eyes. When we take time to appreciate nature, I am more interested in how what we see integrates into the natural world. My wife sees a bunny in the road, stops to smell the flowers beside our path, and gets totally immersed in the setting, while I am more apt to seek the end of the path, wondering where it leads. We have discovered that neither of us is "wrong," but that we are simply different.

Shakespeare puts it well: *"Nothing is either 'right nor wrong,' but thinking makes it so."* Life is much richer when it can be appreciated from another's perspective. However, to be effective this must be achieved through an *"I-Thou"* relationship without attempting to change the other person.

Guardians

A different perspective on life is that of *guardians*. They make up the largest number of personality types, which Meyers and Briggs found in approximately forty-five percent of society. Guardians expect everyone to abide by "the rules," and they expend significant effort assuring that they do. Guardians make wonderful schoolteachers, police officers, homemakers, ministers, nurses, and physicians—occupations in which dependability and their need to provide for others are their primary concerns. They get things done instantly, without question, because they feel obligated, since it is the "right thing to do." In turn, they also make sure that everyone else is doing their job. Guardians need constant praise for their services, however, or they will resent having to serve.

Artisans

The rest of society may be classified as artisans. People with this personality type can see the world without restraint. Artisans are found in about thirty-nine percent of the population. They do not like routine. and may ignore social norms, because they cannot accept living "Inside of the box." Artisans obviously make great artists, but they are also frequently good musicians, actors, advertising agents, or politicians. Many artisans, however, are also incorrigible criminals and social deviants. Artisans can really frustrate guardians, who feel that no one should ignore the rules. By contrast, a rationalist can ignore an artisan unless they are imposed upon. An idealist can appreciate the creativity of an artisan but will have little tolerance for any deviation that does not move toward a positive goal.

How different types work effectively together

For example, if a church dinner is being organized. guardians are the ones who should manage it. But do not misspell their names in the church bulletin! If the church fails to provide recognition, the rationalist may not notice, but the idealist would stop participating. The guardian would resent it but would begrudgingly continue to serve out of a sense of duty. In the meantime, guardians would be infuriated with the idealist for quitting. The rationalist would still be washing the dishes, ignoring everyone else doing the job just because it needs to be done. The artisans may not show up to prepare for the dinner at all— and if they did, they would be decorating the tables.

Why do I need to know this?

So, what does all this have to do with the quality of our life? Everything! Success can only be measured personally. Increasing our self-awareness will in turn increase our opportunity for living a successful life. Not knowing who we are leaves us vulnerable. Assuming others think from our perspective, or personality type, could be disastrous for any relationship. Thus, first knowing ourselves becomes essential to our own happiness. Understanding and appreciating the differences in others improves the quality of our own life.

When our companion stops to examine the flowers, for example, idealists can react in one of two ways: they can become irritated and impatient to get where they are going, or they can see an opportunity to expand their own horizon. One approach limits their existence; the other enhances their life. It all starts with their current attitude. Is the idealist open to new discoveries, or is their attitude closed and the opportunity to grow thereby lost? Understanding the differences between ourselves and another can only expand our experience and enrich life far beyond what each of us could achieve individually.

The rationalist asks the idealist, artisan, or guardian to "stop and smell the roses." The idealist expands the other types of horizons and goals. The guardian can feel more genuine with the idealist, inspired by the artisan, and more genuinely understood by the rationalist while they diligently serve others. The artisan may create works of art and beauty for all to enjoy and not care that they act differently than everybody else. Interaction with each type will provide a different result. Combining personality types in a relationship enhances both, but only if each can accept the other, as they are in an *"I-Thou"* relationship.

Keirsey, in amplifying the Meyers/ Briggs theory, found that although we each have only one primary type, most of us will have a predominant secondary characteristic. This characteristic incorporates one of the other types, which will modify our behavior with some influence on our primary type. Thus, people may be best understood by recognizing in which of the sixteen categories they live.

By understanding psychological types, we can reduce the chance of a personal weakness becoming dominant and causing barriers in our relationships with others. By understanding each category, we can be even more effective in maximizing the quality of our own life. Others can help us discover new paths around our own barriers better than we could ever accomplish on our own. We created a barrier for some reason. It takes others providing new information for us to be able to bridge or circumvent our own barriers.

By fully utilizing our individual strengths, and by bridging our weaknesses with the strengths of others, we can enhance both our own existence and our relationships. The effect is like a spiral. We are better able to fulfill our own life when we share our journey with others. As we share, we grow. As we grow, we are better able to actualize our own existence, and to help others maximize theirs—but only if we are willing to allow others to be their genuine selves. Thus, a successful life is a spiral that continually grows upward through our relationship with others. The opposite, however, is also true. Thus, it pays us to understand what all of this means for our own lives. A few minutes reading Keirsey can make a real difference in the quality of your own life.

Chapter Twenty-Four

Why Should We Make Our Lives Significant?

Many of us focus our lives on our financial gains. Lester and Maria Mondale, first mentioned in Chapter One's Introduction, showed us that our real wealth is so much broader than that. It encompasses our own personal development, which includes our own physical and mental health, the joy we have in the relationships we create with others, the mastery of new skills we learn as we grow, the support we receive from the community in which we live, the thrill of new experiences. And, as we mature, the fulfillment we feel when we learn to give back to others. All of these help us grow and lead to a more balanced, content and abundant life. They are what leads to each of us becoming Fully Alive.

After years of contemplation, for me personally, I have found that ultimately only two aspects of life hold relevance for me. First, **our own life is meaningful to the extent we share in happiness**. By achieving actualization in the manner articulated by Maslow, we can reach the pinnacle of our own existence. However, that alone can cause one to become selfish and to miss the greater values in life that come from sharing our existence with others. Therefore, the second relevant element is equally necessary. Those are the people who are then, Fully Alive.

Simply stated, **our lives become significant to the extent the world becomes a better place because we have lived.** Thus, we are responsible for not only actualizing our own existence, but also for assisting others to achieve the highest quality of life they can attain, both now and in the future. Acting together, we can achieve far more than anyone could accomplish individually. **The healthy person keeps both values in balance.**

My philosophic approach to life is consistent with Maslow's hierarchy of needs. **Living one's life to the fullest by actualizing our existence makes our life meaningful.** Extending our own existence by transcending ourselves, so that we may **contribute to the lives of others, helps make our own life significant** for ourselves. It also adds immense value to us and, even more importantly, to the lives of others. That is Maslow's sixth level of living.

Many contributions can be made by collectively working to improve our world. our own life effort should be to add value. By focusing our attention on constructive issues, and by providing solutions, we raise our awareness of opportunities to serve. We hopefully motivate Ourselves to action in the process, and we also influence others to act whenever such an opportunity to make a difference is presented to them.

How do we apply all of this?

I know a person with a mental disability whose life is dependent upon Goodwill Industries. If they did not exist, my friend could be among the homeless and wandering the streets upon the loss of his support network, or he would not survive. By himself, he could not exist above Maslow's basic level of existence. Even now, with the continual assistance of others, he barely lives on the lower social level—although, this is at least two need levels above what he could accomplish by himself. Does this make his life insignificant, or not worth living? Not to him.

For my friend, his own existence may be all that is relevant— and yet he still cares about others. He feels he is doing a good deed by smiling and saying 'hello" to everyone he meets. He knows no strangers. He does not need to write a book or play a piano to make his own life meaningful. As a matter of fact, it may be easier for my friend to actualize his own existence than for anyone else I know.

Although he has some intellectual obstacles, he does not create many psychological barriers for himself. Non-disabled people have different barriers, because we absorb cultural limitations and establish artificial goals my friend not necessarily perceive.

Moreover, because my friend is so good-hearted, those who care for him can recognize they enhance their own lives by helping him. The guardian's effort to enrich my friend's life gives them a sense of purpose. The idealist gains satisfaction from serving on the Goodwill board or fundraising for the organization. The rationalist finds value in buying or donating products sold at the Goodwill store. An artisan probably designed the brochure that helped raise money for the institution.

The real purpose for each person's participation is not only to serve my friend; it is for each person to fulfill their own needs or purpose through that effort. Everyone continually struggles to improve their current position in life, socially and economically, and to enhance their own sense of self-worth. No action is entirely altruistic. We are also motivated to help my friend to gain fulfillment for ourselves, each in our own way. As a side benefit, we all know that we are doing something worthwhile for a good person who needs our help.

Chapter Twenty-Five

What Can We Do Collectively?

One purpose of formal education should be to reduce cultural barriers that inhibit normal growth and actualization—if not for the public at large (with whom we are trying to communicate), then at least for the more informed people who more easily recognize such barriers. Since the masses are typically uniformed, if not ignorant, on any given subject, organized humanism can help by developing the path to actualization so that it is available for those with enough vision to become aware, and for those who are willing to grow.

This may be the best that we can accomplish with the current elder generation. But it is very important. Hopefully, their children will have more vision. We need to create their opportunity to learn and to eliminate obvious cultural barriers so that they can rise to their full potential, if they will only try. Very few parents can give their children this vision. We can provide a vision for them. That should be a primary purpose for organized humanism.

Provided with the opportunity—without physical, cultural, and self-imposed barriers—people tend to actualize at their own rate, and in their own manner, based upon their own unique personality, educational opportunities, and needs. We cannot change all of society. But the opportunity must be available, and cultural and environmental obstacles to growth must be identified and eliminated (at least for those who are capable of actualization) for anyone to be able to live on the highest levels. All of us do not have to actualize our own lives to be successful, but a successful society must allow each person to have the opportunity to do so.

Many people feel entitled who are unwilling to earn the right

Our constitutional form of government, as proclaimed in the Declaration of Independence, claims that we have "**the right**" to *life, liberty and the pursuit of happiness*, but it does not require our government to give us the means for achieving it. The Declaration does not say that we are entitled to achieve happiness. It is only our right to acquire the pursuit on our own. Our government should protect our rights and eliminate the legal and institutional barriers that would prevent the opportunity. Government should not provide the means, or it will cease to have value for us, and will be expected as an entitlement. To have value you must earn it through your own effort.

No one should be guaranteed success. That will not work, and the attempt to require others to provide our success risks creating lazy people. We must earn success for ourselves for it to have any value in our own lives. Humanists should endeavor to cause the government to reaffirm and support the dignity of everyone by utilizing its welfare and educational policies to encourage individual responsibility and growth, rather than to cause recipients dependence that ultimately creates barriers to the fulfillment of their own lives.

Personality Temperament Types

Our educational system should take into consideration that one very significant cultural barrier is the lack of public awareness of the fact that different personality types exist, and the implication that has for understanding each other. As previously stated, understanding our differences in thinking and motivation can improve everyone's quality of life by reducing miscommunication between people with differing views of life and providing opportunity to learn the benefits of their perspective. Accepting the diversity in other people has great personal value. Understanding and accepting the differences between us can help each of us grow.

Understanding the effect of people living on other levels of Maslow's hierarchy of needs

Another barrier is most people's limited ability to relate to those living on other psychological levels of need. Even governments operate on differing need levels on Maslow's scale. It is unrealistic, for example, to expect the Russian public at large, with many generally existing on the high security/mid-social level, to appreciate the cultural concerns of Americans, who more frequently exist on a high social/ low ego level. Nor can the typical Afghan citizen living on a security level be expected to appreciate our way of life.

People must first be taught to recognize these differing levels, and then how to speak more effectively to those with whom we wish to communicate by first speaking on their level of living. Like Maslow's test of understanding a joke, or appreciating music, communication must begin on the lowest need level of those with whom we are communicating. Teaching the public to identify and understand others' need levels could make a significant difference in meaningful communication.

What about our current educational system?

Another barrier is caused by our educational methods. This can be effectively challenged without threatening anyone's belief system. Frank Goble, author of *The Third Force*, a book amplifying Maslov/s Humanistic psychology, proposes an educational philosophy optimizing human awareness. He proposes we help all people to create, grow, and control their own choices, goals, and he suggest the means of creating an educational system that allows all children to achieve the maximum of their ability to grow, thus improving our current system that assumes: "one size fits all", at least for core subjects.

Frank Goble contends that understanding Humanistic psychology can help provide early educational opportunities tailored to each child's needs, rather than using pre-established educational patterns that may be inconsistent with individual needs of many. By designing our educational strategies to approach everyone within their own temperament type, we will enhance their learning. Making everyone fit into the same square box does not effectively work to maximize growth. If Goble is right, this change in how we approach education, could dramatically enhance the opportunity for our children to fully actualize their own existence, each in their own way.

To make matters worse, our society no longer demands appropriate behavior from our students. Our cultural drift protects the individual student, but the students that lack enough discipline are protected by society today resulting in unacceptable behavior that diminishes the growth of others, and our school boards do not back our teachers by providing them the power to control their own students. That is just plain stupid.

The problem starts at home. Many parents protect their children and do not demand discipline for their negative behavior. Our laws protect the individual and not the school system and, as a result, today's rate of graduation in many high schools is deplorable. School Boards need to back discipline if they expect positive results. The military has proven that discipline improves attitudes and self-worth and increases performance. That is a good model to improve our youth, many of whom lack any sense of self-worth. And, as a result our society continues to decline.

How do we make a difference in our own life?

The message for each of us is to fully become ourselves—but first we must know ourselves. Only then can we become authentic and achieve a meaningful fulfillment of our own life. Maslow contributed by providing a means for understanding the process by which each of us can become fulfilled. We must provide the goals, or path, for ourselves. The way we apply our lives to make the world better and provide meaning to our personal lives will be unique for each of us. We each need to start toward our own actualization by defining our own mission in life. Otherwise, day-to-day living or other people will define us, and because of cultural limitations we easily could miss the opportunity for us to fulfill our own lives for ourselves. It is never too late to make a real difference in our own life. We should constantly improve the quality of our own life, if for no other reason, than for our own life to become fulfilled. We will soon learn that happens best by our serving others.

Sharing our lives with others enhances our opportunities. We can now understand that the differences in each of us are what make our own life challenging and exciting. The world would be a dull place if we were alike. It is never too late for you to make a difference in the life of another person. It should be a daily objective for each of us.

Happiness is the feeling of contentment we experience living momentarily in the node of our needs while following the path toward our own total fulfillment. When all our needs are resting in their node, and we have actualized our own existence, we will have the feeling of becoming fulfilled. At the moment of a peak experience, we will have an exhilarating, and possibly scary, feeling of total awareness—we will gain a rare insight into our personal universe, in harmony and resonating with our own reality. At those moments we will then know that we are fulfilled and have discovered the path to actualize our own life.

Now that we know what conditions have produced our fulfillment it will be easier to reasonably retain those conditions daily as we live our lives, keeping our life and all our needs in balance. This balanced condition enhances our ability to continue to grow. Our own growth should be our constant goal. As we grow, we enhance our ability to achieve even more in our lifetime and to make our own life significant for others. As we learn to unselfishly give of ourselves to others, our life fulfills the purpose for our own existence. Our lives will become significant to the extent the world becomes a better place because we have been here. To the extent our accomplishments live on after our life is over, we will have achieved what for a Humanist is the only valid form of our own immortality we know for certain really does exist. It certainly is a valid, and even scientifically provable, life after our own death—which exists even for a Humanist—is our reflection on the effect we have on those that follow us, and whether we made our world a better place for them because we have been here. Nothing else has much value after we are gone.

Chapter Twenty-Six

What Values Ultimately Are Important for My life?

Only you can answer that question. However, as you consider what is important in your own life, I will give an example. I have previously stated only two aspects of life are relevant for me as a Meyers-Briggs "Idealist":

(1) **My life is meaningful to the extent I am able to achieve actualization**; and

(2) **My life will be significant to the extent that the world is a better place because I have been here**.

To be healthy, I must keep both in balance.

Considering these values, only two of the many leading to a successful life, others will respond very differently to the same circumstances. The response to additional values will be equally different; thus, there are multiple approaches to a successful life. To illustrate the point using only these two values:

If you are an artisan, you might say: *"My life is meaningful to the extent that I am creatively engaged, and to the degree that I am excited about life's opportunities. My life is significant when I have made a uniquely creative work that is really mine and is genuinely prized by others."*

A guardian may say: *"My life is meaningful when I am accepted by others I care about, when I know that my family and loved ones are safe, and when my world feels in order. My life is significant when I am in charge of what I do, and I am appreciated by others for what I provide."*

A rationalist could say: *"My life is meaningful when it is peaceful, when I know what is true, and when I am fully functioning in the world—at least to the degree that I am comfortable in my role, My life is significant when I feel my own contribution has succeeded better than my previous efforts, and when I know that my efforts are right and what I believe is true."*

These statements may be valid only momentarily and will typically vary as we mature, and as our mission in life becomes continually more focused. The younger rationalist, for example, may be more concerned with understanding how they are to accomplish a specific task. Upon aging, however, the need to know grows, and they eventually may want to know how everything works. Goals for all other personality types similarly change. Nothing human is etched in stone, nor should it be, including our own religious and philosophic views. We should always be growing and open to new opportunities for our life to become the most successful one we can achieve.

Although everyone's approach to life is "hard wired," what we as individuals find important at any given moment will only be tentative. All truth is momentary. Only the method by which we process information remains reasonably consistent through our lifetime. That we cannot change. Our individual method of processing information is similar only to others with the same psychological temperament type. However, the means we use to implement our actions will differ from others, even those of the same type. Normally because of our level of growth, maturation, level of education, and our own prior experience. Thus, we will all appear different, even though those of the same temperament type will always process information in the same way.

Fortunately, there is no universal truth that all must accept, and no single answer to life's purpose. However, most of us will continue to assume everyone else understands us, and should agree with us and, therefore, must think like we do. Fortunately, they do not. Imagine how boring the world would be if everyone had to agree. Our personal mission statement is only valid for ourselves, but even that should change as we mature. There are very few absolute truths that we can all accept. The fact that each person will approach their actualization in a different way is good for society, because these differences enhance the quality of all our own lives by expanding our vision.

Chapter Twenty-Seven

So, What Can I Do Now That I Have Discovered: I Am a Humanist?

If you can, now look at life from the perspective that this life probably is the only life for you. What you do next is very important. Recognizing your immortality comes from what you leave behind— those contributions to those surviving or following you, and thus live better lives because of you, or from the product or family that you have produced, —you begin to look at life from the perspective of Maslow's actualized existence. Your motives may still have some selfishness because you want your life to mean something, but that contributes only minimally. Your actions become altruistic because you are intent on doing the best for others that you can achieve in the life you have left. You can contribute to making our world a better place in any way you choose. You too can make a difference in the world today. You do that to make something lasting for others, not to benefit yourself.

As I previously said, John Shelby Spong, Former Bishop of the Episcopal Church for New Jersey, stated: "I look at the 20th century, which in many ways was a secular Humanist century... in that very century, the emancipation of women occurred, the end of colonial domination of the less developed third world nations was largely ended, the civil rights movement broke the back of segregation, and homosexuals began to overcome the prejudice that has prevented them from achieving full membership and justice in the social order. Each of these is a powerful achievement... A study of the history of that century ... reveals that most of the Christian world, expressed through the leadership of institutional Christianity, resisted each of these changes. A study of the history of that century also reveals that these accomplishments were achieved, by and large, through the work of secular Humanist forces." The vision and leadership of Humanists are still making a difference in the world today.

Most of these changes in our society started because one Humanist saw an unfulfilled need and became passionate about resolving it. They were willing to take on the task and to provide the leadership necessary to make it happen. The real point is that each of us can make a real difference in the world, and Humanists continually prove that it can be done. All you need to do is to be open and receptive to the contribution you are willing to personally make to solve a problem affecting others beyond yourself when you see it.

Your vision of what would solve a problem, and a positive attitude that can make a difference to improve the problem you see, is all it takes to start the process. Once committed, others necessary to bring your solution to reality will join you if you explain your goal and properly ask for their help. The result is that you can make a real difference that will survive you. That is an actual form of your own immortality that we know really exists.

One of my grandsons, Braeden Stanley, is a third-generation Humanist. Braeden entered Drake University as a freshman in the fall of 2011. At the end of his freshman year, he and twenty other students signed up for a three-week summer study class abroad. This course was conducted by three professors, one of whom was born in the rural community of Kikandwa, Uganda, located in east central Africa.

The professor took the students there to experience life from a different perspective. Drake has as its mission statement "to provide an exceptional learning environment that prepares students for meaningful personal lives, which results in professional accomplishments, and responsible global citizenship." The university agreed to give the students college course credit; their goal was to see how they could make a difference as a result of their trip, and for each student to be able to write a paper explaining their view of what could benefit others. Drake students in prior classes had each proposed their own plan showing what the community they were visiting that year might do to improve the quality of their own citizens' lives. All their efforts had been theoretical, mostly without considering the lack of their community resources to fulfill their proposed plans. The elders of this community Braeden visited identified that their major need was for some form of a medical facility.

No one previously had considered that the students could personally actually address any community need. There were over 30,000 people in the rural area surrounding Kikandwa. The Uganda government provided some clinics in their country, but these were subject to corruption, were poorly staffed, and were not maintained. The nearest competent clinic was in a metropolitan area many miles away, and most people had to travel on foot. For someone ill, it could be a three-day walk. Even for those with a bicycle it is over one day's journey if you were fit enough to ride there. There was no effective commercial transportation in the heart of rural Uganda and, even if there were, no one in this community could afford it.

Braeden was impressed that the people of Kikandwa were very welcoming and friendly. They invited the Drake students into their homes and shared what little they had with them. Many had not encountered Caucasians before, let alone Americans. One man, the students learned, had taken his pregnant wife to the distant clinic. Because they did not have the equivalent of five dollars to purchase a delivery kit, consisting of gloves and scissors, his wife was refused acceptance by the clinic. They had to deliver their baby boy by the roadside alone. Both his wife and baby died. That was too much for Braeden. He decided that "he would build Kikandwa a medical clinic if it took him the rest of his life".

Once Braeden's declaration was made that he was going to personally accept the responsibility of fulfilling this need, other students willingly joined with him to participate in this project. Their faculty leaders then felt compelled to join them. Within the span of three weeks, the students had met with the community leaders, located a site, and developed a plan. They returned to Drake the next fall and

Braeden personally took on the responsibility of raising the funds necessary to build the medical center, while other students accepted the challenge of deciding what else would be needed, and how those needs would be resolved.

One of the students was the daughter of the head of Character Counts in Iowa. He is very active in Rotary and chaired the International Committee of his Club. The Club accepted assisting with the Drake Student's project. That assured the students' success. Braeden and several other students returned to Uganda during their January break. These students contacted a Uganda Rotary Club that agreed to supervise construction, they had a member who was an architect who drew plans for the medical center, and a contractor who provided a quote for the cost of its construction, and who would be able to build it.

Upon return to Drake for the spring semester they were joined by other Drake students who had also traveled to Uganda with prior classes. They all met weekly during the school year to plan for the operation of their clinic. Braeden and those helping him were able to raise the necessary funds. At the end of Braeden's sophomore year, they broke ground, and construction of their medical center commenced. By the end of Braeden's junior year, the Kikandwa Medical Center was near Completion, but needed to be staffed and supplied. The students located a doctor willing to be Medical Director of the Center and arranged for a local Methodist Church in Uganda to staff their facility.

It takes many different elements to create a successful medical center. However, when you are focused on a goal you see opportunities that otherwise you may never consider. These people in that region of Uganda wanted a clinic. They simply did not know how to get one. Once Braeden provided the initiating leadership, and everyone focused on the task to create a clinic, many community members certainly were willing to contribute their efforts to help, even though they did not have the wealth to help fund its construction. It takes a leader with a vision of success to create momentum. Momentum attracts others to the leader's cause.

Braeden's momentum even affected me. I was the attorney for the Iowa Great Ape Trust, where six of the one hundred thirty African bonobos in captivity in the world today are located. These bonobos think at about an eleventh-grade level. The Des Moines bonobos have lived with humans daily for their entire lifetime who spoke to them in English from the day that they were born, and therefore they easily understand us when we speak to them. Since they have no voice box that would allow them to respond, it only took creating a symbolic language for them to be able to talk back to us.

Since Des Moines is now the only place on Earth where humans can actually conduct an intelligent conversation in the English language with another species of life, these bonobos attract people from around the world. Through that organization, I luckily encountered another lawyer from Minnesota who represents a non-profit company that accepts excess medical supplies and used equipment from hospitals and doctor's offices. This company's mission is to place this used equipment and surplus supplies with needy hospitals in third world nations. Focused on Braeden and his fellow student's project, I realized what this organization could do for their efforts.

The Uganda Clinic was not a hospital, but it was close, and it had the same needs. I introduced the Drake Uganda clinic to this Minnesota lawyer, who was greatly impressed with the Drake students' project. She agreed to help. The students presented their case to her client's board and were able to acquire over $375,000 in equipment and medical supplies for free—if the students in the next two weeks would raise an additional $15,000 for shipment of a 40- foot semi- trailer full of supplies. Even though they were in semester finals, the students worked diligently to accomplish this goal. Thus, Kikandwa would make medical services available to benefit 30,000 people who have never in their history had such services immediately available to them before Braeden and his fellow student's visit.

Drake University President, David Maxwell, announced at a fundraiser Braeden held that "This will give me bragging rights among university presidents." This region of Uganda will now not only have medical care available within a short walk from where these 30,000 people are living, but because of the man who first inspired Braeden, the supplies needed for a delivery will be free to those who cannot afford to pay, so that no women will risk losing her life or baby because they are denied care due to the lack of five dollars.

This clinic must be sustainable, but the community leaders have agreed that people will only be charged for their clinic's medical services based upon their ability to pay. Because of the free supplies it has available, this clinic is now becoming one of the best and most popular medical clinics in the region.

The Kikandwa Medical Center will be easily accessible and available to serve the needs of people who do not have the personal resources to afford private medical care that is otherwise only available in metropolitan areas of Uganda. Thousands of people in the world today will have better lives because a Humanist cared and had the vision and the courage to commit to fulfill a need. It only takes the leadership of one person to start the momentum necessary to complete any task. That is how all Humanists can still make a real difference in the world today, each in our own way. It only takes becoming passionate about something beyond us.

Recently one of the Drake professors visited the Kikandwa Clinic. What she wrote back to Drake expressed it all for me:

"Greetings from Uganda! —from Dr. Deb Bishop, Drake University Associate Professor of practice in Management, Director (Email message dated June 9, 2015) Meeting baby Rebecca this afternoon made it all worthwhile!! I went with two students to meet Dr. Dickson at Mukono today.

On our way back we stopped by Kikandwa. We walked into the patient room that contains three hospital beds and a tiny infant bed. Asleep in that crib was a baby a few months old named Rebecca. She was sleeping quietly. She had been coming to the health center for a few days—the first day desperately ill. Using the lab equipment and supplies, she was diagnosed with both malaria and pneumonia. Each day her mother has been bringing her in to spend the day on an IV drip. As we were standing there, Rebecca opened her eyes and my eyes filled with tears. It was the most incredible sight - a tiny, beautiful life saved and restored to health. That alone was worth all we did!

There is still much to do. The electricity should be complete this week. They have no overnight care at the moment, and it will be most helpful. Please pass this on to those that might want to know. Gratefully, Dr. Deb Bishop"

That message brought tears to my eyes, because it said two things to me:

1. The effect that Braeden has had by declaring that he "would spend the rest of his life seeing that these people would one day have modern medical care available to them." Once he made that commitment, other students and the Drake faculty who sponsored the trip agreed to join him. Soon others, including Rotary Clubs, joined in this effort. That made his goal possible. Four years later, his dream was realized, and it is making a real and serious difference in the world today.

2. To the Ugandan people, their Clinic is the most important thing they have today—yet the Clinic was operating tentatively, without electricity, and may be missing some of the basic resources that we take for granted. We would be objecting if the electricity went off, or if there was a shortage of water, or if there was no toothpaste. They are thrilled just to have medical services immediately available to them that they have never had in their lives before. Perhaps our priorities could be reconsidered when we compare our lives to the lives of most of the rest of the people in our world.

Even though their new clinic may not yet be perfect from our perspective, their clinic is "wonderful" to them. They are so excited about what they have today because a Drake student committed himself to solving their needs. Baby Rebecca, who probably would not have survived, is alive today because Braeden cared. Once his decision was made, he had the perseverance to see that his goal was reached. **One of the two guiding principles in my life is that our lives become significant to the extent that the world is a better place because we have been here**. That is an acceptable form of immortality, even for a Humanist. To these people, Braeden will live forever.

Braeden saw a need and he accepted solving that need as his own personal goal. He had no idea at that moment just how he would get it accomplished. He only knew he was dedicating his life to accomplishing that goal. Once he made that commitment he saw, and took advantage of, all opportunities that moved the project toward its ultimate solution. He simply provided the leadership to reach his goal. Others were necessary to make it happen. He focused on the result. That opened the doors for others whose skills and talents were needed for the evolution of reaching his objective.

Braeden motivated me to help when I saw an opportunity to supply the medical equipment and supplies necessary to operate his medical clinic. It only takes one person to provide the vision and leadership to cause those things to happen collectively. As a result of Braeden's commitment, he made a real difference in the world today for over 30,000 people who do not know his name, but whose lives are better because he has been here. You too can do that, if you only open your eyes, see a need, and resolve to fulfill it. But, to accomplish that, you must be committed to do so. That is what Humanists do, and why our world is a better place today because we have lived. We each create our own immortality. You can too.

Once you view life from a humanist perspective, it will open your eyes. You will see opportunities to contribute to the lives of others for whom you might otherwise be reluctant to expend the energy. Believing that this life is all that there is for you is what motivates you to make the most of it that you can in every way that you can.

For another example of what you could do

The Masonic Fraternity is the world's largest fraternity. There are four million active Masons in the world today, with two million in the United States. The fraternity is also the largest philanthropy in the world today. Masons in the United States alone give between two and three million dollars a day for charitable purposes, without insisting that any Mason contribute a dime. I am a 33° Mason, which is the highest degree in Masonry. I was having dinner at a Masonic event with the Potentate (president) of our local Shrine Temple. He told me that the 22 Shrine children's hospitals had a serious problem today because their in-patient population was no longer paying for their hospital's maintenance.

Masonry is totally serious. The Shrine is a parody of masonry. Masonry is over seven hundred years old. The Shrine was created in the United States in the middle of the 1800's to provide a "fun" organization for Masons. After many years of overdoing fun at their annual conventions, they agreed they must have a positive purpose that benefits our society. One hundred years ago they built 22 hospitals throughout our country. Today they primarily serve children suffering from orthopedic issues and children that have been severely burned. Beyond their insurance coverage, the families of the children they serve are not charged anything for their care. I learned that in 2018 alone they met the needs of 345,000 children visits.

I have volunteered on hospital boards for 50 years, during my entire legal career. I saw immediately what the problem was. The Shrine was functioning on a forty-year-old medical model that was no longer sustainable. Today 85% of the children they serve must have been as outpatients. On any given day, only a few of the children in each of their hospitals may need hospitalization over night for their treatment, even following surgery. The more I thought about the Shrine's plight the more I saw a perfect solution.

After getting the approval of Blank Children's Hospital's president, I took my idea to the president of the UnityPoint Hospital — Des

Moines system, where I have served on at least one of their boards for twenty-four years. The UnityPoint board owns six hospitals in Central Iowa, one of which is Blank Children's Hospital. Blank is the only hospital that was built during World War II, and it took an act of President Roosevelt personally to accomplish it being built. I was glad it was. When I was nine years old at the end of that war that hospital saved my life. I owed it something.

I explained that I wanted to offer to the Shrine the creation of a better means of their offering care by creating the very first Shrine Children's Clinic in Blank Children's Hospital. The Shrine could then see they could better provide their services for children in already existing community facilities that are more closely located to each of their Shrine Temples.

By doing this, instead of the Shrine that is currently spending 80% of their budget supporting bricks and mortar that are no longer needed, they could then turn the unused portion of their hospitals into Masonic Nursing Homes that would pay for their current hospital facilities. The president of UnityPoint Health System that owns Blank Children's Hospital system liked that idea.

So instead of wading through the hierarchy of the Shrine starting on a local level and having to convince hundreds of unknowledgeable people to get a decision made, I called the International Imperial Potentate ("president") personally and presented my idea. He thought about what I was saying and said, "You know, that might just work." He presented my idea to his board, and they agreed that it merited consideration. They sent five of their top officers from their warm offices in southern Florida to Iowa during a snowstorm in the middle of January 2019 (when everyone else from Iowa goes the other direction that time of the year) and they liked what they saw.

Blank has a worthy history. As an example, Blank was able to save all seven McCaughey children born at the same time by one woman, even though they each only weighed a pound and half at birth. Today they are all seven healthy adults. The Shrine worked with the Blank Hospital staff to make this new children's clinic model happen.

This model has proven itself to be very successful. In the first two years it had already exceeded its clinic's space. If the Shine were wise, they would have adopted this model, and all other Shrine units would have their own Clinic ore immediately available for them. These clinics allow access to medical care in a community close to the children's homes instead of their now having the problem the Des Moines Shrine unit previously had requiring Shriners to have to pick up a child at their home, and to deliver the child to the closet hospital in Minneapolis, Chicago or St. Louis, wait for the child to be treated, and then deliver the child back to their parents. And, as I previously said, the Shrine could then turn the underutilized portion of their hospitals into nursing homes for Masons that will pay for the maintenance of the bricks and mortar that previously was eroding of their budget.

Those funds no longer necessary to maintain their hospitals would then allow the Shrine to serve all children, regardless of their medical need. Everyone benefits. But it is the children that benefit the most. Instead, the boards of local Shrine hospitals are struggling today to keep in existence their existing structure so that the board members have their role to play – even though they lack the ability to solve their own budget issues. But a lack of effective growth is what happens from a lack of effective leadership. Organizations that simply keep doing what they have always done, even though times cause change as society advances, as a result those organizations deteriorate.

If managed correctly, the Des Moines Shrine Clinic should be able to raise the local public image of the Shrine within the Des Moines community, which should then result in increasing its membership when more people want to participate. And then, in return the local Shrine Temple will proudly advertise their Clinic in Blank Children's Hospital to improve their public image. By providing quality care for "their children," in the Blank Clinic, it is a win/win for everyone, but especially for the children the Shrine Children's clinics serve.

Wow! Why had no other Shriner thought of doing this first? First, because they do not have the background to see how all the pieces of the puzzle necessary to solve this problem fit so smoothly together, and second, even if they thought of it, they did not realize that they could get this accomplished. I am a member of the Shrine and have been a member of the UnityPoint Health board. I have been a volunteer serving on the boards of hospitals for fifty years, and I realized that the Shrine's problem was that they were operating out of a 40-year-old medical model. And I personally knew the people who could make this happen. In other words, I could see all parts of this puzzle. But it all happened because I was willing to commit myself to do something about their problem.

Putting all the pieces to the puzzle to solve problems is what I do for a living. As an attorney, in my practice I resolve complex structure, relationship, and legal problems for my business clients. As a result, today five of my clients, three of whom I helped clients start working with in their garage, are now the world leaders in what they do today. Not because I am so great. It is because, as an "Idealist," I am able to specialize in seeing how to help maximize opportunities for my clients. However, I just cannot see myself, so I cannot do for myself what I am able to accomplish for my own clients. Therefore, I like to play in other people's sandboxes.

Just to give you another example so that you can see how easy it is to find opportunities. I am accomplishing more looking at life and opportunities that exist all around us from the point of reference of a Humanist because I actively seek them. Not to give the wrong image of Masonry, since it actually does more-good than any other single non-profit non-religious organization in America., but to make my point of the necessity of effective leadership to make any organization successful. I have represented the Des Moines Masonic cemetery for years. As the Masonic membership has declined, their resources and market diminished. The maintenance of their cemetery was nil from decreasing cash flow and increasing costs. They only had one full time and one half time employee to mow the grass of a square mile, open and close all graves. I have told their board for years that they need to transfer the ownership of their cemetery to the City of Des Moines to maintain it. The cemetery board ignored me.

because they really enjoyed their free dinner and drinks before their monthly meetings.

A number of years later, and the dandelions growing on my mother's grave took over my ability to clear them, I finally got angry and wrote a nasty letter to the cemetery board. By then none of the members knew me, but fortunately they took my threatening letter to the two Masonic Lodges that own the cemetery, and the leadership of those Lodges knew who I was, so they told the board they needed to do what I say. The Lodges voted to give me authority to present the cemetery to the City.

I knew that if I called the Park Board that manages the city cemeteries and told them what I wanted to do, they would have taken a look at it and said, "Hell NO!", it had deteriorated to that degree. So, instead, I called the mayor, and told him that the city would soon have an embarrassment if the city did not accept my offer to take the cemetery. He drove through it and agreed. So, I asked him to call a Park Board meeting to tell them that he wanted them to take the cemetery. They did all that they could to rapidly please the mayor. They took possession last year, and today there are no more dandelions on my mother's grave. To put frosting on the cake, the city did not want the residence at the cemetery entrance formerly used by the cemetery manager, so the board sold it and each Lodge received $75,000 they otherwise would not have, and they no longer have the risk of their having to fund replacement of the cemetery roads were no longer theirs. So, today, everyone is thrilled with this result. My point being, that we each can create positive change if we only look around ourselves and are willing to act when we see an opportunity, just as Braeden did in Uganda.

This did not happen because I am so special. It happened because I saw an opportunity to solve a problem that will help others have a better life, especially those that will live on after me. Humanism causes me to differentiate from looking at life seeing only what is good for me. Just the opposite of the many people that currently look at their life solely for their own preservation today. It happened because my perspective in life is on the level of Maslow's hierarchy where the opportunities that I see for making a difference may have no personal benefit. With the Shrine Children's Clinic, I was in a unique position to see all the pieces of the puzzle, so I acted. You are a unique person, and you will see opportunities that I would not be able to see. The difference between us may be how do you respond?

As opportunities become apparent, you will now realize that you could do something about solving the problem you now see exists, if you will only accept the responsibility of causing change to occur. Hopefully you are now motivated to make a real difference in the world every time you see the opportunity. Doing that will make a huge difference in your life, and by solving that problem you will add to your immortality in a way that may well be far beyond what you would otherwise have acquired before reading this book.

Think about my small examples. What the Blank Children's Hospital Shrine Clinic has done for Blank is that their Clinic helps Blank serve children on a level that they otherwise were not able to serve. Before the help of the Shrine, Blank did not have the experience, equipment, nor talent to serve children with severe orthopedic problems. Today they are handling everyone with those needs. In addition, the Shrine pays for the care of all their children, so the hospital does not have to worry about how they get paid. The local Shrine Temple will market Blank without any cost to the Blank budget. And more importantly, children will get good care in a facility that can provide services successfully without having to travel outside of their state to see quality doctors to meet their needs. It clearly is a win/win for everyone.

My wish is that now that this has proved successful, the other four Shrine Temples in Iowa will want to develop their own relationship with existing medical facilities in their community to serve their children. What I really would like to do is to light a brushfire across the nation, so that in the future we can have Shrine Children's Clinics where children with all medical needs can be served close to their own families immediately available for all local Shrine Temples. The Shrine's children's hospital program could grow to be viewed by the public as being bigger than St. Jude's in its ability to benefit our children.

How to overcome other people, or even local boards who are managing any facility with no significant business skills, is a fertile field for your making a difference. Even a local church board may be participating simply because they enjoy their free meal, to even realize the benefit change can produce for the entity they serve. Your participation may make a very significant difference helping them solve problems they cannot see. Armed with what you now know, you should be willing to look for our own opportunities to make a difference. One will appear right in front of you if your eyes are open and your receptive attitude will let you see them. You now have the perspective and motivation to act when you see an opportunity to make a difference. I have just given you some examples. You will see your own for you to make a real difference in the world that will survive you. That is a form of immortality for you that we know really does exist.

My point is that each of us has unique skills and insight in something. Now that you are motivated as a person who is looking for opportunities to make a difference in your life, you will know when you see an opportunity where you can add value. To the extent the world becomes a better place because you have been here, you will have achieved your own immortality. If you are motivated to do something, you only need to open your eyes to seek opportunities where you too can make a difference. Although that is the only one form of immortality, we do know for sure it does exist. Seeking means of making a difference in the lives of others can become a fun endeavor for you. It can become a significant motivator for all of us. Therefore, look around you and see what you might contribute to the lives of others. You will be surprised how opportunities will appear that you would not have previously considered addressing.

Even if you saw the same need before, you may not have thought that you could solve it yourself, because you were not in the habit of accepting such a responsibility. Or you felt that you did not have the time today, or for whatever other excuse you might have, you missed an opportunity. Most people would ignore the problem that was not otherwise their own, wishing someone else would do it. However, once you learn how to view the world from a Humanist perspective, you soon become eager to solve whatever you can by providing the leadership to at least initiate the project, even if you cannot fulfill it on your own. Once you commit to solving whatever it might be, you will see opportunities for others to help that never before occurred to you. It works much like putting the pieces of a puzzle together one step at a time. You will soon have fulfilled whatever task you have committed yourself to resolve. The feeling of pride and fulfillment you then have will motivate you to seek the next opportunity. Your life becomes fulfilled as you gain success. As a result, the world becomes a better place because you have lived. You will arrive at a point when you feel that the meaning of your own life is fulfilled. The difference you have made in the world becomes your immortality that we know might not otherwise exist.

Look at all the hundreds of people today that can take pride in what they contributed to the result of Braeden's Uganda project he initiated before he had any idea of how to accomplish his goal. There is nothing that we collectively cannot accomplish. Acting together, we can all make a difference in our world today that could benefit thousands of people who will live on after we are no longer here. That provides purpose for our own lives and the result of our efforts makes our own life immortal—not necessarily because your name will be remembered. Like with Braeden, what you have created that benefits others will live on. And that is the only thing that truly matters. There is no better way to be sure that your own life will have been significant than to commit yourself to a task that you know will add value to the lives of those that live after you.

If you are now able to view life from the point of view of a humanist but, at age 96, getting out of your wheelchair is a big task, or you are 98 and restricted to bed, there are still lots of ways to ensure your having lived will improve the lives of others. Possibly you have grandchildren. Perhaps they are more apt to listen to you than they are to their own parents, especially if they are late teenagers and not yet 40.

Telling your grandchildren of your errors, and what resulted, can be very meaningful to them. They will remember forever whatever you tell them. They probably have never considered that your life may have been just like theirs, except with the awful revelation that you did not grow up with cell phones that tweeted, and that you had to look at and actually talk to your date. How did you do that? Even so, you have a lot of life experience to share. This can be a huge influence on their lives, especially if you weave these stories into a normal conversation so that it does appear like a lecture. It even works best if you can end up laughing at yourself. Your lineal descendants will always remember those moments. They provide an additional form of your own immortality. Anything that you do say can motivate them.

Another suggestion is if you can write something that is circulated to all members of your family, so it does not appear to your teenage grand-daughter that you really are focusing on her. Your thoughts can make a huge difference, just as the great-great uncle of Tony Hileman changed his relative's life four generations later. Or by my helping my grandson change his attitude about himself significantly increasing his wrestling ability when he was in high school. In other words, there are all sorts of opportunities for you to make a real difference while you are still alive regardless of your age, health and circumstance if you only open your eyes and see.

It is not too late to change your estate plan. Instead of taking the easy path of leaving everything to your children and let them make their own family decisions—which means their children must wait until their parent's demise to benefit from you, consider leaving each grandchild something, a specific sum is typical, but if it is a large amount a percentage of the residue of your estate is safer. If you need most of your money, specific amounts take precedence over a share of the residual, and if you need almost all your assets you will have no assets remaining to distribute to your own children if the specific bequest to grandchildren requires all your remaining money.

Leaving everyone at a percentage assures that you provide something for everyone.

My best advice for my clients is to retain the share of each beneficiary in trust. This is not hard-earned money, so it is easier to spend. Provide no right to invade the principal until each beneficiary is at least twenty- five years old. If they have a real need, such as acquiring a home, the Trustee can invade the principal and own the home in the Trust for your beneficiary. The funds are your beneficiary's, it just makes a difference in who decides they how and when they may be spent, (by an impulsive child, or a wise Trustee, treating your child as they would their own.) I learned as an estate planner of a life insurance statistic that the average 21-year-old will go through 90% of their inheritance in eleven months. I do not know if that is accurate, but I do know that I have seen that result frequently. More important, for all my clients' children I have seen money negatively impact the lives of beneficiaries. I have had three clients that won the lottery. It effectively ruined the life of each of them because they ceased to contribute to their own life and, in one case, it even caused a divorce.

If a beneficiary has passed age 25 let them take out ten percent, but no more than one-third of their share, holding the rest in trust with the right to remove one-half of the balance perhaps five years later and the entire balance ten years later. If your bequest remains within your trust their creditors cannot touch their shares, nor can their spouse in a divorce. More importantly, if you use a professional Trust Company, they will learn how to invest and protect their inheritance. Your money will make a bigger impact on their life and if they need the funds earlier, such as to acquire a home, the trust can buy and own the home for them. Most well-prepared trusts provide the Trustee distribution discretion.

You could take some of your resources and apply them now to help a grandchild get on a career path. The fact that you reach out to your grandchild is a memory that they will never forget. The advice I frequently suggest to a client is that their children can spend 90%. or 80%, or 70% of their inheritance about as fast as they can spend 100%.

Taking the 10, 20, or 30% and leaving that to charitable organizations that have made a difference in your life will have a much larger impact on more people in the years ahead, while also helping assure the future of that organization. However, we also caution our clients not to leave large sums of money outright to their Church or our client will have met next year's budget, thereby relieving the Congregation of their obligation. The following year it will be impossible to get the members to restore their original level of giving. If benefiting their Church is their objective, put their funds in a restricted fund to meet some future beneficial objective.

The immortality resulting from supporting a charity important to you significantly surpasses the result of what you leave your children.

An even better idea, you could consider leaving a significant portion of the wealth you have accumulated to a community foundation where your children, and ultimately their children, could direct the specific charities that benefit by receiving grants the Foundation awards annually from the earnings off the family fund you have created. That gives each of your descendants who participate in making the annual distribution decision a unique sense of family pride and identity that I have not found duplicated in any other way.

One benefit provided by the Humanist Foundation that is popular with older members dependent on their limited income sources is to turn some of their investments currently earning 2 or 3% in bonds or certificates of deposit into an annuity. By contributing the principal to the Humanist Foundation in exchange for an annuity, a person in their eighties may receive an annuity providing no less than 8% annually, depending upon the economy the month of the contribution. This amount is payable for the rest of the donor's lives. For the first twelve years or so up to three fourths of their annual payment is not subject to income tax. Even more important for many is the immediate charitable income tax deduction they receive for the portion of their donation that ultimately will go to the charity upon their demise, together with the other tax benefits means that almost half of their annuity contribution they will have gotten back the first year. In addition, their annuity donation will continue to do good forever. That certainly is an acceptable form of immortality for a humanist.

I have often wondered why anyone who understands what is happening would ever even consider buying an annuity from a life insurance company if they knew that the rates of interest insurance companies are willing to pay leaves no less than one half of the value of the amount of the purchase price for the annuity they acquire for the life insurance company. That is why the insurance company pays such a high commission for their insurance agents to sell their annuities. Normally the commission is 20% of the cost you pay. A well-managed fund frequently results in 100% of the investment in the annuity being retained by the life insurance company after your demise. Why would you want to benefit an insurance company? When, if you buy an annuity from other than a charity, you get no tax benefits. And your money does no good for extending the meaning of your life after you are gone.

For specific information on how you might benefit all you need to do is go on-line or call the American Humanist Association. The Humanist Foundation annuity offers a form of immortality that we know really does exist. Your church cannot even guarantee that.

Chapter Twenty-Eight
How Do I Begin My Own Journey?

The first thing you might consider doing is joining the American Humanist Association, to acquire more information and to see how you may participate in their collective endeavors to make our world a better place because you have been here.

One example of how the Association can make a difference is because our society has deviated so far from our natural environment, our culture is no longer in resonance physically or psychologically with the world around us, and so it slowly deteriorates. Humans are consequently now in danger of self-destruction. Consider our nuclear arsenal. We give Pakistan billions of dollars annually and yet they had allowed Osama bin Laden to build his compound within one mile of their military academy knowing that he was our number one enemy. Why do we do that? Because they have nuclear bombs, and we appease them. One hopes that it is not too late to recognize our negative path and for us to move closer in harmony with nature.

Donald Johansson, PhD., was Director of Science Research at the Cleveland Museum of Natural History when he co-authored *Lucy: The Beginnings of Humankind.* He pointed out in an interview with *U.S. News and world Report* where he stated that human beings developed over four million years in ways which would help them survive in their environment. This evolution played a major role in the general biological makeup of our human behavior—a large part of which is therefore genetically determined. Dr. Johansson states that it is his view that the deterioration in society, such as crime and the breakup of the family, is a reflection of the fact that we are removed from our natural setting." That might be why many people feel several aspects of our culture are beginning to crumble. Living closer to our natural environment would make our lives healthier and more "normal" as our society relates to nature.

Our landfills and our seas filling with plastics that are not biodegradable are prime examples. We have fish ingesting plastic that in turn we eat today. That cannot contribute to our health. One person from a farming community in the Midwest recently moved to a Pacific coast community. He saw what was happening to our seaside, and he created a company that collects plastic from the ocean and, with the use of three-dimensional printers, is now making human prosthetic parts from this plastic. That is the sort of behavior typical of Humanists. Many of us see a need and then turn it into an opportunity by getting creative and thinking outside of the box about better solutions.

Consider once more the lives of Lester and Maria Mondale. They were in tune with nature and their lives helped develop the Humanist philosophy that resulted in the essay that you are now reading. Their life was significant. And they have earned their immortality. Will you?

Even if global warming is not accelerated by us, it is a problem we must face together

Our societies' reluctance to accept global warming and the effect that glaciers and iceberg melt now raising the level of our oceans so that our shoreline cities could flood during our lifetime is serious. Yet we give away billions of our tax dollars away to nations that have become dependent upon us to keep the middle east calm, while they grow our terrorists. In the meantime, our highways and bridges are deteriorating. Makes little sense, when you put our priorities in perspective.

Over Population

Dr. Jonas Salk is the distinguished research scientist that found the vaccine to eradicate polio from most of the world today. In his speech accepting the 1976 Humanist of the Year Award from the AHA, I was fascinated he was concerned with the effects of overpopulation. Dr. Salk compared the behavior of humans with experiments using the fruit fly. Place a small population of fruit flies in a jar with sugar water on the bottom and they will lazily multiply until their population fills the jar, until they run out of food. As their numbers multiply their behavior becomes increasingly frenzied. He compared the frantic behavior of the fruit flies that filled their jar with the population now living in Manhattan. Salk demonstrated that the number of people will grow to fully utilize the resources of their environment and they remain until diminished by conflict or lack of resources. Dr. Salk believes that the food supply is a major factor that will control world population growth.

Dr. Salk pointed out that the negative psychological effects of population growth can be predicted when one observes the behavior of citizens in our larger metropolitan centers. Many people who are confined to small spaces become neurotic. According to Dr. Salk, this behavior is no different than that of the fruitflies within a container. He pointed out that, given enough food, the number of fruit-flies will fill a container, displaying increasingly agitated behavior as they become more and more crowded. He explained that 'Type A" behavior develops when people, crowded in an ever more restrictive environment, become more dependent upon others for their basic-necessities and therefore feel less and less secure.

It was Dr. Salk's opinion that the neuroses currently experienced by the masses in the more highly developed nations stem from population growth. We can predict that pressure caused by large dependent populations could cause further deterioration in the human condition. Thus, we can easily see the need for a voice in society that represents humanity. One effort that could provide a partial solution that would make a significant difference would be for all Catholics to rise up and collectively insist upon a change in the policy of the Catholic Church regarding birth control, recognizing that their policy has been a significant contributor to the problem. Collectively calling public attention to the effect of their policy over time could cause change. That change must start with the membership. It will not start with the clergy. They want more Catholics for their own support.

How does Maslow add to this discussion?

Abraham Maslow, who 1 previously introduced as the founder of Humanistic psychology, was the 1967 recipient of the American Humanist Association Humanist of the Year Award. In his acceptance speech Maslow showed us that the purpose of each life is to become more and more human: for each person to actualize their own existence more fully. By now, recognizing that individual needs can be divided into at least six categories, each with different behavior characteristics, we can easily see all sorts of ramifications in our understanding of the world in which we live. The differing need levels upon which a society exists helps us better understand why we have global conflict today.

Maslow's Humanistic Psychology and his Hierarchy of Needs is widely utilized in education and in personnel management. Its applicability, however, has a far wider range for the understanding of societies, countries, economics, and politics. Like individuals, institutions and governments also polarize, or exist primarily on different need levels, depending upon their development. Our understanding whether another society is traumatized on a level of need, or whether their growth or maturation has been stifled, is of even greater importance for the very survival of our own society. The only way we can ultimately be safe from world conflict is to see that all cultures have a path for their own growth.

As Maslow demonstrated, one's basic needs must first be satisfied before one can grow further as a human being. Many countries necessarily expend all their energy seeking salvation from hunger. People who lack food, sleep, warmth, or shelter generally act to procure this needs satisfaction—even if it means taking from those who have those resources with violence. Overpopulation may make it impossible for some human beings to grow collectively beyond this point. It is conceivable that humankind may be doomed to strangling itself before our societies living in our world today can universally attain a better way of life.

Maslow pointed out that, when it becomes possible, people, institutions, and governments seek security once basic needs are resolved. We "feather our nests" to assure subsequent satisfaction of these needs and to secure ourselves from the threat of their removal by others. When operating effectively, economics should provide for the basic needs level. Governments are necessary to provide the security level. Only when we are secure can we establish the social level, which Maslow tells us is the predominant posture or level of the United States today. Those who live on the social level recognize the futility of living a basic existence. We can say that war is ridiculous, and that people should behave differently; however, until the level of living is universally raised, such beliefs cannot become effective.

Having satisfied the social level, individuals, the same as institutions and governments, can extend outward to satisfy their ego self-awareness level for recognition. Only after achieving reasonable satisfaction of their needs from the basic level through the ego self- awareness level can people, intuitions and societies become fully functional and in tune with reality without fear of negative behavior. According to Dr. Maslow, only six percent of human beings have achieved the level of actualization so far. No country has reached this utopian state of actualization, and very few people today even understand its meaning. To bring about this understanding and fulfillment of this objective for everyone, is one goal worthy of effort from organized humanism. It is a goal that everyone would seek if they were only aware of its existence.

Although few may attain this level, we each must have the opportunity for anyone to succeed in actualizing their own life. Maslow reminds us that the purpose of livin g is for each of us to become fully functioning human beings in resonance with the universe in which we live, living on the highest level that we can attain. For anyone to achieve actualization, our society must provide us the freedom and culturally unobstructed opportunity to do so. For this reason, a principal concern of organized humanism should be how to improve the quality of life for each person here on Earth. Making the public aware of the effect of the hierarchy of needs as a natural part of their growth would be a good starting point.

The question was asked of Donald Johannsson, "If behavior is closely related to genetics, and much of our behavior is inherited, were our ancestors' blood-thirsty killer apes or were they cooperative sharing creatures?" He replied, 'The answer is not at either end of these two extremes; humans are capable of both kinds of behavior. Cooperation played an important role in the success and survival of early humans in the sense that they lived in groups and shared responsibilities, but provoked, the human being can do things that are unsurpassed in the animal world. There are no other groups of animals that systemically wipe each other out the way humans do. E.

O. Wilson, in addressing this issue, showed us the need for balance between those who are selfish, especially those living on lower need levels, and those who become altruistic as they enculturate in larger groups for their mutual protection.

In a society where our technology has accelerated faster than our ability to absorb its effect upon our society, Humanists can be a major cause of cultural awareness regarding our responsibility to be human and to develop the values necessary to sustain human existence. A nuclear war created because our science has exceeded our culture today, could very well extinguish life on earth.

Prison Reform is necessary.

During my own lifetime I have seen our society seriously deteriorate. Looking for how we can make a difference to help society take control of reversing our cultural evolution into a more violent environment, which has resulted in our children today no longer being allowed to play outside in their own neighborhood, or to walk alone to grade school, is worth our effort. How we solve these problems can have an enormous effect in all aspects of control of our society. Prison reform is one area that should be addressed. One concern I have recently discovered is that the quality of life of many who are now incarcerated is limited to a point that rehabilitation is not easily accomplished. Yet, with prison overcrowding, prisoners are being released back into society more violently than when they entered their penitentiary. That makes no sense.

Many who have committed a serious enough crime to merit prison are not really the same person a few years later, yet our society really considers the penalty for crime from a "black or white" mindset when our legislatures create minimum prison sentences. That is a "one penalty fits all" standard that lacks realistic thought. The maximum sentence for any crime in Costa Rica is thirty years, even for murder.

We incarcerate more people in the United States than in any other country in the world today. Why do we do that? We treat those that prove a diminished mental health association with their crime from a totally different perspective. We do not imprison them; we place them in a mental health facility without a term requirement. Instead, we allow that person's being cured as the determinate of when they are returned to society. They are treated from a rehabilitation perspective, as opposed to regular prisoners who are treated from a retribution perspective. That differentiation makes absolutely no sense.

I think of one offender who is currently incarcerated for life because he was tried as an adult while a teenager. He engaged in a robbery with an older person who had control of the youth and insisted that he help the adult rob a store because the older person needed money for drugs. Unbeknownst to the minor, the older person was armed. Under the stress of the robbery the adult shot and killed a person. The minor who was only there out of fear of the adult now also serves a life sentence in prison because of an archaic rule of law that all who participate in a felony are equally guilty if a murder occurs, regardless of who did the killing. That really makes no intelligent sense, but that is the current state of our laws. It happens because those who make the laws do not have sufficient knowledge and experience to fully understand the effect of the laws they create. They respond emotionally saying, "we do not want them, so lock them up and throw away the keys," That thinking has resulted in more crime.

Our system may be better than China's. There, if you are caught committing a crime you are locked up until you prove you are innocent. Once imprisoned you may never be heard from again. Since they do not have that many the Government must feed it is your guess what happed to the rest? But, as a result, they have very little street crime today in China. Is that system better than ours, where is South Chicago you best not be alone walking the streets at night?

For many currently incarcerated in our prison system, the form of rehabilitation provided to mental health offenders would best serve society in many ways. It would reduce our hardcore prison population dramatically. Maximum security penitentiaries are very expensive, particularly those housing a death row population. Such a change in our system of incarceration would give those in prison hope of getting out that would encourage their rehabilitation. It would leave our prisons for those not able to rise above violent behavior, who really are a threat to society.

The possibility of creating a rehabilitation system in all prison facilities would be an incentive for those in treatment to succeed, rather than the prisoner spending their entire life in permanent incarceration. Solitary confinement reduces some prisoners to animal behavior. The threat of arriving in solitary confinement is not enough of a deterrent to justify its existence. It is pure punishment, and hardly rehabilitates anyone. It should be abolished today as a means of rehabilitation. Even electro-convulsive therapy would be somewhat more humane. Although for some people with no hope of rehabilitation it still may be better than our society ever releasing them back into the public.

There are some people that are living on a basic or low security level and, for whatever reason, have no likelihood of advancing above that level. They cannot effectively socialize even in a prison population with a rehabilitation perspective. Even if our goal is simply to punish, incarceration for life certainly is far more effective punishment than banishment to death row, which unnecessarily costs our society millions in managing the court appeal process, established to ease public fear of executing an innocent person (which still happens anyway).

Our science is beyond our society today.

Our tenure on Earth has been slight in comparison with the age of the universe. Today with dams, within our lifetime we could eliminate the Grand Canyon. With hydrocarbon fumes we are destroying in one generation the Great Pyramids, which have survived more than three thousand years. With several nuclear bombs we can annihilate life on Earth. In this short time, humans have developed the capacity for their Own destruction without the wisdom to control these forces.

We humans do not have the ability to avoid conflicts with nature, nor the means to avoid conflicts with countries and cultures still existing on the basic or security levels. It is perhaps unfortunate that many scientist's function on the ego, or for some even on the actualized level, because the results of their research are beyond the maturation or psychological level of the masses of people living on Earth today. Because our societies have become extended, collectively living on at least three different psychological levels, we are not only out of tune with nature; our governments are out of step with reality, especially in more sophisticated countries. The most serious problem is that the masses are out of step with their natural environment— and with their own psychological level of living. As a society, we have become our own worst enemy. Humanists can lead the way in educating the public. After all, it was a Humanist that identified the hierarchy of our needs.

What happens when we run out of natural resources?

We are consuming the world's resources at a dangerous and unsustainable rate. People in countries on a security or basic level are rightfully hostile because of the contrast between their lives and those living in the large consuming countries. None of us can ensure survival for future generations by hiding our head in the sand. We must be concerned and cooperative, preserve and replenish our natural resources, and, consistent with nature, raise the level of living of all peoples in our world, if we are truly to be safe. This is how we may actualize our own lives today and assure that our great grandchildren have the same opportunities.

We must encourage new methods that link and unite the individual with the natural environment. If we are to survive, we must encourage mental and physical health, and develop a spirit of cooperation among all humankind. This is a global effort available for Humanists. That is because we Humanists are among the very few people that have the perspective to see and truly appreciate what this means for our life here on Earth. If everyone lived the life of Lester and Maria Mondale, who lived the life of Epicurus—needing little and wanting nothing but for each moment to be truly lived and appreciated, enjoying what each day brought to them—then everyone might be able to actualize their own life. Instead, as a society, we live today more like the life of A1 Capone and those who can barely rise above the security level of our existence.

As I previously mentioned, I have visited the home of Lester and Rosemary Mondale. They have stayed in my home many times. Humanism, as we know it today, was young when I was President of the American Humanist Association in the late 1970's until the mid1980's. Lester was a Unitarian minister. At that time, Lester was one of only seven of the original thirty-four architects of Humanist Manifesto I (1933) still living. Today all are deceased. The Mondale's really did not need society for their existence. But society needed them. They were leaders, in their own way. They showed us the path, not only for human survival, but for how to actualize our own existence, regardless of our wealth.

Sharing the Mondale's lifestyle shook my values and caused me to reconsider alternatives for a quality life. The Mondale's were not hermits. They were caring people, and they shared their lives with many throughout the world. Lester created the Society of Religious Humanists, which still exists, as an organization within the American Humanist Association, for those Humanists wishing to look upon our philosophy from a Christian religious perspective. The important lesson is that they wasted nothing. They wanted nothing and needed little. They restored what they took from nature and were fully actualized people living in harmony with their environment. They were a model of Humanist living worth considering as we look for ways to save human existence on Earth for future generations, hopefully forever.

Our Humanist values differ from that of many religious fundamentalists. How do we drag them out of the dark ages?

Humanists constitute collectively one of the few voices which unselfishly asks: "What about life on earth, today?" We each differ in our approach and specific concerns, because Humanists are individualistic. But, because of our Association, together we can speak with a collective voice—not merely to respond to any pest attempting to malign our good name for their own selfish purpose, as Jerry Falwell and Tim LaHaye did in my day, but to those control people, wherever they may be, that would deny people the right to live their own lives to the very fullest that they can attain.

Reverend LaHaye was the fundamentalist minister of a church of over 3,000 members in San Diego. He wrote an awful book condemning "Secular Humanists," essentially claiming that living a life that is not "controlled by God" is immoral. On behalf of humanism, as president of our Association, I challenged LaHaye to a two-hour debate which was carried live on CBS in Southern California on a Saturday afternoon in the early 1980's.

1 used a member of my AHA Board, Gerald LaRue, PhD., Professor Emeritus of the University of Southern California, whose specialty was Biblical Archeology, to speak for humanism, so that if discussion dissolved to the Bible by LaHaye, we could effectively respond. LaRue was one of the archeologists who participated in

the excavation of Qumran in Israel, where the Dead Sea Scrolls were written. He knew what he was talking about when he opened his Bible.

When the debate was over, Reverend LaHaye acknowledged that he had the wrong view of humanism. Carl Sagan leaned over and said to me "I do not believe that LaHaye has heard a word that we have said today." He was right. Two months later LaHaye left his church and joined Jerry Falwell to help him form the "Moral Majority" (which, you may remember, is neither). Many of us thought that LaHaye was following his 'Ultimate Concern": money. As a result, together they empowered the most unenlightened of the public to become an organized political force intent on taking control of our government to impose their religious values. The American Constitution was intended to protect government from religion. As a result, our government has become increasingly negatively polarized.

Control People that view life from a primitive narrow perspective, whether from religion, or irresponsible citizenship, are still today a serious threat to our society's ability to raise the public awareness to higher levels of living. Some of this problem is caused by our system of public education, which today tolerates negative behavior in our classrooms and fails to provide our children with an in-depth understanding of our history and the values upon which our country was founded. Many people no longer have enough educational foundation to create the necessary values for our society to become in tune with our environment. Many people today look at life from a selfish perspective and are unwilling to consider the greater good. Those of us with a Humanistic perspective need to become more vocal.

What is the advantage of a group effort?

Through our collective voice, we can assist each person to recognize their individual responsibility for improving the quality of all life for all people to assure the survival of human existence. As I have said before, I look upon the American Humanist Association as *"the mouse that roared."* If some voice is not heard in our governmental and cultural decision-making institutions saying, "We must be aware of what is best for all human beings," we may continue to deviate from what is truly natural for humans and, consequently, human life on Earth easily may not survive. A nuclear holocaust could be the result.

A common goal all Humanists can agree upon, regardless of their personal discipline or view, is the removal of barriers to the actualization or growth of the individual, our institutions, and even our governments. Humanists can encourage all people to assist all cultures to be in tune with reality and to live consistently with nature whenever we observe cultural deviation. As Humanists, in addition to what we can do collectively, we individually realize that we must work to make the world a better place for our having been here.

We can collectively designate specific concerns common to our related disciplines and make an even greater impact in the improvement of world conditions. Regardless of whether a religious or a personal ethic directs our individual lives, until all people accept as part of their ethic a recognition that **those things are good" which improve the human condition, and those are 'bad" which deter improvement of the human condition or hinder a responsible individual's ability to achieve actualization for their own life,** Humanists will continue to have a job of educating all who we encounter. There will remain a place for humanism as a separate philosophic view of life that is distinct from other belief systems guiding the lives of the masses of people living in our world today.

With examples, such as my grandson whose decision resulted in a medical clinic for 30,000 people living in Uganda who never had such care immediately available to them, we can each make a significant difference in our world today. In doing so we may save our world and our descendants' existence as human beings.

The American Humanist Association has created a Caucus in the United States Congress to assure that issues related to the ability of everyone to fully live their life here on Earth are addressed and incorporated in our laws. This Caucus is growing and today it is significant to address lobbying is provided by corporations, and religious organizations that would deny the rights of each individual. Having an organization that looks at all legislation from the perspective of protecting the freedom of each person being allowed to fully live their life here on Earth is very important. Few look at all legislation from that perspective. Its voice needs to be protected and preserved. You can help in that endeavor.

Chapter Twenty-Nine
In Conclusion

What all of this means is that—even recognizing that we ultimately will physically become space dust—our existence still has meaning for ourselves. Should we say that the Sun has no current value because its light will eventually become extinguished, even though it has existed for billions of years? The Sun's value is providing sustenance, contributing to Earth being able to sustain life, thereby offering all of us a chance for us to live. It gives us the opportunity for happiness and meaning in our own lives. The Sun does not have to exist forever for it to have value. Why should we be any different?

The truth is that we really know very little about anything. We know even less about how and why our own life came to be. We can only act upon what we know, or what we are willing to believe. Even though humans might not be immortal, our individual lives are valuable to ourselves today. To exist for any interval of time requires us to contribute as if there will always be a future. Life is enough justification for itself. Nothing else is necessary for our own life to have meaning. Whatever else we may choose to believe can only add to the meaning of our own life, if only for ourselves.

Instead of feeling that they are giving up something valuable,

know for certain does exist. On the contrary, people with this view find that they must put even more effort into their life on Earth. Because this may very well be all that there is, they feel a greater need to achieve actualization, thus fulfilling their own life's purpose.

All that anyone really can verify is that we live our own life today for ourselves, for those we love, and for those for whose lives we make a difference. Anything more is essentially a matter of "blind faith," and not of fact. However, those who choose to believe there must be an afterlife, if there is one, especially benefit by fulfilling their own existence while here on Earth. They may well experience the best of both this life and the next one. No one knows for sure. Humanists do not see any evidence that such an afterlife exists, so they simply do not worry about it. Most Humanists recognize that their own immortality may come solely from their good works for the benefit of others and their posterity that follows them. There need not be more for our own life to have value.

We may be here through a fluke of nature, but we do exist. Humans are part of the natural evolution of life. It is not possible to know whether individuals exist only to foster the evolution of the human species, or whether there may be a deeper, more specific purpose for each of us as individuals. We only know what feels right for ourselves. All that we really do know for certain is that, as individuals, we only have one opportunity to live. Our immediate objective should be to live our own life here today to the fullest, striving to be the very best that we can become as an individual and doing our best to help our society grow out of the dark ages in which we are currently living.

By showing us that higher levels of living exist, Maslow has helped us understand how to enrich our own lives by providing a path to actualize our own existence. By eliminating barriers and fulfilling all our needs on all levels of living, we can grow and expand our own lives and teach this to our posterity. We will then live on through them.

We know now that we must each discover the specific path for ourselves. When we achieve a peak experience, we will then know we have fulfilled our own life, at least for that moment. When we have done our best to assist others in their journeys, our lives will have significance. By fulfilling our own mission statement—e.g..: **"our lives are meaningful for ourselves and significant to others", -- our own life will then have served its own purpose** .

At some point, death is inevitable. For those who believe that the soul and body separate after death, actualizing their existence while here on Earth should only enhance this opportunity. By actualizing their existence, their life will not have been wasted by missing an opportunity to live primarily for a life hereafter that may not exist. This approach to life should not conflict with any intelligent religious view. If it does, an educated person should question the value of such a limiting view provided by those controlling their life. They should by now realize that they did not acquire those beliefs on their own, so they at least have made the effort to make the very most of this life. Those with faith in a life hereafter may win even more by actualizing their existence here on Earth—particularly if they are correct. Today many people are content with believing that this life is all that exists. No one knows for certain. Hopefully for all of us, by actualizing our own existence—and thus knowing that we have lived a full life while we are here—we should be able to peacefully accept the end of our own life when the time comes. We should need nothing else for our own life to have had purpose and meaning.

As the Humanist Manifesto states in the Appendix, **"The responsibility for our lives and the kind of world in which we live is ours and ours alone.** The challenge is great. The reward is a slice of Humanist immortality."** To leave the world better than we found it, Humanists will all agree, is an acceptable form of immortality. Like our sun, or a flower in the forest, when we have lived this life to its fullest, there need be nothing further for our own life to have been important.

For us, at least, if we are then **Fully Human /** and have become **Fully Alive**, our own life will then have purpose. If we can then go out like we were making the winning run by sliding safely into home plate shouting, **"Wow! What a trip!"** we will know that our own life has been fulfilled, and we were **Fully Alive**.

Our Road Through Life

Our road through life goes far past
With some perhaps not seeing,
That moments spent upon our sacred
soil Lasts forever in our being.

As examples set for us new
heights We grow more rapidly.
As barriers fade, we gain insight,
Tuning ourselves to reality.

Our lives are richer for each day
We stretch our inner worth..
Fortunately, we have passed by this way.
The closest place to any heaven is Earth.

As experiences here result in change
That threads throughout society.
While those that extend their future range
Share in immortality.

Lyle L. Simpson, 1981 President,
American Humanist Association

Appendix

A DECLARATION OF HUMANISM
A Humanist Ethic

I.

Humanism is a philosophy, or an approach for fully living this life on Earth. It starts with the premise that we are part of nature and only know for certain that we are living this life today. Certain aspects of life have value for living a good life. Consistent with this philosophy, I personally believe that a healthy person grows through the following stages, normally in the following order. This is my philosophic and ethical approach for living my life:

1. **Existence.** My body is my temple of life, and health is essential for my existence. This life is all that I can say I possess for certain.

2. **Responsibility.** I must assume the primary responsibility for my own life. My behavior is within my own control. I can only make my choices as I allow myself to live in the present. My personal attitude at any given moment is within my control. A positive attitude enhances my chances for success. At the same time, I benefit from allowing others within my defense mechanisms who are willing and wanting to assume the responsibility of sharing their life with me. The balancing of responsibility for meeting

another person's needs with our own greatly enhances life for both of us.

3. **Meaning**. My life is meaningful to me to the extent my own needs are satisfied, and I achieve the homeostatic state of happiness. not be a universal purpose for my life to have meaning. My own life has sufficient purpose for itself. My goal for living my own life is to achieve all that I find possible.

4. **Security.** I must support justice for all, and respect the freedom of choice of everyone else, for me to secure the opportunity for equal justice. Justice is a progressive attainment of equality, limited only by the unique constraints of each person. Force should be tolerated only to suppress force that would otherwise inflict one person's unwarranted will over another. However, I must contribute to making our way of life safe from others who would prevent my family from having the same opportunity to live their lives to the fullest.

5. **Social Relations**. Human interdependence is essential for my health and growth. I must be willing to give mutual respect and trust to maintain close personal relationships. I recognize the relationship of inter-need dependence with others as love. I allow those I love within my defense mechanisms so that we might share our lives together for our mutual support. I must allow all others to be themselves. I strive to maintain I-Thou relationships with all others with whom I interrelate.

6. **Actualization of Life**. My purpose for living is to experience the joy of my life, and to actualize my growth to my fullest potential as a human being, consistent with my responsibility to others, and within the personal, environmental, and social resources available to me. I have an awe and spiritual reverence for nature while living my life as a part of the natural universe, and I recognize that I am a steward of its resources each day while I am living on Earth. All life is

sacred. I do not live my life on Earth with any expectations of or a need for a life after my death.

7. **Commitment to Others.** My life becomes significant to the extent I assist others to actualize their own lives. I believe that achieving the highest quality of life as a healthy, mature person means balancing the meaningfulness of my life with my significance to others. Only in consort and harmony with others will my own life reach its maximum potential.

8. **Knowledge.** I feel that it is essential to maintain the conditions of free inquiry and an open society to encourage the expression of all ideas. The expansion and expression of all knowledge can ultimately result in the best choices for the growth of everyone. I support using all means available for ascertaining the truth, and applying the results obtained to improve the welfare of all life on Earth. My values and standards are relative and malleable as new experiences and information shape my world view. There are no absolutes, except that one day I too will die.

9. **Social Institutions.** Within my own resources, I encourage people I encounter, as well as governments and other institutions, to reduce and eliminate all barriers for personal growth, and to provide optimum conditions for the healthy development of all people. The democratic process assures the greatest opportunity for the most people. We live in a world economy. World governments should assure peace from physical conflict for all people on Earth.

10. **Interdependence of Life.** We are only stewards of what we possess here on Earth for a very short duration. I should protect, enhance, and preserve all I have for the benefit of those who follow me. I affirm the wonder and beauty of nature as the creative process from which we humans have evolved; and I thereby recognize the unity and interdependence of, and feel respect for, all life on Earth.

All people must share responsibility for the maintenance of the natural order of our planet. All life is sacred. However, overpopulation of any species may threaten the opportunity for a quality life for all species. Humans are not an exception. Nature attempts to maintain a healthy balance. All living creatures On Earth must share our world together in harmony and balance if we are to survive and grow to our full potential.

II .

Additional expressions, such as an emotional attachment to a religious view, are very personal. They arise from previous experiences that have oriented our individual lives. We are each entitled to have our own. Therefore, our own religious views of life should not be imposed upon others.

My Goal

My Goal in life is to want nothing and need little, and to be able to fully appreciate the environment in which I find myself at that moment.

Then I will know that I am **Fully Human**, having actualized my own life, and when I leave this world a better place because I have been here, I will realize that I am finally **Fully Alive.**

If I have lived as much of my life as I am able above the level of actualization my life will have been meaningful to me. And if I have made the world a better place through my endeavors, my life will have been significant for others.

Lyle L. Simpson

1960

Humanist Manifesto III

Thirty-four people, primarily Unitarian ministers and philosophers were in discussion regarding their unique view of life in 1933. They reduced their collective thoughts to writing and adopted the first Humanist Manifesto, expressing the central points of their Humanistic philosophy of life. That document was made more contemporaneously relevant with the adoption of a second version in 1973. This is the third version, adopted in 2003 by the American Humanist Association as the current guiding consensus statement of philosophic principles that are agreed upon by most Humanists:

Humanism is a progressive philosophy of life that, without supernaturalism, affirms our ability and responsibility to lead ethical lives of personal fulfillment that aspire to the greater good of humanity.

The life-stance of Humanism—guided by reason, inspired by compassion, and informed by experience—encourages us to live life well and fully. It evolved through the ages and continues to develop through the efforts of thoughtful people who recognize that values and ideals, however carefully wrought, are subject to change as our knowledge and understandings advance.

This document is part of an ongoing effort to manifest in clear and positive terms the conceptual boundaries of Humanism, not what we must believe but a consensus of what we do believe. It is in this sense that we affirm the following:

Experimentation, and rational analysis. Humanists find that science is the best method for determining this knowledge as well as for solving problems and developing beneficial technologies. We also recognize the value of new departures in thought, the arts, and inner experience— each subject to analysis by critical intelligence.

Humans are an integral part of nature, the result of unguided evolutionary change. Humanists recognize nature as self-existing. We accept our life as all and enough, distinguishing things as they are from things as we might wish or imagine them to be. We welcome the challenges of the future and are drawn to and undaunted by the yet to be known.

Ethical values are derived from human need and interest as tested by experience. Humanists ground values in human welfare shaped by human circumstances, interests, and concerns and extended to the global ecosystem and beyond. We are committed to treating each person as having inherent worth and dignity, and to making informed choices in a context of freedom consonant with responsibility.

Life's fulfillment emerges from individual participation in the service of humane ideals. We aim for our fullest possible development and animate our lives with a deep sense of purpose, finding wonder and awe in the joys and beauties of human existence, its challenges and tragedies, and even in the inevitability and finality of death. Humanists rely on the rich heritage of human culture and the life-stance of Humanism to provide comfort in times of want and encouragement in times of plenty.

Humans are social by nature and find meaning in relationships.

Humanists long for and strive toward a world of mutual care and concern, free of cruelty and its consequences, where differences are resolved cooperatively without resorting to violence. The joining of individuality with interdependence enriches our lives, encourages us to enrich the lives of others, and inspires hope of attaining peace, justice, and opportunity for all.

Working to benefit society maximizes individual happiness.
Progressive cultures have worked to free humanity from the brutalities
of mere survival and to reduce suffering, improve society, and develop
a global community. We seek to minimize the inequities of
circumstance and ability, and we support a just distribution of nature's
resources and the fruits of human effort so that as many as possible
can enjoy a good life.

Humanists are concerned for the wellbeing of all, are committed
to diversity, and respect those of differing yet humane views. We work
to uphold the equal enjoyment of human rights and civil liberties in an
open, secular society and maintain it is a civic duty to participate in the
democratic process and a planetary duty to protect nature's integrity
diversity, and beauty in a secure, sustainable manner.

Thus, engaged in the flow of life, we aspire to this vision with the
informed conviction that humanity can progress toward its highest
ideals. **The responsibility for our lives and the kind of world in
which we live is ours alone.**

*"Humanist Manifesto" is a trademark of, and its contents are copyrighted by,
the American Humanist Association and is replaced here with permission.*

Maslow's Hierarchy of Needs

The revised Maslow's Hierarchy of Needs expands the original five levels to include a sixth level, which addresses the need for self-transcendence. Here are the six levels in the updated hierarchy:

1. Physiological Needs: Basic necessities for survival such as food, water, warmth, and rest.

2. Safety Needs: Protection from elements, security, order, law, stability, and freedom from fear.

3. Love and Belongingness Needs: Intimate relationships, friendships, trust, and acceptance, receiving and giving affection and love.

4. Esteem Needs: Self-esteem, respect, status, recognition, strength, freedom, and feeling of accomplishment.

5. Self-Actualization Needs: Achieving one's full potential, including creative activities, personal growth, and self-improvement.

6. Self-Transcendence Needs: Connecting to something beyond the self, such as altruism, spirituality, and the pursuit of higher meaning.

These levels represent a progression in human motivation, from basic physiological survival to the fulfillment of higher psychological needs and, ultimately, self-transcendence.

www.ingramcontent.com/pod-product-compliance
Ingram Content Group UK Ltd.
Pitfield, Milton Keynes, MK11 3LW, UK
UKHW051023240225
455495UK00018B/262